PLUNDERING
LONDON
UNDERGROUND

To Lynn
Best wishes & solidarity

Janine

PLUNDERING LONDON UNDERGROUND

NEW LABOUR, PRIVATE CAPITAL & PUBLIC SERVICE 1997-2010

Janine Booth

MERLIN PRESS

© Janine Booth, 2013

First published in 2013 by
The Merlin Press Ltd.
99B Wallis Road
London
E9 5LN

www.merlinpress.co.uk

ISBN. 978-0-85036-617-4

British Library Cataloguing in Publication Data
is available from the British Library

Printed by Imprint Digital, Exeter

This book is dedicated to everyone who fought against the
Public-Private Partnership and for a fully publicly-owned and
publicly-funded London Underground.
History proved you right.

TABLE OF CONTENTS

Chapter 5 – Learning the Lessons from PPP Past   163

Chapter 6 – A Socialist Alternative   181

FOREWORD

The London Underground Public Private Partnership (PPP) was one of the biggest political cons in post war British History.

Exploiting concerns about a system that had been starved of investment for decades, the 1997 New Labour Government promised the PPP would deliver a new expanded Underground.

Ministers even claimed the PPP would need no public money at all. Somehow the private sector was to magically and benignly plough money into the Tube.

Despite opposition from the overwhelming majority of the public, tube workers, the London Mayor, and a range of experts and politicians the Government ploughed ahead. Gordon Brown and John Prescott in particular were determined to see the PPP in at all costs. It was, after all, arguably the biggest of all PFIs.

Yet, a decade after it was implemented, the PPP had collapsed and in the process squandered billions of pounds of tax payers' money, leaving a legacy of cuts, job insecurity and some of the highest fares in Europe.

The critics, not least the RMT, had been proven right. The PPP remains a national scandal and it is a national disgrace that the privateers and politicians who did so much damage to our Tube have not been held to account.

Yet as with all struggles the battle around the PPP produced positives. There were tremendous displays of solidarity and unity between workers and their unions. The industrial and political mobilisation was inspirational.

And the fact that the trade unions, which began as an isolated opposition, eventually won and were proven right has lessons for us today in the debate about how we resist austerity and fight for a better society. This book is an important contribution to the history of the PPP and that wider debate.

Bob Crow is General Secretary of the RMT

ACKNOWLEDGEMENTS

I would like to thank everyone who gave their time to be interviewed by me; Tony for repeatedly making me rewrite the book, each time improving it; Adrian and Glenda for putting it all together; and my partner John and sons Alex, Joe and Harrison for allowing me to disappear into research and writing for many hours at a time.

GLOSSARY

Abatement – money deducted from the fees paid by London Underground Ltd to an Infraco due to the Infraco's failure to meet standards

Ambience – measure of the 'quality of the customer environment'

ASLEF – Associated Society of Locomotive Engineers and Firemen: trade union organising the majority of London Underground drivers

Availability – time cost to passengers by delays caused by the Infracos, measured in Lost Customer Hours

BCV – Bakerloo, Central, Victoria lines

Bonds – debt securities, bought by a person who thereby loans money to a corporate or government body for a defined period at a fixed interest rate; the issuing body sells the bond, and owes the buyer a debt, paying interest and repaying the purchase price at a later date

CAN – Corrective Action Notice: a contractual remedy served when an Infraco has defaulted in the performance of its obligations under the PPP Contract, and requiring the Infraco to undertake corrective action to remedy the default

CATP – Campaign Against Tube Privatisation

CSEU (or Confed) – Confederation of Shipbuilding and Engineering Unions: trade union group organising a small number of London Underground engineering staff

DETR – Department of the Environment, Transport and the Regions

DfT – Department for Transport

Directions (Draft, Interim, Final) – findings of the PPP Arbiter on matters within his power e.g. the level of the Infrastructure Service Charge

Dividend – payment made by a corporation to its shareholders, usually as a distribution of profits

Extraordinary Review – a review carried out by the PPP Arbiter at a time other than the 7½-yearly Periodic Review points

GLA – Greater London Assembly or Greater London Authority (the Authority is the Assembly plus the Mayor)

GLC – Greater London Council

HM Railway Inspectorate – body responsible for overseeing safety on Britain's railways and tramways; from 1990 to April 2006, it was part of the Health and Safety Executive; it has since been replaced by the Railway Safety Directorate at the Office of Rail Regulation

HSE – Health and Safety Executive; public body responsible for the encouragement, regulation and enforcement of workplace health, safety and welfare

Infracos – Infrastructure Companies

ISC – Infrastructure Service Charge: the fee paid by London Underground Ltd to the Infracos

JLE – Jubilee Line Extension

JNP – Jubilee, Northern, Piccadilly lines

LINC – consortium which bid for PPP contracts but which was unsuccessful

LPTB – London Passenger Transport Board

LU – London Underground

LUL – London Underground Ltd

Metronet – consortium which won two contracts: for the Bakerloo, Central and Victoria lines (BCV); and for the sub-surface lines

NAO – National Audit Office: the government's spending watchdog

Opsco – the Operating Company: London Underground Ltd

Periodic Review – see Review Period

PFI – Private Finance Initiative

PPP – Public-Private Partnership

PSC – Public sector comparator – an estimate of how much it would cost a public-sector body (in this case, London Underground) to carry out the same work that the private sector was being invited to do: used to test 'value for money'

Quango – quasi-autonomous non-governmental organisation

Review Period – 7½-year periods of the PPP contract for which the Infrastructure Service Charge and Terms are set in a Periodic Review. (RP1/RP2/etc. – First/Second/etc. Review Periods)

RMT – National Union of Rail, Maritime and Transport Workers: largest trade union on London Underground, representing workers in all grades

Shadow Running – the period from September 1999 until the start of the PPP, when London Underground operated a structure of Infracos and an Opsco in preparation for the PPP's structure

SSL/SSR – Sub-Surface Lines/Railway: Metropolitan, District, Hammersmith & City, Circle and the former East London Line

TfL – Transport for London, body appointed by the Mayor of London to run London's transport

TSSA – Transport Salaried Staffs Association: trade union organising a minority of London Underground station staff, and administrative staff

Tube Lines – consortium which won the contract for the Jubilee, Northern and Piccadilly lines

TUC – Trades Union Congress

LIST OF KEY PERSONS

Malcolm Bates: one of Geoffrey Robinson's team of four to choose London Underground policy, 1998; Chair of London Transport 1999-2001 and 2001-2003.

Tony Blair: Labour MP for Sedgefield; Prime Minister 1997-2007.

Chris Bolt: PPP Arbiter 2002-2010; economist; stand-in Rail Regulator 1998-1999.

Gordon Brown: Labour MP for Dunfermline East / Kirkcaldy and Cowdenbeath 1983-present; Chancellor of the Exchequer 1997-2007; Prime Minister 2007-2010.

Mike Brown: London Underground Ltd: joined 1989; Chief Operating Officer 2003-2008; Managing Director 2010-present.

Stephen Byers: Labour MP for North Tyneside 1997-2010; Secretary of State for Transport 2001-2002.

Martin Callaghan: London Underground Ltd: PPP Director 1999-2003.

Howard Collins: London Underground Ltd: joined 1978; manager from 1985; Chief Operating Officer 2008-2013.

Bob Crow: National Union of Rail, Maritime and Transport Workers (RMT): Assistant General Secretary 1991-2002; General Secretary 2002-present.

Alistair Darling: Labour MP for Edinburgh South West / Edinburgh Central 1987-present; Secretary of State for Transport 2002-2006.

Gwyneth Dunwoody: Labour MP for Crewe / Crewe and Nantwich 1974 until her death in 2008; Chair of the House of Commons Transport Select Committee 1997-2008.

Dean Finch: Tube Lines Chief Executive 2009-2010.

Stephen Glaister: transport policy expert: Professor of Transport and Infrastructure and Director of the Railway Technology Strategy Centre, Imperial College London 1998-present; previously non-executive member of London Transport Board, 1984-1993; member of Transport for London Board 2000-2008.

Keith Hill: Labour MP for Streatham 1992-2010; Parliamentary Under Secretary for Transport and Minister for London 1999-2001.

Glenda Jackson: Labour MP for Hampstead and Highgate / Hampstead and Kilburn 1992-present; Minister for Transport in London 1997-1999; unsuccessfully sought selection to be Labour's candidate for Mayor of London, 2000; former actor.

Simon Jenkins: journalist; columnist for the *Evening Standard*; London Transport Board member 1984-1986.

Boris Johnson: Conservative MP for Henley 2001-2008; Mayor of London 2008-present.

Bob Kiley: Commissioner of Transport for London 2001-2006; former Chairman and Chief Executive Officer of the New York City Metropolitan Transportation Authority (MTA) 1983-1990.

Jimmy Knapp: National Union of Rail, Maritime and Transport Workers (RMT): General Secretary 1990-2001; previously General Secretary of the National Union of Railwaymen 1983-1990.

John Leach: National Union of Rail, Maritime and Transport Workers (RMT): Council of Executives, London Transport Region representative 1999-2001 and 2005-2006; National President 2007-2009.

Ken Livingstone: Mayor of London: independent 2000-2004, Labour 2004-2008; previously GLC leader, 1981-1986; Labour MP for Brent East 1987-2001.

John McDonnell: Labour MP for Hayes and Harlington 1997-present; previously, Deputy Leader of the GLC 1981-1985.

Terry Morgan: Tube Lines Chief Executive 2001-2009; Chairman, Crossrail 2009-present.

Steven Norris: defeated Conservative candidate for Mayor of London, 2000 and 2004; Jarvis plc Chairman 2003-2010.

Tim O'Toole: London Underground Ltd Managing Director 2002-2009.

John Prescott: Labour MP for Hull East 1970-2010; Deputy Prime Minister 1997-2007; Secretary of State for the Environment, Transport and the Regions 1997-2001.

Geoffrey Robinson: Labour MP for Coventry North West 1976-present; Paymaster General 1997-1999; businessman.

Steve Robson: civil servant; Second Permanent Secretary at HM Treasury 1997-2001.

Derek Smith: London Underground Ltd Managing Director 1999-2001.

Tony Travers: academic and journalist, specialising in local government; Director of the Greater London Group at the London School of Economics and Political Science.

Denis Tunnicliffe: London Underground Ltd: Managing Director 1988-1998, Chairman 1998-2000; London Transport Chief Executive 1998-2000.

Shriti Vadera: special adviser to Gordon Brown; formerly of UBS Warburg bank.

John Weight: Metronet Chief Executive 2003-2005.

Christian Wolmar: railway historian, journalist and author.

INTRODUCTION

This book tells the story of the Public-Private Partnership (PPP) on London Underground – the policy that put the infrastructure of 'the Tube' into private hands. First announced by the new Labour government in 1998, it was implemented in 2003, supposedly to last 30 years, but by 2010 it was already over.

There are arguments for and against PPP, and I consider some of them, but I have written this book as someone heavily involved in campaigning *against* this policy. I have seen the damage done! So do not expect me to praise the PPP policy. In my view, lessons need to be learnt and conclusions drawn from this episode in the history of London's Tube system.

I set out a case for public ownership. London Underground does best when it is:

- publicly-owned
- unified
- under the control of a (preferably, elected) London body
- adequately funded
- allowed to operate as a public service rather than a commercial business

By 1997, a general election year, London Underground barely met any of these criteria. It had consequently fallen into a very poor state. London voters helped to elect Labour in 1997; they had come to despise the Conservative Party and they wanted a change, including renewed support for public services such as transport. Labour's manifesto promised a 'public-private partnership' for the Tube, and voters thought they saw in PPP a policy that contrasted with the Conservatives' policy of full privatisation. But when the nature of the PPP was revealed, many felt a sense of betrayal. 'New' Labour had ignored the lessons from London Underground's history and the views of its own party members and trade unions.

London Underground workers and some trade unions fought the PPP. But they were hampered by anti-trade-union laws, and by weaknesses and divisions within the trade union movement. They also faced press hostility, particularly from the *Evening Standard*. The unions had some genuine allies, but some of the opposition was technical or opportunistic. Ken Livingstone, a London Mayor elected on a platform of opposing PPP, quickly embraced private finance and moved to accept – as a compromise – a policy he had claimed to oppose.

Labour in government used undemocratic methods to sideline critics. Notable examples include grossly manipulating the process of selection for Labour's candidate for the newly-created post of Mayor of London and fiddling planning figures to 'prove' that the PPP was a cheaper option than public funding. The Labour government ignored opposition. It was so determined to impose PPP – on any terms – that it set out amazingly generous terms in its negotiations with private companies. The government forced PPP through. But such was the strength of the resistance that it took five years to put it in place, instead of the two years that it had foreseen.

The years in which the PPP was in place saw a catalogue of failure. The 'Private Finance Initiative' projects which preceded PPP still haunted London Underground, but PPP seemingly made problems worse. The Underground was not properly maintained, let alone improved. Critics said the PPP would undermine safety; they were proved right. The first year saw several trains derailed. Critics said that fragmentation and contracting-out would lower standards, and numerous incidents showed that this was also right. Critics said that the PPP would allow the private infrastructure companies to fail to deliver on their promises to maintain and improve the Tube: there were some achievements, but critics were proved right and performance targets were missed. There were also numerous late starts to the morning train service due to engineering overruns. The target of making London Underground accessible to disabled people was missed. Critics said that the PPP would make life worse for workers while allowing the private companies to enrich themselves: this prediction also came true.

New Labour was not listening. Money drained out of the Tube to pay for PPP's failures and its costs, and London Underground made cuts to make up the losses. Ken Livingstone betrayed his past record of opposition to privatisation and turned privatiser himself. The East London line became part of London Overground, operated as a private franchise.

The PPP's collapse was a predictable result not just of the particular infrastructure companies' failings, but of the Public-Private Partnership policy itself. The infrastructure companies extracted vast sums of money but failed to deliver what they promised. PPP was a particularly poor policy, and some contend that its failure exposes only the flaws of this specific model. But I argue that, whether by PPP or otherwise, private-sector involvement introduces the profit motive into London Underground and de-prioritises safety, services and workers' rights. The solution lies not with a better form of privatisation, but with London Underground being unified, publicly-owned, democratically run under the control of a London body, adequately publicly funded, and operating as a public service.

This book draws on documents, reports, contracts and campaigning materials, books and contemporary news coverage. I also draw on my own experience – I worked on London Underground during this time and campaigned against the PPP. In preparing the book, I talked at length with many of those involved, including London Underground's top managers and many of its workers, including engineers, drivers and station staff. Where not otherwise referenced, quotations are from my interviews with these people. My views are my own, and should not be taken to be those of London Underground, Transport for London or the Rail, Maritime and Transport Union (RMT), of which I am a member.

The unions – particularly RMT – continued to battle when the PPP was in place. They were at their most effective when militant, united, outward-looking and rank-and-file-led. I consider why the Labour Party, born of the workers' movement, chose to pursue a policy such as PPP, and how it was able to do so despite huge opposition. I contend that 'New Labour' was motivated by a desire to prove its credibility to the employing, rather than the working, class. It was able to impose its policy because our democracy is inadequate – and so too is the functioning of the Labour Party, which fails to respond to the concerns of its members.

The first chapter of the book begins with John Prescott's announcement of his PPP policy. I then look back on the 150-year history of the Tube. The basic case for the PPP policy is set out in its announcement by Prescott, and so the first chapter looks at arguments for and against this case and records the first episodes of opposition.

Chapter 2 charts the growing opposition to the PPP, which became near-unanimous by 2003. Objections grew as the flaws of PPP became increasingly obvious – complexity, falling safety levels and steadily falling expectations for performance and improvements.

Chapter 3 examines the PPP in practice.

Chapter 4 records the collapse of PPP. The Metronet Infraco (infrastructure company) fell first, going into administration in 2007 with debts of £2bn, and leaving improvement works in chaos. The Tube Lines consortium followed it back into public ownership three years later, after spectacularly messing up the Jubilee line upgrade.

Chapter 5 examines the legacy of PPP: one of underfunding, cuts and fragmentation. The people who were responsible walked away, unscathed and enriched, whilst workers and passengers had to pay for the consequences of their failed and unwanted policies.

A final chapter considers alternative policies for London Underground. I argue that London Underground needs not just 'old-style' nationalisation or public ownership, with all its faults, but a workers' and passengers' plan to improve and maintain the Tube, along principles of a socialist transport policy. The workers' movement and its allies should fight for such a policy.

This is a complicated story involving many institutions and persons. A **GLOSSARY** on pages xi-xii lists many of the terms and organisations involved, and **APPENDIX 2** on pages 200-201 lists significant public posts and their holders, including secretaries of state with responsibility for transport, and managing directors of London Underground. There are also timelines at various points in the book to help situate events.

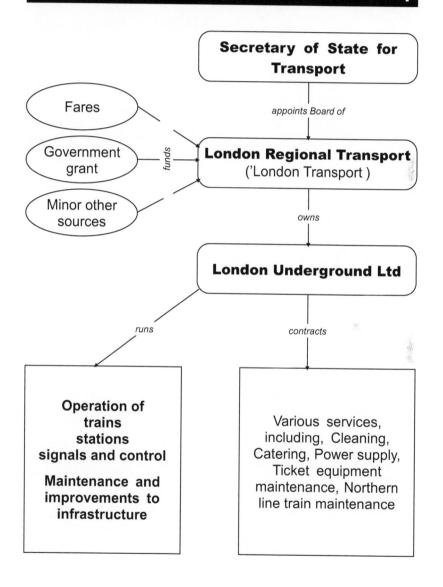

Outline structure of London Underground governance prior to the Public-Private Partnership

Secretary of State for Transport

appoints Board of

Fares

Government grant

Minor other sources

funds

London Regional Transport ('London Transport)

owns

London Underground Ltd

runs

contracts

Operation of trains stations signals and control

Maintenance and improvements to infrastructure

Various services, including, Cleaning, Catering, Power supply, Ticket equipment maintenance, Northern line train maintenance

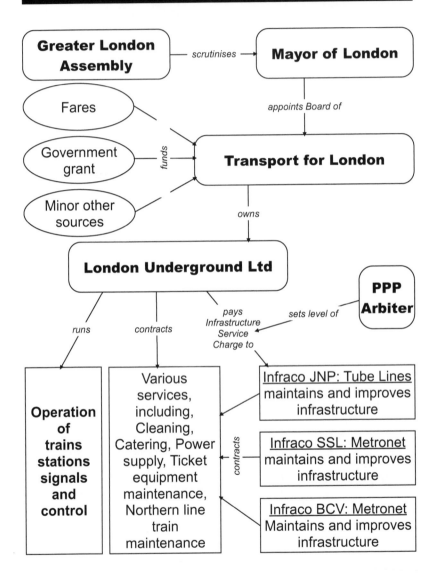

Outline structure of London Underground governance under the Public-Private Partnership

Greater London Assembly — scrutinises → Mayor of London

Mayor of London — appoints Board of → Transport for London

Fares, Government grant, Minor other sources — funds → Transport for London

Transport for London — owns → London Underground Ltd

London Underground Ltd — runs → Operation of trains stations signals and control

London Underground Ltd — contracts → Various services, including, Cleaning, Catering, Power supply, Ticket equipment maintenance, Northern line train maintenance

London Underground Ltd — pays Infrastructure Service Charge to

PPP Arbiter — sets level of →

Various services — contracts → Infraco JNP: Tube Lines maintains and improves infrastructure

Infraco SSL: Metronet maintains and improves infrastructure

Infraco BCV: Metronet Maintains and improves infrastructure

CHAPTER 1 – LABOUR PAINS: THE CONCEPTION AND BIRTH OF THE PPP, 1863-1998

This book is about the 'Public-Private Partnership' (PPP) policy on London Underground, implemented by the Labour government – which branded itself as 'new Labour' – elected in 1997 and led by Tony Blair and John Prescott. This first chapter starts with Prescott's announcement of the PPP policy in March 1998, ten months after his Party's election to government. It then retraces London Underground's history beginning with its first journey in 1863, explaining previous policies for the Underground's ownership and financing and how the Underground came to be in need of a new policy by 1997. This chapter surveys the reasons that Prescott and his government gave for choosing this particular policy. But not everyone agreed with New Labour's choice of PPP: this chapter also looks at some of the initial objections and efforts to dissuade the government from this course of action.

A PUBLIC-PRIVATE ANNOUNCEMENT: MARCH 1998

London Underground – known as 'the Tube' – is the world's oldest subterranean railway, and one of its largest. Passengers made some 800 million journeys in 1997, travelling along its 244 miles of track through its 267 stations and using its twelve different lines. That year 38,840 trains ran late, 4,000 more than in 1996. Of the five service performance targets London Underground set itself, it missed three. Passengers wanted something better from Tony Blair's new Labour government. So how would the new Labour government rescue the Tube?

At 11am on Friday 20 March 1998, Deputy Prime Minister John Prescott rose to announce Labour's plans for London Underground to the House of Commons. Prescott had been elected Labour's Deputy Leader in 1994. Son of a railway signaller, and previously a merchant navy steward and trade union official, he was presented as a working-class voice in a Labour Party leadership increasingly dominated by professionals like leader Tony Blair. Prescott would be a key figure in the future of the Tube. That day he told Members of Parliament that he had come up with 'a radical, modern and imaginative solution ... an entirely new approach – a third way'.

He explained that 'for many years, investment in the underground has simply been too low to ensure that the worn-out assets are properly replaced', and that the Tube needed funds to catch up with its investment backlog and improve its services. Prescott outlined a 'Public-Private Partnership' (PPP). London Underground's operations – the running of trains, stations and signalling – would remain as a 'single, integrated entity' in the public sector. He would award the job of maintaining and modernising the Tube's infrastructure to private companies, with groups of lines packaged into contracts. For the two years it would take to prepare the PPP, the government would give the Underground an extra £365m grant. The PPP would deliver £7bn investment, 'aimed at creating a first-class underground for London'.

Some 'new Labour' stalwarts shared the Deputy Prime Minister's enthusiasm. Streatham MP Keith Hill gushed: 'This settlement has secured for Londoners a tube system of which they can be proud for a generation.' Several MPs looked forward to improvements to those parts of the Tube that ran through their own constituencies. But although MPs hoped for improvements, this did not mean that they all supported the PPP policy. John McDonnell, left-wing Labour MP for Hayes and Harlington, recalled that MPs 'welcomed any new investment in the Tube, but neither I nor a number of others in the House wanted another form of privatisation such as the PPP'. The Conservatives advocated full privatisation – selling London Underground to a new private owner or owners. McDonnell told the House that 'it beggars belief that anyone could urge wholesale privatisation of London Underground ... a number of us favour wholesale public ownership'. Conservative spokesperson Norman Fowler described Prescott's proposals as 'an unsatisfactory and inadequate compromise' which accepted the principle of privatisation but still clung partly to nationalisation, 'which almost everyone now thinks is an outdated and failed model'.

The Department of the Environment, Transport and the Regions (DETR) – a new mega-ministry set up for Prescott to head – explained that London Underground Ltd's operating surplus (the amount by which its fares and other revenue exceeded its spending on running the train service) could not meet the Tube's need to prevent its trains, stations and infrastructure deteriorating ('steady state maintenance'). Neither could

LUL's operating surplus address the Tube's backlog of repair work.[1] By 1998, London Underground needed an extra £1.2bn to catch up with outstanding repairs.[2] As the section below[†] will explain, previous governments had starved London Underground of funds. Passengers were enduring a 'grisly ritual of squeezing on to overcrowded Underground trains'.[3]

The story of how London Underground came to be in this condition is a journey in which five factors come together. These are: *ownership* varying between private and public, *control* between local and national, *funding* between inadequate and a little better, *integration* between fragmentation and unification, and *ethos* between public service and commercial business. These five factors, influenced and accompanied by the effects of workers' and sometimes passengers' campaigning, have determined the Underground's development.

A JOURNEY THROUGH TUBE HISTORY: 1863-1979

TIMELINE 1863 – 1979

1863: First London Underground journey, operated by the Metropolitan Railway from Bishop's Road, Paddington to Farringdon Street (3¾ miles).

1908: The various private companies agree to jointly promote their services as 'the Underground', with advertisements, a free publicity map and a logo that would evolve into the famous 'roundel'.

1921: Trade Facilities Act provides for government financial guarantees for private operators to promote employment.

1933: London Passenger Transport Act creates the London Passenger Transport Board (LPTB).

1937-48: New Works Programme.

1948: Nationalisation of the railways; control of London Underground passes to British Transport Commission (BTC).

1963: Control of LU passes to London Transport Board, appointed by Secretary of State.

1968: Victoria line opens.

1970: Control of LU passes to London Transport Executive, appointed by Greater London Council.

1977: Piccadilly line extended to Heathrow.

1979: Jubilee line opens.

† THE THATCHER AND MAJOR YEARS 1979-1997, page 6-11

The world's first railway to carry passengers underground did so for the first time on 10 January 1863. Thereafter, private companies built and operated several new lines, creating a railway web beneath London. From 1908, the companies began to jointly promote their services as 'the Underground'. In the 1920s, governments gave the companies financial support to improve services and create jobs, but the competing private owners nonetheless failed to provide a coherent and reliable service.

In 1929 Herbert Morrison, Minister of Transport in a minority Labour government, drafted a Bill to unite the Underground in public hands, later recalling that, 'Here was I, without a socialist majority, determined to go into some scheme of public ownership'.[4] He recommended that London's passenger transport should be run by 'a small board of business men of proved capacity', and that the dispossessed private owners should be paid compensation. Morrison's plan was implemented in 1933.† A new public corporation, the London Passenger Transport Board (LPTB), now ran London Underground. Previously separate 'railways' became 'lines' of a single London-wide Underground service: for example, the Central London Railway was now the Central line.

The chair of the LPTB was Lord Ashfield, until then leader of the Underground Group of private companies. In its first year, the LPTB's stockholders – mainly the former private owners – received dividends of nearly £5m.[5] Because of the continuing involvement of the private companies and their chiefs, some trade unionists and Labour left-wingers felt that Morrison's scheme fell short of the full public ownership and industrial democracy that they wanted.[6] Ernest Bevin, leader of the Transport and General Workers' Union called it 'positively the worst form of public control'.[7] By 1936, there were reports of a 'rising storm of protests' by passengers and a 'seething discontent' among workers about poor services and worsening conditions.[8]

Matters improved with the New Works Programme. From 1937, the Programme provided substantial new investment and created jobs at a time of high unemployment. It extended the Central, Northern, Piccadilly and Bakerloo lines, electrified the Metropolitan line north of Rickmansworth, and built new tunnels, stations and escalators. The programme slowed during the Second World War, but nonetheless led to

† The London Passenger Transport Act was passed under the 'National government', which had replaced the Labour government in 1931.

services running 18 per cent faster in 1947 than in 1933.[9] For transport writer Christian Wolmar, this period was 'undoubtedly the London Underground's heyday'.[10] For the first time, some degree of each of the five key factors – public *ownership*, London *control*, adequate *funding*, *integration* and *public service* – were all in place together.

London Underground was run by a London body until 1948, when Labour's first majority government brought the whole railway industry into public ownership. London Underground was placed within the new British Transport Commission. This new body prioritised reconstruction of the mainline railway and shelved unfinished parts of the New Works Programme. This 'nationalisation' meant that a *national* authority, rather than a London one, now had ownership and control of the Underground. Christian Wolmar wrote in 2002 that 'if any period could be identified as the source of the state of the Underground today, it is the immediate post-war period up to the 1960s when, quite literally, nothing was invested. The system has been playing catch-up since then'.[11]

After fifteen years of national control, the Underground returned to the control of London bodies from 1963, and investment began to grow again. The Victoria Line opened in 1968. In 1970, the new Greater London Council took over, and according to Underground worker Dave Welsh, 'It began to be possible to articulate a strategic policy for the tube with cheaper fares as the keystone'.[12] The 1970s saw the Jubilee line (originally named the Fleet line) built and the Piccadilly line extended to Heathrow airport, funded partly through government finance and partly through by the new London Transport authority (LT). But the second half of the 1970s saw real-terms public funding of London Transport fall off. Martin Eady, who worked at Ealing Common depot, explained that:

> by the back door the public expenditure cuts are having serious effects on tube workers and passengers.
>
> The cuts in capital spending mean not only that much-needed extensions are not built (remember the Fleet line extension, the River line, the Hackney-Chelsea line, etc.). Renewals of outworn rolling stock, decrepit station buildings and appalling staff facilities are held back, resulting in severe discomfort for passengers and staff alike. Many spare parts have to be robbed from one train to keep another in service, so repairs become make-do-and-mend jobs, especially on the older pre-war stock.[13]

Government – both London and national – was about to change hands, with dramatic consequences for London Underground.

THE THATCHER AND MAJOR YEARS: 1979-1997

TIMELINE 1979- 1997

1979: Conservatives win General Election; Margaret Thatcher becomes Prime Minister.

1981: Labour wins GLC election; Ken Livingstone becomes Leader; Fares Fair policy.

1984: Livingstone's GLC begins to remove guards from LU trains.

1984: London Regional Transport Act transfers control of LU to London Regional Transport.

1 April 1985: London Underground becomes a limited company, London Underground Ltd (LUL).

1986: Conservative government abolishes GLC.

18 November 1987: King's Cross fire; 31 deaths.

1991: Monopolies and Mergers Commission report on LUL.

1992: LUL Company Plan.

1993: LUL publishes plan for 'Decently Modern Metro'.

1993: Railways Act privatises British Rail.

1994: Prime Minister John Major appoints P&O Director Peter Ford as Chair of London Transport.

In the late 1970s a Conservative Greater London Council (GLC) faced a Labour national government. By the early 1980s these positions were reversed. The Conservatives under Margaret Thatcher began an offensive against local government, driving policies that starved it of reliable funding, and removing the control of London's transport by an administration accountable to Londoners. The network was divided up and sold piece by piece. Thatcher's government set about dismantling public ownership, control, funding, integration and a public service ethos: the factors that made for a healthy Tube.

In 1981, Ken Livingstone's Labour GLC brought in a hugely popular 'Fares Fair' policy, cutting bus and Tube ticket prices by a quarter, attracting many more passenger journeys[14] and easing London's road congestion. Conservative-run Bromley Borough Council asked the courts to declare the policy illegal. Failing at the first court hearing, Bromley council successfully appealed, and the Law Lords then deemed Fares Fair unlawful. The GLC acquiesced: fares doubled, passenger journeys fell dramatically, and congestion gripped the capital's roads once more.[15] The GLC planned cuts to services on most Underground lines, but backed down in the face of trade union opposition.[16]

Howard Collins, later Chief Operating Officer of London Underground Ltd, told me that he recalls:

We were on a trajectory to go bankrupt because central government weren't giving Ken [Livingstone] the money to bankroll this reduction in the farebox [revenue raised through ticket sales]. Loads of people were using it but we didn't have the investment cash, and the government had almost forced us into a position where we couldn't operate any more. We were literally tight for cash to pay people their wages. It became a big scrap, and that ended up with the government of the day deciding to abolish the GLC. It was quite a tough time.

Collins was then on the first rungs of the London Underground management ladder. He would go on to become a more senior manager and later a director, and would play a significant part in London Underground's story in the years that followed.

In 1984, the London Regional Transport Act took the Tube away from GLC control and gave it to London Regional Transport (LRT), a new quango appointed by the Secretary of State. Mike Brown, also a junior London Underground manager then but later a senior manager during the PPP years, told me he noticed a change:

Central government was in direct control, so you were going to be yelling at the same people who were going to fund you. You were at risk of one day yelling at someone 'give us more money' and the next day, thanking them and pleading with them and adopting a different style.

The Act required London Regional Transport to set up subsidiary companies for each element of the capital's public transport, one task of which was 'to involve the private sector in the provision of services'.[17] Labour transport spokesperson Robert Hughes MP described the new law as 'a prelude to the privatisation of what profitable parts may be extracted from London Transport'.[18] London Underground became London

Underground Limited and, though still publicly-owned, was expected to act like a private business. Paul, a station worker who joined the Underground in 1985, explains that:

> When I started, the cleaning was still done by uniformed staff and everyone worked in-house. The canteens were part of London Underground life, they were unionised, everyone was directly employed, everyone used the canteen facilities, they were renowned for reasonable quality food, very good price. But there was frustration because they were being run down. There was a big campaign organised by the NUR [National Union of Railwaymen, predecessor of RMT] against Compulsory Competitive Tendering of catering and cleaning. There was a workplace ballot: the union people came round with a ballot box. It was a big topic of discussion at work. Then it got privatised. The staff wore different aprons, and the food changed. You used to be able to buy a hot dinner or breakfast, but a lot of it now was being warmed up and was less appetising.

Compulsory Competitive Tendering was a Conservative government policy which required public bodies to invite private companies to bid to deliver services. London Transport disbanded its Works and Buildings Department, which had employed around 1,700 construction workers, and contracted private firms to take on its work. Paul describes how the Department worked:

> [It] would come to your station and fix things. They had a huge workshop at Parson's Green, like a small factory, plus remote workshops. People did apprenticeships there – I tried to get one – but it was wound down and had gone by the mid-80s. That now is all outsourced, all profits going out of the company for a much shoddier service. It was much better before: it could have been tightened up and perhaps it should have been, but it didn't need to be privatised to do that.

Government grants to London Transport shrivelled from £190m in 1984 to just £95m in 1987. Historian Philip Bagwell comments, 'The passengers, as well as the staff, were being made to feel the 'squeeze' as a result of the Thatcher government's starving an essential public service of necessary funds.'[19] The Tube was in a dire state. London Underground manager Howard Collins described:

> The things we put up with! If it rained on a Thursday, you couldn't use the telephone system to talk to anyone east of Tower Hill, because the telephone didn't work. There was radio of sorts on trains, but nothing on stations. I can remember when about a quarter of the Northern line fleet was out of service because it was awaiting spare parts and staff. No-one wanted to work for us because we didn't pay very well, the hours were difficult, the conditions were pretty poor.

Only the tragic deaths of 31 people in the fire at King's Cross station in 1987 made politicians consider the need to improve rather than neglect the Tube. London Underground shelved plans to cut station staffing, and QC Desmond Fennell's report into the fire[20] recommended 118 safety improvements.

Enter Denis Tunnicliffe, former pilot and British Airways manager, appointed Managing Director of London Underground Ltd in 1988 as a new broom to sweep the Tube clean. He told me that the London Underground he took over 'felt like a slum':

> You waded through litter, everywhere was dirty and graffitied. Between the end of the Second World War and the late '80s, essentially the Underground was 'decapitalised': you take assets and sweat them and you take value out of them by not looking after them or not replacing them. We needed a dramatic turnaround in investment to try and put that right.

Denis Tunnicliffe would preside over major changes to London Underground. Ten years later he would help devise the PPP. London Underground Ltd manager Mike Brown believes that the company's changes in response to the King's Cross fire 'transformed the place – it's almost unrecognisable from those days in the 1980s when safety was seen as almost something separate from the running of the place rather than as an integral part'. Conservatives often argue that only the private sector can bring about radical change. These transformations – made by the public sector – after the King's Cross fire show that this is not true.

In 1991, the Monopolies and Mergers Commission – a public body since replaced by the Competition Commission – produced a report[21] which damned 'an erratic, overcrowded and poorly maintained service' on the Underground and blamed, among other things, 'chronic underinvestment'. The report recommended more – and more stable – funding, and accused London Underground Ltd's management of not fighting the government hard enough for the money it needed. The government responded by increasing its grant to LUL by 60 per cent, but pledges of adequate funding for further years proved hollow. Just a year later, the government cut the grant from a promised £860m to just £562m.

Each November, the Secretary of State told London Transport what grant it would receive for the following financial year, a practice called 'annuality'. Mike Brown says:

> You couldn't have any kind of meaningful plan that you could implement. You ended up spending money on relatively small-scale, often cosmetic, improvements like decorating a station – which is important, you've got to have the place looking decent – but it was never going to sort out the fundamental pieces of kit on the system. Sometimes, you didn't even get the funding settlement until the start of the calendar year when the financial year finished in April, so you had to make assumptions about where you were going to spend money without knowing whether you had any or not.

The government tossed a yearly scrap to a hungry London Transport, enough to keep it alive but hardly healthy. The government demanded that London Underground Ltd cut costs. In a major reorganisation in 1992, called the Company Plan,[22] LUL slashed the workforce from 21,000 to 16,000 and made all staff sign a new contract. The Company Plan reduced planned maintenance in favour of mending things when they broke. The following year, LUL published a plan to become a 'Decently Modern Metro',[23] which promised that it could run without government grant within a decade. All it needed, it claimed, was enough government funding over that decade – but the government refused.

The Monopolies and Mergers Commission report recommended that London Underground allow more private companies to bid for work – perhaps not surprisingly, as the Commission's role was to investigate 'uncompetitive' practices in industry. But LUL itself did not necessarily see private-sector involvement as the way forward. Denis Tunnicliffe told MPs that:

> I cannot see a scenario where the private sector would be interested. I have had my talks with the private sector and I find them remarkably risk averse. They are in the business of getting a reward for their money and they want me to make warm statements about there not being a real risk and sign them.[24]

Managing Director Tunnicliffe opposed straightforward privatisation, but, however reluctantly, he followed the government's policy of inviting private companies into the Tube, using labour supply agencies, increasing contracting-out and adopting a 'Make or Buy' policy.[25] London Underground now embraced Private Finance Initiative (PFI) projects (something I explore further in the next section). Tunnicliffe told me, 'There was a general presumption by government for us to prove that we were as efficient as the private sector. It was a policy that was not credibly reversible. We tried to use that policy in as intelligent a way as possible.' He would return to this theme a few years later when drawing up the PPP.

By 1994 government funding was so low that London Underground Ltd restricted its plans to 'minimis[ing] risks from declining asset health by more inspection and repair'.[26] The Conservative Chancellor of the Exchequer from 1993 was Kenneth Clarke. Journalist Jonathan Prynn believed that Clarke was 'Part of the 'Midlands mafia' with little sympathy for London's commuters' and that he saw London Underground as 'an irritating begging bowl, almost the last of its kind in the public sector'. Prynn reported that Clarke's last Budget before the 1997 General Election 'slashed London Underground's subsidy', which came as a 'hammer blow' for the Tube.[27]

PRIVATE FINANCE INITIATIVE: 1992 ONWARDS

In November 1992, the Conservatives introduced a new policy for levering the private sector into public services: the Private Finance Initiative. Throughout the 1980s and into the '90s, Conservative governments sold great chunks of the public sector. Gas, water, electricity and telecommunications were privatised; state-owned companies, land and property were sold. The rail network was privatised and franchised, and competition was imposed in all public bodies through contracting-out. Private pensions, care homes and other services were encouraged. Private companies and shareholders made a fortune, while the state received £71bn.

But there were some public services that even the Conservatives could not simply sell. For these, they devised the Private Finance Initiative (PFI). Under PFI, a private company would take on the task of, say, constructing a public building, and the public sector would pay the private company a fee to lease back the building over several years. Conservatives argued that the private sector was more efficient, but most often fees paid to private companies were greater than their outlay. Private companies made profits while the public sector paid more.

The Treasury ruled that PFI payments were not to be included in the Public Sector Borrowing Requirement (PSBR). If the government had borrowed the money to pay for projects directly, that would count towards the PSBR, but PFI was not taken into account. PSBR limits were 'observed' and although measured by common sense, costs were rising, public spending was presented as being lower.

TABLE 1: PRIVATE FINANCE INITIATIVE PROJECTS ON LONDON UNDERGROUND

YEAR	PURPOSE	COMPANY	VALUE	DURATION
1995	Provide and maintain new Northern line trains	General Electric Company (GEC) plc /Alstom plc	£400m	20 years; option to extend for 16 further years
1998	Power supply	Seeboard Powerlink Ltd	£1bn	30 years; LUL exercised option to cancel after 15 years
1998	'Prestige' smartcard ticketing	TranSys consortium	£1bn	17 years; contract terminated early, August 2010
Announced 1998	Piccadilly line extension to Heathrow Terminal 5	British Airports Authority	£70m	Completed 2007
Contract 1999, operational from 2003	Accommodation for British Transport Police	AP Services Ltd	£13m	23 years
1999	'Connect': integrated radio system	Citylink consortium	£475m	21 years

MD Denis Tunnicliffe recalled to me that PFIs 'were all the rage at the time. We were under political pressure to do the PFIs, so we did the PFIs. It got us new trains, it got us new systems.' London Underground's first PFI project was for new Northern line trains, with depots at Morden and Golders Green transferred to Alstom plc's control along with their train maintenance staff. When it was signed, transport writers Tony Travers and Stephen Glaister described the contract as 'a good illustration of the benefits of competition in procurement'.[28] It did not turn out so well in practice: Christian Wolmar reported that in its first years, 'the contract worked badly and performance deteriorated'.[29] The new trains made their debut on 19 August 1998, more than a year late. Alstom plc took old trains out of service, but after the company cut back on staff, a backlog of work built up and many new trains remained in storage. Alstom plc borrowed engineers from the Bakerloo and Victoria Lines, with LUL paying the bill.[30] 40-year-old trains continued to run, while new trains repeatedly broke down. London newspaper the *Evening Standard* reported that, '[Northern line] General manager Wilben Short has been reduced to handing out apologetic leaflets rather than hailing a success.'[31] But however badly Alstom plc performed, the PPP contract set a limit – 'commercially confidential', but believed to be around £20m – on how much it would have to pay in compensation for its failure to deliver.[32] Train maintainer Kevin describes the difference that the PFI made:

When all underground staff were part of London Underground Ltd (LUL), we worked as a team and shared the same service. Now we have to make our own arrangements for jobs that need to be done around the depot and at our outstations ... Employing outside firms means we often have to haggle and work inevitably gets delayed ... once privatisation takes place on a wider scale, a huge range of jobs will be sub-contracted out. Corners will be cut to save money and we'll end up with shoddy work that takes ten times longer to complete.[33]

Further PFIs followed (see **TABLE 1**), with accompanying problems. The 'Connect' project was commissioned to install a modern radio system to enable communication between Underground staff across all locations and emergency services, but was repeatedly delayed. The 'Prestige' contract – to develop, install and maintain London's automated fare collection system including the Oyster card – was awarded to the TranSys consortium (an association of four companies: Cubic Transportation Systems, HP Enterprise Services, Fujitsu Limited and WS Atkins plc). The contract gave TranSys more money if it installed new machines quickly. It brought system failures. Howard Collins admitted that TranSys was 'always in a hurry to install them, even in cases where they may not be adequate'. New ticket barriers at Southgate station had to be removed and reinstalled because TranSys had placed them in an unsafe location.[34]

The biggest PFI project was the Jubilee Line Extension, which ran chaotically: late and over budget. Supporters and opponents of private-sector involvement in London Underground both cited the extension as a case which proved their point (see box below). While the Jubilee Line Extension was still mired in problems, the 1997 General Election was approaching.

JUBILEE LINE EXTENSION: 1992-1999 – PUBLIC OR PRIVATE FAULT?

The 9.93-mile Jubilee Line Extension (JLE) linked Westminster to the new business centre in Docklands, jumping the queue to be built ahead of other projects, such as the East London Line Extension, which would link working-class residential areas. Its construction was beset by delays, difficulties and a huge overspend. Conservative Transport Minister Steven Norris believed that 'The JLE convinced crypto-Tories like [Tony] Blair, who had always suspected that this was the case, that the public sector could not manage big projects and that in future they were going to have to get the private sector in'.[35] But an examination of the project's story suggests that it may have been private involvement that caused the project's problems.

The Conservative government insisted on private-sector involvement in extending the Jubilee line, and Olympia and York (O&Y) – the property company that was developing Canary Wharf in Docklands – agreed to contribute £400m. But in April 1992, when its first £40m instalment was due, O&Y was close to insolvency and six weeks later went into administration. The government put the JLE project on hold for eighteen months, a delay which Christian Wolmar claims cost more than the sum eventually obtained from the private sector.[36] The European Investment Bank gave some money to the project, and in October 1993, O&Y Properties Corporation emerged from the bankrupt O&Y. Its contribution, spread over 25 years, was now worth just £186m in real terms, meeting only 5 per cent of the

JLE's eventual bill.

Work on the Jubilee Line Extension was beset by technical difficulties. A noise ban restricted work at Canary Wharf; Big Ben shifted a little; a series of accidents slowed the job down; there were serious problems with tunnelling; contractors lodged £200m claims for extra work on design changes; a 100-tonne crane collapsed at Canning Town; the track had to be ground because the new trains' wheels did not fit; and problems with 'joining up' the line meant that the extension would open in three sections. Denis Tunnicliffe told me that London Underground 'simply didn't know how horrendously complicated and diverse the first two metres are when you go down in London. At London Bridge, we found a sewer that had to be suspended from girders. There was an enormous array of old material in the ground.'

The biggest technical hitch was the new 'moving block' signalling system supplied by private contractor Westinghouse Signals Ltd. With 'considerable technical difficulties' developing, engineers were redeployed to the JLE from the Central line, which was also suffering problems with a new Westinghouse Ltd signalling system. In February 1998, John Mills left his post as Chief Executive of Westinghouse, some saying he jumped, others that he was pushed.[37] Westinghouse admitted later that year that its signalling system would not be able to run on the whole Jubilee line. Wolmar contends that LUL 'could have sued Westinghouse and put them out of business over their failure, but it was felt that would not help ... progress the new line.'[38] Claims for the efficiency of private capital overlook the fact that when foul-ups happen the private sector has evaded responsibility and fails to pay compensation.

John Prescott admitted: 'London Transport was not to blame for the failure in the signalling system; it was the fault of a private company that did not live up to its contract to produce on time'.[39] Steven Norris blamed London Underground Ltd: 'they bought the idea of moving block signalling even though there was not a single example in the world where it was working in practice'.[40] By Norris's logic, if a shop sold you a new product that did not work, it would be your fault for buying it, not the shop's fault for selling it to you. Howard Collins says that it was the government's decision, not LUL's, to buy a new signalling system for the extended Jubilee line from Westinghouse Ltd rather than from, for example, Canadian company Alcatel, and believes that it may have chosen Westinghouse Ltd to help preserve the company's 3,000 jobs at Chippenham in Wiltshire.

London Underground Ltd put Collins in charge of delivering the JLE on time, now minus the new signalling system. He described the task to me as:

> like flying a balloon across the Sahara. Someone would say, 'We're losing height, throw out the ability to run an automated train service, and we can gain a bit of height and get a bit further'. Then we would start sinking again because the programme was running late, so throw out the decent accommodation and we'll make do with a few Portakabins.

The Jubilee Line Extension project was in so much trouble that London Transport paid top dollar to US firm Bechtel Corporation to crack the whip and according to Collins, it 'sort of wrestled it into submission and got it working'. Bechtel Corp. had a reputation as the 'SAS of the engineering world'.[41] It had also faced trouble with the US authorities for concealing cost overruns and avoiding safety controls at nuclear sites. Journalist Nick Cohen wrote that '[t]he salient features of Bechtel's record in the US are the lavish contributions to the campaign funds of politicians who can give it business and the hounding of whistle-blowers who complain about health and safety'.[42]

The Jubilee Line Extension would eventually open just in time for the new millennium, 21 months late and having cost £3.5bn, nearly double its initial estimate. Supporters of private finance blamed the public sector, but an LUL manager explained:

> it is not so much that the public sector were involved too much, it is the other way round ... We were always getting information off the contractors far too late, as they did not liaise with us and that meant a lot of the designs were wrong and there had to be expensive late changes. There were always communication difficulties, as I was not allowed to talk to subcontractors directly but only through contractors.[43]

Senior LUL managers took differing views, Mike Brown pointing the finger at the private sector, Howard Collins at both public and private, Denis Tunnicliffe describing both options as 'gross over-simplifications'. Tunnicliffe argued that, 'Broadly speaking, every cookie that could crumble, crumbled the wrong way', and cited poor contracts between LUL and the private firms as one of many problems. But Tunnicliffe was keen to point out that despite its overspend and lateness, the technical problems have since been corrected, and he described the JLE as 'the most transformational piece of construction to hit London in almost forty years'.

GENERAL ELECTION: MAY 1997

So far this chapter has surveyed the story of London Underground from its beginning in 1863 until the eve of the 1997 General Election. I contend that through this history, London Underground did best when five factors were in place: control by a London body; adequate and reliable funding; unified structures; a public service, rather than a commercial, approach; and public ownership. (Appendix 1 sets out in table form how these five factors varied at each stage in the Tube's history.) As the 1997 General Election approached, how was London Underground measuring up? It was no longer under the control of an elected London body; it was required to function as a commercial business; its funding was both low and unreliable; and it was not wholly unified, contracting-out and PFI having separated several parts from the rest. But London Underground Ltd – the 'core' business operating the train service and maintaining the infrastructure – was still owned by the public sector. Much of it was in a woeful state, starved of cash, crying out for new funding, for a new policy and direction. What were the policies on offer to improve the Tube?

The Conservatives sought re-election on a manifesto pledging to privatise the still publicly-owned London Underground Ltd. Transport Secretary George Young predicted that this policy would 'deliver a Tube that puts passengers first',[44] but admitted that 'uneconomic stations and services may face closure as part of the sale'.[45] A London Underground worker wrote:

What it will really mean we can see from the fate of British Rail: bidding-down of wages, conditions and jobs in a drive for private profit and a worse service ... The Tory plan means, in effect, a public subsidy paid straight into the pockets of profit-hungry private owners.[46]

Glenda Jackson, Labour's Shadow Transport Minister and MP for Hampstead and Highgate, predicted that, 'If the Tories get their way, images of fat cat controllers lapping up the cream while commuters face delays and cancellations will become as part of the Tube as they are of the railways. It is a desperate act from a government that has given up on public transport.'[47] Jackson cut a Tube map in two with giant scissors, declaring to the assembled media that Labour would not do this to London Underground as the Conservatives planned to. It was a theatrical performance from Oscar-winning former actor Jackson; perhaps she did not know then that her Party's leadership would go on to cut the Underground into three.

Labour's manifesto decried the Conservatives' privatisation policy as 'a poor deal for passenger and taxpayer alike', and promised instead 'a new public/private partnership to improve the Underground' and that it would 'retain London Underground in public ownership and give it the right to seek private finance for new investment'. It also pledged to restore a London-wide elected body, something lacking since the abolition of the Greater London Council. Labour produced a specific business manifesto, pledging to sell 'unwanted' state assets and take a 'tough stance' on public sector pay, spending and borrowing, and that 'public/private partnerships will play an increasing role in procuring public services and investment'. Tony Blair told a City audience that 'if you vote Labour you are getting a pro-business, pro-enterprise government'; Gerry Robinson, chairman of media conglomerate Granada Group, declared that 'business can do business with new Labour'.[48]

Which party did London Underground's managers and workers support? MD Denis Tunnicliffe was (and remains) a Labour Party member; but Howard Collins told me he voted LibDem, whilst Mike Brown said he does not remember which party he voted for. For London Underground workers, there seems to have been only one choice; everyone I spoke to voted Labour. Emergency response worker Tom said, 'there weren't really any alternatives for me. The only option was to vote Labour.' Bakerloo line driver Jock recalls that 'we'd gone through eighteen awful years of the Conservative Party who were anti-working-class and anti-trade-union, so I voted Labour in the hope that things might change for the better, be more progressive, with more rights for ordinary working people'.

On 1 May 1997, voters gave Labour a huge Parliamentary majority. In and around London the swing to Labour was higher than elsewhere.[49] The unpopularity of Conservative plans to privatise the Tube may have influenced many voters. London Underground staff, a workforce which from January 1997 included me, told of feeling 'elated' and 'relieved' at Labour's win, but nevertheless concerned. For Tom, 'Their victory felt really good. My children had never seen a Labour government – the Tories had been in for as long as I could remember, and they never knew any different. But I was concerned about what they were saying about privatisation, because I knew they were going the wrong way.' Trackworker Sam recounts that, 'When Labour got elected, people became more hopeful. There wasn't a huge euphoria, but people felt pretty much that we were going to be better off and that was probably going to be the end to any plans to sell off the Tube.' *Guardian* columnist Hugo Young pointed out that 'Tony Blair had two objectives during this election. The first was to win, the second to minimise every expectation of what would happen then'.[50]

The outgoing Conservative government had set London Underground Ltd's grant at starvation levels for the next three years: £650m for 1997/98; £310m for 1998/99 and £150m for 1999/2000. LUL had to find a further £280m because the government withdrew its commitment to fully fund the Jubilee Line Extension. LUL was so short of funds that it suspended plans to renew track and signalling, replace escalators and refurbish stations and trains. The incoming Labour government could have undone this budgeting, injected much-needed funding and started improvement works, but it did not. Labour's Chancellor of the Exchequer Gordon Brown pledged to stick to Conservative spending plans for two years after winning the election. Brown seemed determined to hold tight on the reins of public spending and to earn a reputation as an 'Iron Chancellor'. Denis Tunnicliffe told me he believed it was the Chancellor's stance, rather the cost overruns on the Jubilee Line Extension, that prompted Tony Blair to seek a private funding policy for the Tube.

'New Labour' embraced spending cuts and private finance. The party that fifty years earlier had nationalised the railway industry now announced the privatisation of London Underground infrastructure via the 'Public-Private Partnership'. John Prescott cheerfully admitted that he had 'long called for public-private partnerships to boost our transport system'.[51] The *Guardian*'s Victor Keegan described how he saw the Labour government leap into the arms of private finance: 'In opposition Labour's view was clear. PFI stank. In power Labour embraced it with evangelical fervour. Suddenly what had been backdoor privatisation became the Third Way.'[52]

PREPARING THE PRIVATE PLAN: 1997-1998

The new Labour government turned to business to devise the detail of its policy for public services. Paymaster General Geoffrey Robinson, a Labour MP and businessman with a personal fortune of around £30m, asked fellow businessman Malcolm Bates (see box page 22) immediately after the election win to conduct a speedy review of PFI, to streamline it and remove obstacles.[53] After Labour's election victory, some senior civil servants cleared their desks, but Robinson and Gordon Brown persuaded another one, Steve Robson, to stay at the Treasury and appointed him second permanent secretary. Robson had been the 'acknowledged privatisation guru' under the Conservatives in the 1980s and '90s,[54] and had largely designed the structure of British Rail privatisation. Journalist Jeremy Warner saw him as 'new Labour through and through, a sort of reformed Thatcherite – like Tony Blair, really ... he fits the new administration like hand in glove.'[55]

There was intense public interest in what Labour's new policy for London Underground might be – at least from that (significant) section of the public which travelled on it. Journalist Jonathan Prynn believed that 'Almost everyone who regularly uses the Underground has a view – usually strongly held – on what must be done to improve the service. The only consensus is that "they" must somehow find more money.'[56]

The government set up a working group on Tube funding in July 1997, including various government departments. The group excluded London Underground Ltd because the government 'considered [LUL's] presence would inhibit a frank exchange of views'.[57] Managing Director Denis Tunnicliffe did not have a 'strong sense' of LUL being marginalised by this exclusion: 'I felt we weren't as in charge as I had hoped we would be, but we felt fairly in charge. The PPP was developed in full consultation with myself and colleagues.'

The government also appointed professional services firm (and Labour Party donor[58]) Price Waterhouse Ltd to report on options for a London

Underground PPP. The government told it to consider several options, excluding both wholesale privatisation and complete public ownership. The criteria for assessing options were: improving passenger service; guaranteeing safety; reducing the investment backlog; attracting private investment; value for money; and contribution to an integrated transport policy.[59] London Underground Ltd also commissioned a report on options, hiring bankers Lazard Brothers Ltd and accountants KPMG Peat Marwick to carry out the task.[60] (KPMG was also a Labour donor, and later recommended the Labour Party contract-out its own membership services.[61]) The LUL-commissioned report, submitted to the government in September 1997, ranked sixteen options in order of preference. First choice was the current structure with more stable government funding and borrowing; second choice was full privatisation, favoured by London Transport Chair Peter Ford. The report ranked the two models that most closely resembled the eventual PPP at twelfth and fifteenth out of sixteen.[62] John Prescott had little time for London Underground's report: Ford claimed that the Deputy Prime Minister had not even read it, only 'sort of looked at it'.[63]

By November 1997, the *Evening Standard* was reporting that 'Ministers can not make up their minds what to do' about the Tube.[64] The working group discarded the option of a partial flotation (selling some shares on the stock market) due to 'lack of market interest', and also discarded public ownership because existing rules would not allow London Underground Ltd to borrow money and the government was unwilling to bend those rules.[65] The Labour government first tied its hands to disallow full public ownership and then ruled out public ownership claiming that its hands were tied!

Tensions emerged between Prescott's department and the Treasury, described by Jonathan Prynn as 'a fascinating struggle between Old Labour Transport and New Labour Treasury':

In the red corner, deputy Prime Minister John Prescott, with his trade union sympathies and private-sector suspicions. In the blue, the Treasury advisers and officials whose priority was getting shot of the crumbling and subsidy draining network. Enter Geoffrey Robinson, the Prime Minister's free-ranging trouble-shooter, to broker a deal.[66]

Robinson appointed a team of four businessmen to review the options (see box below). The team's deliberations led to John Prescott's announcement of the Public-Private Partnership on 20 March 1998. Prescott explained that 'Over the last 10 months, we have undertaken a thorough and careful analysis of all the options for developing the public-private partnership' and that he had taken advice from 'expert sources' including financial advisers.[67] Critics noted that this advice came not from Labour's rank and file, but from bankers and business managers, people with expertise and interest in profit-making rather than in public transport provision. Such was the background to Labour's new policy.

GEOFFREY ROBINSON'S TEAM

Malcolm Bates had been Deputy Managing Director of GEC plc, already involved in London Underground with the Northern Line PFI. The Conservative government had appointed Bates to its energy deregulation taskforce and Private Finance Panel.

John Roques was Chief Executive of accounting and consultancy firm Deloitte and Touche plc, and had been senior accounting adviser to the Conservative government on its privatisations of gas, water, electricity and coal.

Graham Hearne was Chairman of Enterprise Oil plc, the company created by the Conservative government in 1982 to run the oil exploration and production activities of British Gas in preparation for its privatisation. Hearne had been Chief Executive of Enterprise Oil plc from 1984, the year that the company was floated on the stock market, and became Chairman in 1991.

Ed Wallis was Chairman of Powergen plc, previously part of the publicly-owned Central Electricity Generating Board (CEGB). As CEGB's head of systems operations, Wallis had helped Margaret Thatcher to defeat the 1984/85 miners' strike by devising the strategy to minimise disruption of electricity supply. Acknowledging that this was 'the making of my career', Wallis went on to become 'One of the major players who helped guide the privatisation and liberalisation of the electricity industry in the 1990s.'[68]

The four were experts in privatising public services and had made gains from earlier privatisations. Between them, they were involved with several companies awarded contracts by the government. Bates and Wallis, having helped to conceive PPP, would go on to hold senior positions in London Transport.

PUBLIC-PRIVATE PROS AND CONS

We have arrived at March 1998, when Deputy Prime Minister John Prescott announced the Public-Private Partnership (PPP) policy. What was the detail of this policy?

The PPP would divide the Tube's infrastructure into three[†] contracts: firstly the Jubilee, Northern and Piccadilly lines (JNP); secondly the Bakerloo, Central and Victoria lines (BCV); and thirdly the Metropolitan, Hammersmith and City, Circle, District and East London lines. This third group was known as the 'sub-surface lines' (SSL) or 'sub-surface railway' (SSR), closer to the surface than the 'deep Tube' lines. Each of these three groups would become the responsibility of an infrastructure company, or 'Infraco', and leased to a private firm or consortium of firms. Initially planned for around fifteen years, the private sector later successfully lobbied the government to double the lease period to thirty years. The government expected the private companies to invest £7bn in improving the Tube's infrastructure. The publicly-owned London Underground Ltd would continue to operate trains, stations and signals, and would pay a fee – the Infrastructure Service Charge – to the Infracos. LUL would be the operating company, or 'Opsco', and would also collect revenue. LUL would retain freehold ownership of the infrastructure, and would regain ownership at the end of the contract. Several arguments were put forward for and against PPP: how did they stand up to scrutiny?

John Prescott told MPs, 'I am advised by people who should know that the new structure could result in considerable efficiency gains'[69] and Chancellor Gordon Brown claimed that the private sector could 'bring a wide range of managerial, commercial and creative skills to the provision of public services'.[70] But while the view that private companies would be more innovative, adept and efficient than public bodies was often asserted, it was rarely substantiated with evidence.

There were concerns that splitting the operation of the Underground's train service from the maintenance of its infrastructure – a division colloquially known as dividing 'wheel and steel' – might cause problems. London Underground Ltd itself did not support the separation of operations and infrastructure, its 1997 report arguing that it would 'reduce the seamlessness of the network ... [and] increase the risk of things going wrong at interfaces.' The Health and Safety Executive also cautioned that the potential loss of safety was greater the more the

† The number of contracts was not yet determined at the time of the announcement.

Tube's structure was subdivided. John Prescott claimed he had the endorsement of expert advisers when rejecting such concerns.[71] The Health and Safety Executive came round to the government's view that the 'horizontal split' between operations and infrastructure could be made to work safely,[72] and once the PPP was announced, LUL found itself supporting the structure. LUL's PPP Director Martin Callaghan[†]'s argument for dividing operations and infrastructure seemed to be how best to lure money rather than how best to run a railway: 'The bit of the railway which needed the money was the infrastructure and not the operations. So is it not obvious that the infrastructure is what you package up to try to get the money – and not the operations?'[73]

The House of Commons Transport Select Committee – an all-party body with a Labour majority, chaired by Labour MP Gwyneth Dunwoody – produce a report on the PPP plans,[74] which expressed concerned about potential friction between the public London Underground Ltd and the private Infracos. The government offered reassurance, telling the Committee that, 'The Minister of Transport hoped that in any disputes between the operating company and infrastructure provider(s), common sense would prevail'. The Committee retorted that its experience of the privatised national railway meant that it could not share the minister's optimism. It described the PPP as 'a convoluted compromise' and demanded that the government 'must demonstrate clearly that its proposals for the Partnership represent the best deal for passengers and taxpayers'. Dunwoody was MP for the railway town of Crewe and had a reputation for hard work, forthright speaking, and some willingness to dissent from her party in government when she thought it wrong. She led the Committee through dogged scrutiny to criticism of the PPP – criticism which ministers would foolishly disregard.

Critics of the Public-Private Partnership feared a repeat of the Conservatives' 1994 privatisation of British Rail. LUL's Mike Brown 'had difficulties with the way [British Rail] was split, and with the blame culture – the operator blaming the infrastructure and vice versa, which was just hopeless for passengers and those who worked in the industry'. Rail privatisation was perhaps the most unpopular of all the outgoing

---

† Callaghan had been an adviser to London Underground Ltd Managing Director Denis Tunnicliffe – who described him to me as 'one of the brightest people I've ever met' – and became PPP Director because LUL wanted him to progress from advising directors to making decisions.

Tory government's policies. Since privatisation, rail services had deteriorated, trains were running later and were dirtier, and the workforce was reduced and depended more on casual labour. Public subsidy and private profit both increased, and outrage greeted revelations of the lavish incomes of rail company directors. An editorial in London newspaper the *Evening Standard* described rail privatisation as 'an expensive, scandalous failure ... perhaps the biggest political scandal of the Nineties' and recommended that Prescott 'think very hard before introducing any form of privatisation for the London Underground'.[75] Bakerloo line driver Jock, who had worked on British Rail before joining the Underground, told me that he 'saw the splitting up of the BR Board into segments so they could hive it off to private companies, and saw with my own eyes the effect of fracturing the industry and the attack on the morale of the workers'. But the Department of the Environment, Transport and the Regions insisted that London Underground's PPP was different from British Rail privatisation in several respects: the public sector owned the freehold; there were no plans for competition between train operators; the public London Underground Ltd would operate signalling and be responsible for safety.[76] Prescott assured Parliament that: 'We are doing everything we can to avoid the mistakes which were made in previous privatisations and were the reasons why we rejected privatisation.'[77]

There were also fears about the cost of the PPP. Journalist Simon Jenkins wrote that 'Londoners will have to pay Danegeld to any private company reckless enough (or indemnified enough) to buy the Tube's stations and tunnels'.[78] Keith Bill of Save Our Railways, a campaign set up to oppose rail privatisation and which now monitored it, warned that 'Londoners had better beware, otherwise they will be taken for an expensive ride'.[79] MPs feared fare rises or service cuts to bridge any gap between LUL's income and its fees to the Infracos, and several passenger groups pointed out that London's Tube fares were already the highest in Europe. The Transport Select Committee suggested a cap on fare rises, but the government said no: fares would be the responsibility of the Mayor of London, a new post due to be elected in 2000.

Anthony Hilton, city editor of the *Evening Standard*, set out the attractions of the PPP and the rewards that might tempt private companies. He reminded readers that London Underground Ltd had turned itself into a profit-making body, and that five years had passed since the Company Plan had slashed jobs. The PPP's 'Infracos' could reap a cash reward:

> Potential bidders will therefore be thrilled to learn that next year's surplus should be bigger again while the year after, with the Jubilee Line operational, a £400 million margin could be achieved. The trick is to cut costs while at the same time finding ways to boost passenger numbers. ... The more prosperous the train operator [LUL] ... the more it can afford to pay for track access and rolling stock hire and therefore the more secure the infrastructure business. [80]

The Transport Select Committee criticised the PPP for failing to provide for new Underground lines or extensions to existing lines, and London Underground Ltd admitted that this was a 'weakness'. But the government responded that it would not be 'appropriate' to include this in the PPP, as extensions and new lines would be the responsibility of the Greater London Assembly, a new body that would be elected alongside the Mayor.

The Committee also considered the duration and number of infrastructure contracts. LUL argued that there could be no sensible cash flows in contracts below fifteen years, but little benefit beyond 25 years; the Committee's report concluded that, 'contract(s) should be no longer than fifteen years'. Railtrack plc – the private company that owned the national railways' infrastructure – argued for a 30 to 35-year contract, and also proposed that there should be a single infrastructure provider – itself, perhaps? In contrast, Brown and Root Ltd, part of a consortium intending to bid, argued for more than one contract, purportedly to allow the government to compare contractors and to 'avoid one dominant bidder deterring other bidders.' (Did it have Railtrack in mind perhaps?) Already, private companies seemed to be arguing for their particular – often antagonistic – interests.

THE ONLY FUNDING SHOW IN TOWN?

For Deputy Prime Minister John Prescott, the key merit of PPP was that it would 'secure long-term stability in the investment programme'. Prescott's 'expert advisers' had calculated that every £500m invested under PPP would deliver £600m benefit, 'simply through the better capital productivity of long-term planning'.[81] PPP's advocates repeatedly claimed that only private money could solve London Underground's problem of low and unreliable funding. But the government could also have chosen to provide adequate and stable public funding: this too could have undone the damage done by 'annuality'. But such an option was dismissed as impossible. The government said it was constrained by Treasury rules; in effect, the Treasury was running the government, rather than the government running the Treasury.

Supporters of public ownership cited international examples of funding underground railways, to show that public funding was a practical option:

- **Paris Metro**: public funding raised through a 'payroll tax' on employers
- **Hong Kong MTRC**: government funding, plus rights to develop property alongside stations
- **New York Metropolitan Transportation Authority**: from 1982, issued bonds (debt securities, similar to loans) secured by ticket and toll revenue, raising two-thirds of the $23bn spent on modernisation, the rest coming from direct government subsidy and fare income.

But there were also groups lobbying for more private sector involvement. Business lobby group London First published a pamphlet in September 1997 suggesting that private companies – the interests that it represented – should be franchised to provide maintenance services.[82] The Adam Smith Institute – a think-tank devoted to promoting 'libertarian and free market ideas' – published a pamphlet advocating awarding concessions (contracts to run Tube services as commercial operations) to private companies, highlighting the attractions of fare increases and staffing cuts.[83]

London Underground Ltd managers were, according to one report, 'deeply sceptical' about the anticipated PPP in the run-up to its announcement, fearing it would be 'time-consuming, costly and distracting'.[84] But once Prescott confirmed the PPP plan, LUL managers seemed to accept that it was the 'only show in town' when it came to fundraising for the Tube. Howard Collins told me:

Whether PPP was bad or good, the one thing it did was allow us to take away the fact that we were going to be a burden on the public sector borrowing bottom line. I sat in that room, believing that this was one way, the only way, that we could get the government to put their hands in their pockets for a long-term investment. We were cash-strapped, batted around from Tory to Labour, Labour to Tory, and we were further down the pecking order than many other public services in dire straits – education, the health service. We were told, whether we believed it or not, this was the only way forward.

Mike Brown told me that he:

> did get excited that there might be some glimmer of hope that it would give a proper, steady stream of funding. That was the fundamental reason why people went for it. People were told that there was a choice: you either continue with this annualised budget and you don't get any more certainty, you limp along, it'll be a fairly awful place to work and travel on; or you've got this potential – it may not be a perfect organisational model, but you do get a guaranteed steady stream of funding, which the government can't change its mind about.

MD Denis Tunnicliffe was more enthusiastic, describing the PPP to me as 'pretty perfect if you were going to have major involvement of the private sector with public money masquerading as private money in a way that satisfied the Treasury'. Moreover, he said, the PPP was 'enormously better than the alternatives – like privatising it line by line'. He might have preferred high and reliable public funding, 'but that wasn't a credible option at the time. The Labour government wasn't going to do it and no other government was going to do it. [PPP] was the right policy in the sense of being the policy that was practical politically, that was a deliverable policy.'

Denis Tunnicliffe briefed London Underground Ltd's top 150 managers about the PPP, and they then passed the message on. Howard Collins 'felt a sense of relief' at the PPP announcement as he, being a manager in the operational part of the company, would remain in the public sector. But Mike Brown was less pleased: 'It was hard for me to conceive of the operational engineering bit not being integrated with the operational delivery bit.' Whatever their reservations, managers conveyed their instructions. Brown remembers briefing his line's senior management:

> We'd all been given a piece of paper on what we had to brief. I couldn't quite see how it was going to work, because the split that I feared was going to happen was now going to happen, and it really did fill me with a sense of dread. We weren't asked to sell, it was given to us as a factual statement to communicate, then there were questions. A lot of my team felt the same way as I did. I responded as professionally as I could, but I don't think anyone could have been under any illusion as to how I felt.

Lifts and escalators engineer Ronnie told me of managers summoning him and his workmates to meetings:

> They might say now that they opposed it all along, but they weren't saying it then, not whatsoever. They were saying it was an opportunity to go forward and make more money in the private sector. Andie Harper [future head of JNP Infraco and later Chief Executive of Tube Lines] was the one who tried to sell it that it was really good, how wonderful it was going to be.

TIMELINE FEBRUARY-AUGUST 1998

13 February: RMT protest at John Prescott's office.

20 March: Prescott announces Public-Private Partnership.

21 April: Prescott sacks Peter Ford as Chair of London Transport; Ford receives 'golden handshake' of around £350,000; 'Perhaps', the *Evening Standard* speculates, 'the Government is looking for someone with more faith in its plans for partial privatisation of the Underground'.[87]

28 April: NOP opinion poll: 51 per cent prefer London Underground to remain publicly-owned, 30 per cent PPP, 13 per cent outright privatisation, 6 per cent don't know.[88]

30 April: Hundreds of Underground workers and others attend RMT lobby of Parliament; rally chaired by Christian Wolmar.

6 May: Mick Rix defeats Lew Adams in ASLEF General Secretary election.

15-16 June: RMT 48-hour strike.

12-13 July: RMT 24-hour strike.

15 July: House of Commons Transport Committee report on PPP. London Underground Ltd places a notice in the Official Journal of the European Communities.

16 July: 400 delegates from interested firms attend LUL's 'market sounding' conference at the Millennium Gloucester Hotel in South Kensington.

14 August: London Transport signs 'Prestige' PFI deal; London Underground's power supply transfers to Seeboard Powerlink Ltd under another PFI; the *Evening Standard* writes that together, these two deals 'mark the first stages of the Underground being sold'.[89]

London Transport Chairman Peter Ford 'welcomed' PPP and enthused to staff that 'These are exciting developments ... The future starts here.'[85] Tunnicliffe was confident that 'working together, we will make a success of the future'.[86] But did London Underground's staff share their employers' confidence?

WINNING OVER THE WORKERS? 1998

John Prescott argued that the Public-Private Partnership was 'like mortgaging. When you mortgage your house, the house still belongs to you but the bank will lend you money against the value of your house. When you have finished the payments, you get back the assets.'[90] But was the PPP the same as a mortgage? After all, when you mortgage your house, the bank does not move in, charge you for doing housework and redecorating, and employ one third of your family! This final section of chapter 1 looks at how the planned PPP would potentially affect London Under-ground workers and how they, and their trade unions, responded to the announcement.

Prescott wrote to all London Underground staff, setting out the structure of the PPP. One sentence alone referred to the PPP as 'new' three times, each underlined and in italics. While admitting that 'Of course it means change', Prescott did not mention that 5,000 infra-structure workers would transfer to private employers. He concluded, 'I know I can count on your support'. But could he? Train maintainer Jim Dickinson told how he and his workmates were 'rock-bottom devastated ... We're seen as the poor relations, we do all the dirty work and now we're going to be kicked in the teeth.'[91] Engineer Ronnie recalls that having expected Labour's election to spell the end of privatisation plans, 'Then we saw the news. You heard that you were being sold, that companies were bidding for you.' Even those staff who were to remain with the public London Underground Ltd saw the dangers of their workmates transferring to new employers. Driver Jock told me:

> It didn't matter what grade you were in, people were all unhappy with the proposal. They could see that once you start to break up the Tube along private lines, it would be salami-style tactics until your job had been hived off to the private sector. If you're a driver, you rely on properly-maintained track and signalling, you rely on station staff giving you support. We work as a team and support each other. We weren't going to allow ourselves to be isolated like that.

For some there was a sense of betrayal by the Labour Party. Tom was 'absolutely appalled' with Prescott: 'It was the biggest stab in the back ever. I genuinely believed, and still do, that he was selling out the people who made him what he is. It was the Labour Party turning on its own people and selling us down the road.'

London Underground workers looked to their trade unions to defend them. The unions had fended off LUL's threat to axe 200 station jobs in the wake of Kenneth Clarke's 1997 funding cut, and, in the run-up to the PPP's announcement, had battled to stop plans to sell London Underground's Railway Engineering Works at Acton. Known as 'Acton Works', this was the only purpose-built train overhaul and modification unit in the south-east. It had been maintaining Tube trains since the 1930s. The RMT trade union held two sizeable protests against the sale of Acton Works outside Prescott's office and named two strike dates. Prescott met a union delegation and then announced that the sale of Acton Works to private company Adtranz Ltd would not now go ahead. RMT claimed this as a boost for those who wanted to stop any privatisation, as 'Until now the privatisation juggernaut has seemed unstoppable',[92] but Acton Works would instead become part of whatever 'public-private' scheme Prescott devised. Underground workers did not wait for the detail of the scheme before beginning their protests against the PPP, and on 13 February 1998, a thousand RMT members and supporters protested outside Prescott's office at the Department of the

Environment, Transport and the Regions. When Prescott refused to meet a deputation, protesters sat down in the road and stopped the traffic.

Nearly all London Underground workers were members of one of four trade unions. In order of membership size, largest first, these were the Rail, Maritime and Transport Union (RMT), the Transport Salaried Staffs Association (TSSA), the Associated Society of Locomotive Engineers and Firemen (ASLEF) and the engineering confederation (Confed, or CSEU). RMT organised workers across all grades in the Tube's hundreds of work locations; TSSA was limited to clerical grades and some operational staff; ASLEF organised a majority of drivers, although a sizeable minority were RMT members; and a handful of engineering workers were members of the Confed, later to become part of Unite. When the government announced the PPP, RMT's General Secretary was an ailing Jimmy Knapp, with Vernon Hince and Bob Crow as Assistant General Secretaries. TSSA's leader was Richard Rosser, a 'new Labour' loyalist later rewarded with a seat in the Lords. TSSA opposed industrial action, and station staff members who joined it were often those who did not want to strike. ASLEF's General Secretary was Lew Adams, a 'close confidant' and 'friend' of Prescott's.[93]

TSSA responded to the PPP announcement by expressing 'serious concerns'.[94] ASLEF's Adams, though, wrote an article headlined 'Only private cash can stop the Tube going under', stating that 'As a union we cannot stand by and issue bland statements that LU must be both publicly-owned and fully paid for by the taxpayer. It is not going to happen ... Aslef [sic] will not play at ostrich and oppose a public private investment package.'[95] Adams acknowledged that 'not all in my own union will agree': true enough, as ASLEF members had not decided on this new policy of embracing private finance. In May 1998, ASLEF members voted to remove Lew Adams as the union's General Secretary and replace him with Mick Rix, a Leeds train driver who thus became the first of the so-called 'awkward squad' of new trade union leaders critical of 'new Labour' and its direction.† The shock result received wide media coverage, newspapers admitting that: 'Anger at Government reluctance to reverse rail privatisation and plans to bring the private sector into the London Underground appear to have been factors in the result'[96] and that Rix's win reflected a 'growing frustration with new Labour among

† More on Labour and trade union criticism of the New Labour's direction in the section CHANGING LABOUR'S MIND? in Chapter 2.

trade union members, who believe that Tony Blair has forgotten his traditional supporters'.[97] Rix did not take office until January 1999, giving Adams time to place an advertisement in labour movement newspaper *Tribune* welcoming the PPP[98] before he took up his new post with Virgin Trains as consultant to its Millennium Drivers Ltd.

RMT opposed the PPP policy, and favoured London Underground remaining in public ownership with increased public funding. Within a few months of Prescott's announcement, RMT (without the other trade unions) began the first round of strikes against PPP – or rather, against 'the effects of privatisation'. Legislation outlawed industrial action for political objectives and restricted union action to the pursuit of 'trade disputes'. RMT therefore concluded that it could not strike directly against PPP, and balloted members for action in support of six demands: one, staff to remain employees of London Transport; two, preservation of terms and conditions of employment; three, preservation of contracts with the current employer; four, opposition to splitting up current work; five, preservation of current disciplinary procedures; and six, preservation of the 'machinery of negotiation and consultation' – practices governing how unions and management negotiated with each other. After a 6:1 majority vote, RMT called a 48-hour strike in June 1998. On the second day, the *Guardian* reported that 'London Underground's claims that it was beating the Tube strike crumbled last night as services were cut, with some lines operating at only a third of normal schedules.'[99] Despite going it alone, RMT members felt that the action was worthwhile, one representative explaining that 'we were getting the campaign up and running, winning hearts and minds, letting the government and the company know that we were not taking this kind of privatisation lightly, that we were putting up a scrap about it. It provided leadership'.

RMT's Annual General Meeting (AGM) in June 1998 endorsed the union's campaign against the PPP. Delegate Diana Udall, a Central line driver, spoke in the debate: 'Glenda Jackson said she really didn't understand why we think we're being privatised. Does she think we're stupid?' The AGM also passed a resolution that 'Those [RMT-sponsored Labour MPs] who refuse to oppose this privatisation should have their sponsorship withdrawn forthwith.' John Prescott was angry but unmoved: 'I can not allow any doubt that such a resolution can be used to influence me ... if it is the union's intention to pursue this course of action I will have no qualms about resigning from the union.'[100]

A further, 24-hour RMT strike in July again saw significant disruption. Members of direct-action environmental campaign group 'Reclaim The Streets' showed their support for the strike by climbing on top of a Central line train at Bank station and unfurling a banner reading 'Private Profit at Public Expense'. Following the strike, a meeting of RMT workplace representatives agreed to put industrial action on hold, wanting time to develop the union's strategy and hoping that ASLEF's imminent change of leadership might see it join future action.

RMT protested outside while Paymaster General Geoffrey Robinson and Denis Tunnicliffe – now Chief Executive of London Transport – addressed a 'market sounding' conference in July 1998, described as 'the start of a six-month consultation programme on the public-private partnership'.[101] The government still believed that it could have the PPP in place by 2000. The following month, London Underground Ltd released the names of the hundred-plus organisations interested in bidding for PPP contracts. Noting that one of these was Porterbrook, a train leasing company whose directors became millionaires through British Rail privatisation, RMT General Secretary Jimmy Knapp said, 'The very fact that the fat-cat companies are bidding for the Tube is an indication that they see the taxpayer as milch cows'.[102]

It was now summer 1998. The Labour government had deliberated over its policy, announced its intentions, looked for support and encountered opposition. Now it had to develop its policy and prepare to implement it.

CHAPTER 2 – DEVELOPING AND IMPOSING PPP: 1998-2003

By summer 1998, the 'new Labour' government had set out its policy for London Underground – a Public-Private Partnership (PPP) – and had met some initial disagreement. It now needed to spend time developing the policy before implementing it: the contracts needed to be drawn up, the private infrastructure companies selected and London Underground's structures reorganised. Despite opposition from some quarters, the government seemed intent on sticking to its policy and proving its support for private business. The policy took five years to put in place, considerably longer than the two years originally intended. From 1998, opposition grew and the PPP's preparation was repeatedly delayed until it was finally imposed in 2003. During those five years, the Labour government disregarded calls to abandon its PPP plan and rejected alternative policies.

DISCONTENT AND DELAY: 1998-1999

TIMELINE: GROWING OPPOSITION TO PPP PLAN 1998-1999

1998

September: Campaign Against Tube Privatisation (CATP) launched.

19 October: CATP leaflets opening of Parliament.

12 November: Malcolm Bates begins second review of PFI.

13 November: CATP begins 48 hours of stalls and petitioning, 'Nightmare on London Underground'.

14 December: John Prescott tells Parliament that PPP will proceed but with no implementation deadline.

22 December: High Court injunction against RMT strikes on New Year's Eve and 3-4 January.

1999

18 January: Malcolm Bates appointed London Transport chair, on an annual salary of £80,000 for a two-day week.

5 February: RMT holds large protest at Prescott's office.

14 February: Start of RMT 48-hour strike.

15 February: Transfer of ticketing maintenance and repair staff to Cubic Transportation Systems under Prestige PFI.

15 March: LUL and government publish progress report on PPP and announce creation of PPP Arbiter.

30 March: Jimmy Knapp re-elected RMT General Secretary.

1 May: 'Reclaim The Streets' protest party on a Circle line train.

19 May: RMT members vote 2,184-70 against PPP.

15 June: Prescott announces 'prequalification' of bidders for BCV and JNP; and that Railtrack plc will work on proposals for SSR.

22 June: RMT, ASLEF and TSSA launch 'Listen to London' campaign.

3 August: Opinion poll commissioned by Listen to London: 66 per cent of Tube users want LUL to remain fully public; 78 per cent believe PPP will result in fare rises; 69 per cent believe Mayor/GLA should be in charge of LUL's funding.

9 October: CATP protest festival in Trafalgar Square.

In September 1998, the RMT trade union's London Transport Region launched the Campaign Against Tube Privatisation (CATP), hoping to encourage Londoners beyond its own ranks to join it in opposing the Public-Private Partnership. The Campaign's name reflected the union's assertion that despite Deputy Prime Minister John Prescott's denials, the PPP was a form of privatisation. The CATP gave out leaflets, held campaigning events, and by summer 1999 had attracted the support of members of nearly a hundred bodies: as well as Tube trade unions, these included 42 trade union branches outside the rail industry, eleven campaigning and passenger groups, eight Constituency Labour Parties and one University Labour Club, and eleven other political groups, mainly Greens and socialists. London Underground trackworker Sam remembers that:

> One of the first real highlights of the campaign against the PPP was a protest at John Prescott's office. There were loads of trackworkers there, and the Disabled People's Direct Action Network turned up as well, because they were campaigning for access to transport. It was great fun, it stopped the traffic, and we ended up with a police officer rolling around on the floor with one of our track-workers who was

trying to protect a protester from being cut free from her wheelchair which was chained to a bus. That got people interested. There was a high degree of interest from the workforce, and people were up for resisting it.

While campaigning against the PPP, RMT also sought protections for workers should the policy go ahead. It published a document, 'Putting People First: The London Underground Public Private Partnership and RMT's proposals for protecting staff', which asked for measures including: retaining working conditions; guarantees that there would be no compulsory redundancies and no subcontracting; and that negotiations between the unions and the employers would take place at councils involving the infrastructure companies (Infracos) and London Underground Ltd. John Prescott told RMT that he could not give the guarantees that the union wanted because working conditions were LUL's business, not his. LUL told the union that it could not give the guarantees because Prescott's policy tied its hands. RMT complained of 'being given the run-around between LUL and the Government'.[103]

Prescott noted trade union concerns in a statement to Parliament in December 1998. He also announced a 'very positive response' from 'a cross-section of bidders' for the PPP contracts, and that he had decided that there would be one Opsco (operating company, London Underground Ltd) and three Infracos (infrastructure companies) based on groups of lines.

Some 'indivisible resources' carried out their function for all of London Underground but could not be split between Infracos, so were each allocated to one Infraco, as follows:

- Transplant (engineering trains and plant): JNP
- Trackforce (track renewals): BCV
- Train Modification Unit: BCV
- Apprentice training: BCV
- Distribution Services: JNP
- Emergency Response Unit: JNP

TABLE 2 – THE THREE INFRACOS[104]

Infraco	Lines	Stations (Section 12 ie. below surface)	Lifts and Escalators	Trains	Track
Subsurface	District Metropolitan Hammersmith & City Circle East London	96 (32)	13 lifts 53 escalators	76 District 57 Metropolitan / East London 46 Circle / Hammersmith & City	366km
BCV	Bakerloo Central Victoria Waterloo & City	76 (51)	23 lifts 145 escalators	36 Bakerloo 85 Central 43 Victoria	298km
JNP	Jubilee Northern Piccadilly	100 (74)	65 lifts 207 escalators	59 Jubilee 106 Northern 87 Piccadilly	370km

With the government poised to invite companies to tender for Infraco contracts, RMT announced two 24-hour strikes, on New Year's Eve and the first working day in January 1999. London Underground Ltd applied for a court injunction banning the strike, and Justice Sullivan granted it, giving as one of his reasons 'the consequences of public disruption'.[105] RMT balloted its members for industrial action again, raising new demands: the contractual right to voluntary severance; no compulsory redundancies; and no employee to transfer to a new employer without his/her written consent. General Secretary Jimmy Knapp explained that 'I have no doubt that LUL's reluctance to introduce modern working conditions is linked to their plans to push through tube privatisation. LUL are terrified of deterring private bidders by introducing job security agreements.'[106]

2,489 RMT members voted to strike, just 436 against, and when talks broke down, RMT called a 48-hour strike stoppage starting on 14 February 1999. The union timed the action to coincide with the transfer of ticketing maintenance and repair staff to their new, private employer under the 'Prestige' Private Finance Initiative (PFI), but did not prevent the transfer going ahead. The strike saw the four busiest lines (Northern, Piccadilly, District and Central) reduced to less than half of their normal service.[107] It seemed that there was some public backing for RMT's action. The union reported that many members of the public phoned its headquarters to express support for the strike.[108] As I picketed with workmates, many passers-by congratulated us for taking a stand against the PPP policy, despite having their travel disrupted by the strike.

London Underground Ltd told RMT that there was 'no question' of it agreeing to the union's demands[109] and rejected them all. Despite this, RMT's national executive decided not to call further strikes and instead held a referendum asking members whether they supported PPP and London Underground's stance: 97 per cent voted 'no'. RMT members also voted in the election for the union's General Secretary, and re-elected Jimmy Knapp against rival Greg Tucker. The *Evening Standard* urged Tube workers to vote for Knapp, but admitted that many union members 'complain that Mr Knapp and Mr [Vernon] Hince should have been exerting more pressure on the Government to re-nationalise the [national rail] network and abandon the Tube privatisation plan'.[110]

Initially, the government intended that the PPP would operate from April 2000 – two years after its announcement. But this timetable for the beginning of PPP soon stalled: partly because of growing opposition and partly because of problems and flaws in the PPP plans themselves. In December 1998, John Prescott told Parliament that the PPP would proceed to its next stage but there would no longer be a deadline for its implementation. Prescott appointed Malcolm Bates – the businessman who had helped devise the PPP – as the new Chair of London Transport. Bates needed to soothe potential private bidders, who seemed to have concerns. The *Evening Standard* wrote:

> The [PPP] plan seems to have shuddered to an unscheduled stop, with private companies quaking at the prospect of taking on an antiquated system vulnerable to unexpected and highly costly disasters, without reassuring underwriting from the Government.

The private companies took up their concerns by lobbying heavily – and successfully – for changes to the PPP as it developed over the next few years. These changes minimised risk and maximised profitability for the private firms.

Critics of the PPP (for example, the Transport Select Committee, as described on pages 24-26) expressed concern that under the proposed set-up, the private Infracos and the public London Underground Ltd would come into conflict with each other. Addressing this concern, in March 1999 the government created a mechanism to mediate those conflicts. London Transport Minister Glenda Jackson announced the creation of the post of 'PPP Arbiter', a role lying 'somewhere between the arbitrator of a contractual dispute and a utility style regulator'.[111] Later the same month, government officials admitted that the PPP might not be in place until after the next General Election. But they also insisted that it remained on course, and one spokesperson even claimed that it was 'going well'.[112] Transport writer Tony Travers warned that PPP 'might not work at all. What the private sector would agree to sign up to would be unacceptable to the Government. What would be acceptable to the Government wouldn't make commercial sense to the companies.'[113]

The Labour government was discovering how hard it is to reconcile private companies' demands for guaranteed profits with workers' and passengers' desire for decent railway services with secure and satisfied staff. Sunday newspaper the *Observer* claimed that '[t]he DETR is struggling to find a formula for the partial sell-off that will attract private sector partners, mollify disgruntled staff, give value to the taxpayer and provide the estimated £7 billion needed to modernise the Tube over the next 15 years'.[114]

Doubts and dissent were growing, but the government was determined to defy them and press ahead with the PPP. This gave the private companies a powerful hand in shaping PPP's development to their benefit. Bidders cranked up the pressure to make the PPP contracts more favourable to them. One complained that, 'This is going to be a bloody expensive thing to bid for, bloody expensive'.[115] Another said that, 'If we don't have much information on the state of the Tube, we would be taking a big risk and would have to charge a high price'.[116] This was their solution: more guaranteed payments to the private companies.

In June 1999, Prescott invited bidders to 'prequalify', an assessment process designed to rule out unsuitable bids. There would be a competitive bidding process for the BCV and JNP Infracos, but not for the Sub-Surface lines. Instead, London Transport and Railtrack plc would explore the possibility of linking the national railway to these lines. This move spelled 'exciting new possibilities' for the Deputy Prime Minister, but others disagreed. The Capital Transport Campaign – a body set up at the time of the GLC's demise to promote safe, affordable and adequately-funded public transport in London – argued that 'Given Railtrack's inability to invest adequately in the surface rail network, the company is unlikely to deliver a decent modern metro system to London's long-suffering communities.' London Underground Ltd's operational managers were not keen either. Denis Tunnicliffe described it to me as 'an absolutely stupid, hare-brained scheme'. Howard Collins recalled that he:

> [tried] to operationally explain that this wasn't a good idea for London. There is a difference between running a mainline service and metro operations. There's a whole philosophy about managing the service, the speed of response, and there were many things about the mainline railway which didn't have that sense of urgency of delivering the service. You would lose focus and attention.

WHERE DOES THE MONEY COME FROM?

The process of developing the PPP continued, and it raised questions about sources of funding.

Evening Standard transport correspondent Dick Murray claimed that PPP was 'a realistic funding policy' to raise the £7bn finance for renewing and improving the Tube.[117] PPP's advocates often used the term 'raising finance' as though this came at no cost. But the PPP looked more like 'raising' money in the manner you might 'raise' some desperately needed cash from a loan shark, not 'raising' money in the manner of a charity coffee morning.

'Funding' and 'finance' are different: funding refers to the *source* of the money, finance to *how* it is obtained. Thus, arguments about how (and by whom) the money is raised miss a more basic point – where the money actually comes from. Whatever financing method the government uses, funds for London Underground come overwhelmingly from two sources: fares and (local or national) government grant. Money may come *through* the private sector, but it does not come *from* the private sector. It comes from fare-payers and tax-payers. With a near-negligible income from other sources such as advertising revenue and rent, London Transport's funding already fell heavily on its fare-paying passengers, as this comparison with New York and Paris in 1998 shows.[118]

TABLE 2 – SOURCES OF METRO FUNDING: LONDON, NEW YORK, PARIS 1998

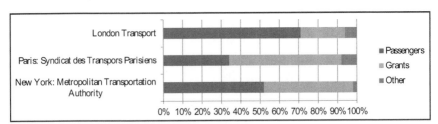

Deputy Prime Minister John Prescott had claimed that the PPP could make London Underground self-financing, that it was 'a sound business that could pay its own way'.[119] But if no money came to London Underground from the government, then all funding bar the single-figure percentage from minor 'other' sources must come from fares. Over the previous decade, London Underground's government grant had shrunk and its fares had risen by more than twice the inflation rate. Removing the grant altogether would be unprecedented: no European capital city funded its underground railway solely through fares. It was also a surprising policy from a Labour government which claimed to support public transport. So it was perhaps to be expected that the government would backtrack on this claim, and Glenda Jackson told MPs in early 1999 that 'Our aim is to avoid paying further grant if possible, but that is not a prerequisite of concluding the PPP'.[120]

The trade unions also entered the debate about funding and finance, through their 'Listen to London' initiative. In June 1999, unions RMT, ASLEF and TSSA held a rally against PPP and launched 'Listen to London' to lobby against the PPP and for public ownership of London Underground. 'Listen to London' commissioned reports, held fringe meetings at conferences and vigorously canvassed MPs and other 'opinion formers'. Its emphasis was heavily on research and lobbying, less on organising public protests.

'Listen to London' asked accountants Chantrey Vellacott DFK to analyse the relative cost of public and private financing for the Tube. The accountants calculated that public funding was the much cheaper option: where the private sector demands a 12 per cent annual return, the public sector could borrow at 4.5 per cent.[121] So it would cost the public sector £11.7bn to borrow the £7bn required, but would cost the private sector £19.6bn. Overlooking direct government spending – under which £7bn would cost £7bn – this still showed that public sector financing would cost nearly £8bn less. John Prescott dismissed Chantrey Vellacott's analysis as 'flawed'.[122]

The following year (2000), another report commissioned by 'Listen to London' claimed that the government had exaggerated the level of investment that PPP could secure:

> Of the £8 billion which is required for capital investment in the network over the next 15 years, LU estimates that **only £2.5 billion will be raised as private finance, while the rest will come directly from fares revenue and would therefore be available even without recourse to private finance.**[123]

London Underground Ltd's own sums showed that with the remaining £5.5bn (70 per cent) having to come from fares, there would need to be a 40 per cent real-terms rise in revenue from passengers. So either 40 per cent more journeys were to be made, for which London Underground did not have capacity (especially as the PPP did not provide for new lines or extensions), or there would have to be big fare rises, which may deter passengers and therefore not achieve the rise in revenue needed, or a government subsidy would have to fill the funding gap. The Infrastructure Service Charge (ISC) would rise whether fares revenue rose or not. So if revenue fell, perhaps due to a recession or fear of Tube travel following a terrorist attack, London Underground Ltd would still have to pay the increasing ISC, leaving it short of funds for its own operations.

By the time PPP began, it was clear that at least £6bn of the investment needed would have to come from the public sector. In the first 7½-year Review Period, 45 per cent of finance would come from the government, 30 per cent from fares and just 25 per cent from the private sector.[124] Even that 25 per cent would eventually have to be paid back to the private sector by either fare-payers or tax-payers.

TIMELINE: FROM SHADOW RUNNING TO BEST AND FINAL OFFERS, 1999-2001

1999

19 September: Shadow Running begins.

5 October: Paddington crash.

7 October: Shortlist of bidders announced.

30 November: Government announces Railtrack plc will no longer bid for Sub-surface Infraco.

2000

24 March: £65m funding injection due to escalator problems.

1 April: Infraco JNP contract takes effect.

4 May: Mayor and GLA election.

21 July: 100 demonstrate outside Prescott's office.

28 July: 600 attend rally against PPP.

18 August: Leaked letter from Railway Inspectorate to LUL warns that Shadow Running raises 'safety issues with potentially serious consequences'.

25 September: Hutton report published.

9 October: Bob Kiley appointed Commissioner of Transport for London.

17 October: Hatfield crash.

11 November: Labour Party Greater London Region votes to oppose the PPP.

13 November: Parliament debates a Conservative Party motion criticising PPP.

20 November: BCV/JNP bidders submit 'Best and Final Offers'; LUL rejects them.

6 December: GLA votes to both oppose and formally scrutinise the PPP.

13 December: Kiley report published.

15 December: National Audit Office report published.

2001

5 January: BCV/JNP bidders resubmit Best and Final Offers.

5 February: Metronet, LINC and Tube Lines submit BAFOs for sub-surface lines.

SHADOW RUNNING: FROM SEPTEMBER 1999

Part of the preparation and development of the PPP was to test it in practice. This was done through 'Shadow Running', begun in September 1999. London Underground adopted the organisational structure it would have under PPP, forming the Infracos in preparation for them being transferred to whichever private companies or consortia won the bidding competitions. LUL divided its infrastructure work into three sections – BCV, JNP and SSL. Each section became an entity separate from the operating company, London Underground Ltd, and operated as though it were the separate business it would become under the PPP. For the Underground's engineering workers, Shadow Running meant being separated from each other. Trackworker Sam explained that, 'We were aware that a wedge was being driven between us. It felt like we were being carved up and we were losing.' Lifts and escalators engineer Ronnie added:

> They announced we were splitting, that they were going to move you into some sort of Infraco, according to where you worked. I worked on the Piccadilly line, so I was JNP. There were management meetings: managers were coming out, some of them were shaking their heads. They were just told to deal with it, they weren't sure themselves what was going on, they were just reporting and handing over bits of paper.

Shadow Running caused problems for London Underground operations too. Bakerloo driver Jock explains:

> Everything slowed down, in terms of getting things fixed. You'd bring up an issue with a fault on the track, and where things used to get sorted out, things gradually seized up – especially with infrastructure issues because they were trying to cut costs, to make things look good for any possible private company to take over. Shadow Running was a mess.

Shadow Running was intended to test the PPP in practice, so this experience might have convinced the government not to go ahead with the PPP. But they continued despite managers' own misgivings. Jock recalls managers telling him privately that Shadow Running exposed PPP's flaws: 'They were banging their heads on brick walls as well. Some of them would say at high-level meetings, this isn't working. But they would be told to shut up, it's the only show in town, we just have to get on with it.'

Mike Brown recounted to me the doubts he had:

Everyone was very clear that the risk transfer, the responsibility – commercially, financially, operationally – would shift to these big consortia, but I just couldn't see how that would work in practice, because the whole presentation of London Underground, the way the world sees us, was going to become just this little Opsco, Operating Company. A lot of the debate we thought was interesting and useful, but the simple reality was that the London Transport Board had been directed by the government to make this happen. So all those comments and input the Directors were making were dismissed as a little bit of noise rather than being dealt with substantially.

PERFORMANCE SPECIFICATION AND COMPLEX CONTRACTS, 1999-2001

The PPP needed a regime checking the Infracos' work, and ensuring that the Infracos were rewarded for meeting the standards expected from them or penalised for falling short. This was called the 'performance specification',[125] and it had a very unusual feature: it was 'output based'. This meant that London Underground could not tell the Infracos what work to do. It could not ask for signalling upgrades, track improvements or new trains. Instead, the Infracos would decide what work to do, and the performance specification would judge them according to various outcomes for passengers, such as their journey time. The idea was 'to give maximum freedom for Infracos' and to 'increase the scope for innovation and flexibility'.[126]

To measure outputs, the PPP's performance specification created categories such as capability, availability, ambience, assets and systems, and fault rectification, and set standards for each of these categories. What did these terms mean, and how were they to be measured?[127]

'**Capability**' was average journey time. This was a passenger's time on the platform plus time on the train. The regime also considered 'consistency' and 'control', aiming to encourage journey times to be steady and reliable.

'**Availability**' was time cost to passengers by delays caused by the Infracos, measured in 'lost customer hours'. Christian Wolmar wrote that 'There is no other contract in the world which has attempted to measure the output and, therefore, the payment levels through such an indirect concept as "lost customer hours".'[128]

'Ambience' was the 'quality of the customer environment', including cleanliness, graffiti, condition of train seating and litter. It was measured by 'mystery shopper surveys': anonymous informants hired to travel London Underground reporting on what they saw. But this system would not incentivise the Infracos to refurbish specific stations, so the PPP allowed London Underground to order them to do so. 'Output-based' specifications could not work for station refurbishments, so an input-based system was used instead.

Similarly, **'assets and systems'** and **'fault rectification'** could not be measured on outcomes, so they too reverted to the more common input-based system: London Underground would tell the Infracos what standards it expected.

Infraco performance in all these areas would be measured against **benchmarks**. If performance exceeded a benchmark, the Infraco would have a bonus added to the payment it received; if performance fell short of the benchmark, an **'abatement'** would be deducted from the payment. For example, the cost to an Infraco of a 'lost customer hour' varied between three bands. Normally, it cost £3 (5p per minute), but if it took the Infraco to a 'poor' performance level, it cost £5.76 (9.6p per minute), and to a 'bad' or unsatisfactory level, £8.84 (14.4p per minute).

The benchmarks were eventually set 5 per cent *below* existing performance levels, so that an Infraco could allow London Underground's services to deteriorate and then earn a bonus for exceeding the benchmark that had been re-set at a lower level! The *Evening Standard* wrote that the government was 'offering private bidders an amazingly generous deal'; the situation was 'scandalous', and if LUL were not allowed to raise money in a different way, through bonds (see **GLOSSARY**), then, 'the disparity between the two sides of the partnership will be like that between the honeymoon limousine and the tin can – with passengers in the tin can'.[129]

There were some services that London Underground Ltd needed from the Infracos where the measures itemised above could not capture inadequate performance. So the PPP ran a system of **'Service Points'**. An Infraco would incur Service Points for failing to fix faults on time, make assets available or achieve target mystery shopper survey scores at individual stations (the Ambience regime dealt only with averages). Each Service Point would cost the Infraco a £50 abatement. 'Service Points' and 'abatements' may sound like 'failures' and 'penalties', but PPP's designers were keen to avoid such punitive-sounding terms. LUL's PPP Director, Martin Callaghan, explained that: 'we invented this word, service points, to get away from the concept of deficiency but it is the same thing'.[130]

TfL described the performance regime as 'replete with terms that are generous to the Infracos'.[131] Two examples illustrate this. Firstly, when trains were tested, the Infracos could exclude up to 40 per cent of their fleet, ensuring that only the best trains were assessed. Secondly, while an Infraco was supposed to receive a £50 abatement (reduction in the fees it was paid) for each Service Point it incurred, it would only be penalised if the number of Service Points exceeded a certain threshold in each four-week period: if the number of Service Points were lower that this threshold, there would be no abatement. This threshold rose during negotiations and was eventually set at a very high level: 40,000 for one Infraco and 30,000 for each of the other two. This meant that the Infracos could make 100,000 mistakes in four weeks without losing any money: equivalent to a waiver of over £5m per month.

The performance specification needed a mechanism for establishing whether an Infraco was to blame for a fault or delay. If London Underground and an Infraco disagreed as to blame, they would have to resolve the disagreement through a process of up to ten steps. LUL estimated the annual cost of this 'fault attribution' process at £677,114.73.[132] Transport writer Tony Travers believed that the PPP's contractual relationships were so complex that it would be 'virtually impossible' to attribute responsibility, with the consequence that 'Everyone ... will end up blaming everyone else'.[133]

The performance specification also needed to address a further issue. What was to stop the Infracos buying, building or maintaining assets in a way that was cheapest for them during PPP's lifetime only for those assets to break down when the contracts ended? The answer was to set **'defined asset condition targets'**.

In an unusual twist, the performance specification addressed the possibility of an Infraco carrying out no improvements to its part of the Underground's infrastructure. What was to stop it only maintaining performance at current levels, knowing that its fees would keep coming in? The document listed seven factors that should deter an Infraco from doing this, but it seems odd that a PPP designed to improve the Tube technically allowed for the Tube not to be improved at all.

As part of Shadow Running, the draft PPP contracts took effect on 1 April 2000. At this stage, they were contracts between one part of London Underground (the Opsco) and another (the Infraco). Although this was the 'start date' of the contract, its 30-year term would run instead from the 'transfer date', the as-yet-undetermined future date on which the successful private bidder took over. Even at the start date, the draft contract was a massive and complex document, the summary alone running to 92 pages.[134] The contract included five Codes, seven Agreements† and five schedules, each with several sub-sections. It covered every aspect of the relationship between separate organisations, from intellectual property rights to the requirement to share information.

The contracts set out how London Underground's operational property, such as stations, would be administered. Each station would be leased to the relevant Infraco, but as LUL needed to use stations to run its service, it would take them back as a sublease. LUL explained that this **'lease and lease back property arrangement'** 'serves the purpose of administrative ease'. LUL had primary access rights to stations and track during 'traffic hours', the times when trains ran; the Infracos during 'engineering hours' at night. An **Access Code** set out the terms on which either party could obtain access outside its hours. Each Infraco would be entitled to a 'base allocation' of minor closures (defined as 'disruptive access during traffic hours, such as closure of a station at a weekend'). It would have to agree with LUL any extra disruptive access.

London Underground Ltd would pay the Infracos a fee, called the **Infrastructure Service Charge** (ISC). A bonus would be added to the ISC payment when the Infraco exceeded a performance benchmark and an abatement would be deducted when the Infraco's performance fell short. LUL and the Infracos would agree the ISC between them, and the figure would be reviewed at regular points during the contracts. It was eventually decided that these **Periodic Reviews** would take place every 7½ years, dividing the 30-year contracts into four Review Periods. At a

---

† Access Code; Property Code; Standards Code; Performance Measurement Code; Risk Management and Insurance Code; Safety Agreement; Dispute Resolution Agreement; Insurance Agreement; Codes Accession Agreement; Inter-Infraco Assets and Facilities Agreement; ERU [Emergency Response Unit] Agreement; Framework Agreement

Periodic Review, LUL could restate, and perhaps revise, what it required from the Infracos. LUL had to give each Infraco at least one year's notice of its proposals for the next Review Period, and the Infraco would then notify LUL of the ISC it felt it should be paid to meet these obligations. If LUL and an Infraco could not agree – and it was surely optimistic to expect them to – the PPP Arbiter would set the ISC. The rules specified that the ISC must be set at a level which did not penalise an Infraco for making excess profit and which ensured that it made its anticipated return. If it wanted its ISC fee to increase, an Infraco could request an Extraordinary Review between the regular Periodic Reviews; the Arbiter explained that this would 'allow charges to be modified ... if Infracos experience cost shocks outside their control'.[135] There was no similar protection for London Underground Ltd from 'cost shocks'.

The contract stated that London Underground Ltd could 'sack' an Infraco if it breached the contract *materially* or *persistently*. If this happened, LUL would issue a 90-day warning. If the problem were not resolved within that time, LUL would issue a mandatory sale notice. If the Infraco could not find a buyer within twelve months, LUL would take over the sale process. If there were still no acceptable buyer a year later, the contract would transfer to a subsidiary of LUL. So even in the case of grave private-sector failure, the road back to public ownership would be long.

There was no provision for TfL or London Underground Ltd to terminate a contract if it were in the public interest to do so, despite such a clause being standard in PFI contracts. The government claimed that LUL gave up this right so that the private companies did not increase their prices because of political uncertainty. However, LUL confessed that it had asked for the 'public interest termination' clause to be included, but the Infracos refused.[136] Metronet's Rod Hoare (see page 77) argued that there was no need for a public interest termination clause because 'everything we do is in the public interest'.[137]

By November 2001, the draft PPP contracts involved 135 separate documents, over 2,800 pages and 2 million words. One set of contracts alone filled ten single-drawer filing cabinets.[138] London Underground Ltd would sign contracts with each of the three Infracos, who would each sign contracts with each other, with their consortium members, their banks and with subcontractors.

The contracts' specifications were complex from the outset, and became more so as the parties picked over the detail. The contracts defined what constitutes litter: anything less than the width of a Tube ticket did not qualify. The *Daily Telegraph* commented, 'So one dropped ticket would count as litter, but 100 tickets torn into pieces would not.' The contracts required measurement of the amount of chewing gum on station walls, and of the relative importance of dirt depending on its location. PPP's 'output-based' contracts had to measure those outputs using bafflingly complex formulae. Literally thousands of measurements had to be input into mathematical formulae such as this measurement of train ambience:[139]

$$TMS = \sum_{j} \left(\frac{QATAS_j \times W_j^T}{\Sigma_j W_j^T + \Sigma_k W_k^T} \right) + \sum_{k} \left(\frac{QATAS_k \times W_k^T}{\Sigma_j W_j^T + \Sigma_k W_k^T} \right)$$

Critics saw the PPP's complexity as one of its greatest flaws. That complexity arose not through coincidence or carelessness, but because dividing up London Underground into different companies meant dividing up the money.

DISRUPTION, DISASTERS ... AND A SHORTLIST: 1999-2002

So far, we have seen the preparations for the PPP proceed through Shadow Running, prequalification of companies bidding to run the Infracos, and the development of specifications and contracts. The PPP was encountering criticism for its cost and its complexity. Meanwhile, the Tube continued to face operating problems, and the national railway experienced tragedy. What could these events tell us about the best policy for the Tube, and would the government learn those lessons or plough on regardless?

During the summer of 1999, the Circle line and the Northern line's City branch both closed for nine weeks for essential repair work. Tube passengers suffered daily disruptions on other lines too. On just one day (8 July), the eastern end of the Central line shut after a defective train damaged signals; a Northern line signal and points fault caused 'horrendous problems' and the Piccadilly line was disrupted when a broken axle hanging off a train smashed twenty trainstops (track-mounted devices which stop a train if it passes a red signal). 1999 also saw London Underground take dozens of escalators out of service and close some stations, after discovering that it had no spare parts to replace

cracked drive shafts.[140] Were these problems a reason to proceed
promptly with PPP, or a reason to abandon it and revisit public funding?

When Denis Tunnicliffe was appointed as Chief Executive of London
Transport, Derek Smith came in as London Underground's new
Managing Director and Chairman. Smith was previously chief executive
of King's College Hospital, where he had been 'a proponent of the Private
Finance Initiative'.[141] During the 1999 summer of his passengers'
discontent, Smith asked them to 'stick with us', pleading that, 'I've no
wish to make excuses, but what *other* industry has had to make do with
so little for so long?'[142] LUL hoped that an additional £517m grant,
announced in July, would tide it over until PPP brought new funds, but
the London Chamber of Commerce derided it as a 'sticking plaster for an
ailing patient'.[143] The *Evening Standard*'s Rowan Moore wrote that public
concern about transport was 'not some perennial gripe like those about
the weather or English cricket, but a real, well-informed sense of crisis',
and predicted that 'The cost of the PPP will inevitably be passed on to
the public, who will also experience the joys of a Tube in multiple
ownership.' It seemed that the PPP policy was not popular. The
Independent on Sunday noted that, 'It is difficult to find many people who
support the concept [of PPP], apart from the companies which may profit
from it.'[144]

Then on 5 October 1999, a tragic event shook public confidence in
both rail privatisation and the London Underground PPP. At 8.11am, a
Great Western train approaching London's Paddington station crashed
into a Thames train on its way out of the station. Fire engulfed Carriage
H of the Great Western train, with temperatures exceeding 1,200C,
melting all the tables and chairs. 31 people died, including both drivers.
The Thames Train had crossed a red signal because the driver could not
see that the signal was red. Drivers had complained about the sighting
problem previously, but the signal had not been moved to a clearer
position. The drivers' trade union ASLEF released minutes of a meeting
showing that Railtrack plc had been asked to look at signal sighting in the
Paddington area and that 'signalling irregularities' had been rising.[145]
The *Observer* revealed 'Railtrack's catalogue of neglect': on the day of the
crash, government ministers had received a Health and Safety Executive
report accusing Railtrack plc of 'lack of depth and technical soundness'
in safety standards; 'lack of strategic safety research', a 'biased view of
priorities' and not drawing safety lessons from previous incidents.[146]

The crash might not have occurred if the trains had used the Automatic Train Protection (ATP) system, which stops trains that pass red signals. The official report into the 1988 Clapham crash – in which 35 people died – recommended ATP be installed across the railway network, but the (then Conservative) government chose not to order this, on the grounds of cost. In 1999, Great Western's annual operating profit stood at £25m, Railtrack plc's at £442m, and ATP was still not being used. Stan Davison of the Capital Transport Campaign berated the private railway companies:

> The only reason they could possibly have for not implementing safety measures is money. Anything that makes inroads into their profit margins leads them to make judgments on maintaining profits at the level they want and they are doing it at the expense of safety.[147]

The disaster made Underground workers nervous. Jock explains that:

> On the Bakerloo line, we run on a section of national rail track. After the Paddington crash, drivers felt more concerned running on the national rail section because the crash showed the dangers inherent in how things were operating up there. Most Tube drivers like to drive in open [non-tunnel] sections, because you get some daylight and fresh air, but one of our drivers said he felt that after that, he preferred driving in the tunnel: it was like safety in the womb.

The government was due to announce the shortlisted bidders for the London Underground PPP Infraco contracts on the day of the Paddington crash. In the wake of the disaster, it postponed the announcement, but by only two days. Anger greeted the decision to name the shortlist so soon: Ken Livingstone – former Greater London Council leader and now Labour MP for Brent East – called the decision 'extraordinary', RMT's Bob Crow labelled it an 'absolute disgrace', and the *Evening Standard* predicted that it was 'certain to cause outrage', especially as the bodies of the dead still lay in the wreckage at Paddington.[148] There was particular concern that Amey plc – the contractor responsible for the signals and track in the Paddington area – was part of a consortium shortlisted for the JNP Infraco. Jonathan Bray of Save Our Railways said:

The Paddington crash raises huge concerns about the safety of the privatised overground railways. Surely the whole question of the Tube could have been put on hold until we are absolutely sure that safety on the Underground will not be compromised.[149]

Around a dozen consortia had sought to prequalify for the 'deep Tube' (BCV and JNP) contracts. Five succeeded, and became the shortlisted bidders. One – NewMetro, comprising Taylor Woodrow, Siemens and Mott MacDonald – withdrew a few months later, leaving four in the running. London Underground reassured the public that 'no bidder will be awarded a public-private partnership contract unless they show a genuine commitment to safety'.[150] But their records gave cause for concern (see box below).

THE SHORTLISTED BIDDERS

LINC was a consortium of the following companies:

John Mowlem & Co had been a partner in the UK Detention Services group building and running private prisons. It sold its shares in that consortium in 1996, a year in which five prison inmates died in HMP Blakenhurst. In 1999, a subsidiary company, Barclay Mowlem Construction, was fined $175,000 for failing to ensure workers' safety at an Australian railway station. One worker had suffered severe head injuries causing brain damage when struck by an electrical wire from overhead pylons.[151]

Fluor Daniel and others were fined $110,000 after an explosion at the Hanford nuclear facility in 1997, having stored chemicals incorrectly, ordered workers to walk through a toxic plume, and not scrutinised radiological tests until a month after the incident.[152]

Ken Livingstone condemned **Alcatel** for 'operation in several oppressive regimes including Indonesia; number 17 on the 1996 list of the top-40 worldwide defence production companies'.

By 1997, **Anglian Water**'s prices had risen since privatisation by 40.8 per cent in real terms, its bills £70 higher than the national average. Anglian had been convicted for pollution 31 times since 1989/90. In 1998/99, it lost 201 megalitres of water per day in leakage.[153]

Bombardier Incorporated had a $710m contract to supply trains to the US railway service Amtrak. But Amtrak complained that the trains were unreliable and plagued with problems, and accused Bombardier

Inc of a 'staggering record of failure'.[154]

METRONET was also a consortium, formed from:

Adtranz Ltd. The company had failed to deliver new trains for the Central line on time. In 2000, the Turbostar trains it supplied to Scotrail suffered breakdowns, causing a quarter of the 24-train fleet to be out of service at any time.[155]

Balfour Beatty plc. It was fined £1.2m over a 1994 tunnel collapse at Heathrow; fined £500,000 following the derailment of a freight train in Essex in 1997; and found guilty of failing to ensure the safety of seven workers killed during the Channel Tunnel's construction.[156]

WS Atkins Consultants Ltd, owned by Atkins plc. In 1998 it had advised Thames Trains not to fit Automatic Train Protection (ATP). The Paddington crash inquiry heard that Atkins Consultants Ltd's cost-benefit analysis made errors and assumptions that skewed the findings towards rejecting ATP.[157]

In 1998, **Thames Water plc** let raw sewage and chemicals pollute the River Thames, flooding some homes, leaving most unfit to live in. In 1998/99, the company leaked a daily 770 megalitres of water, and received 40,000+ written complaints, both the highest of any water firm.[158]

SEEBOARD plc was fined £4,000 after a worker received a shock from an 11,000-volt live line in April 1999. Friends of the Earth rated SEEBOARD plc as having the worst commitment to renewable energy.[159]

TUBE LINES was a consortium of:

Bechtel Corp, the 'troubleshooter' brought in to rescue the Jubilee Line Extension (see box on pages 14-17) and **Amey plc,** the contractor responsible for signalling in the Paddington area (see pages 52-53).

Hyder plc was fined £50,000 in 1999 after an electrician lost both arms following a 33,000-volt shock from cables to which the company 'forgot' to attach warning signs.[160]

Jarvis Fastline was fined £500,000 after two freight train derailments in 1999; and was fined £7,000 after a contractor lost an eye.[161]

This book has already mentioned **Alstom plc**'s shortcomings on its Northern line PFI contract (see page 13).

TUBERAIL was a consortium of the following companies:

Brown and Root Ltd paid £750m compensation for its mismanagement of the South Texas Nuclear Project. In 1993, it was involved in a corruption scandal, with twelve people jailed for colluding to obtain a $173m Taiwan sewage works contract at an artificially high price.[162]

AMEC plc was part of a consortium contracted to build a 474-bed Carlisle hospital. It claimed £1.5m extra; when refused, it proposed a smaller hospital with 90 fewer beds. Refused again, it crammed the 474 beds into the smaller space, making it 'clinically unworkable'.[163]

Carillion plc formed as the construction and facilities management business of **Tarmac Group Ltd**; the two 'demerged' in 1999. Tarmac Ltd engaged workers as 'labour-only subcontractors' and paid no sick pay. It supplied materials to the Newbury bypass and built the M3 extension through Twyford Down, opposed by environmental campaigners.[164]

Ken Livingstone commissioned the Ethical Consumer Research Association to report on the bidder firms. When he announced the findings, Livingstone described the firms as 'Companies that have presided over the deaths of their workers, companies that have polluted our water supply, taken risks and supplied arms to oppressive regimes ... the worst scum of capitalism.'[165]

The government confirmed Railtrack plc as the sole bidder for the Sub-Surface Infraco despite its involvement in the Paddington crash. ASLEF commented that this news 'sends a shudder up the spine of the rail unions', and that the public would want Railtrack plc 'to keep its sticky fingers off the Tube'.[166] The trade unions' 'Listen to London' campaign urged people to lobby against Railtrack plc's uncontested bid for the Sub-Surface Infraco, and in November 1999, the government scrapped the plan. The PPP would now be delayed again, to allow other bids to come forward. PPP was wounded, but it soldiered on.

One year after the Paddington disaster, there was another fatal rail crash. On 17 October 2000, a train shattered a rail near Hatfield, derailing and killing four people. Railtrack plc was in charge of the track, and Balfour Beatty plc was its main contractor in the area. The previous December, workers had reported wear and tear, but repairs were delayed by an argument about which company would pay for them. Railtrack plc and Balfour Beatty plc eventually had to pay £13.5m fines for breaching safety regulations at Hatfield, although charges of corporate manslaughter were dropped. While Railtrack plc was no longer bidding to take over Tube maintenance, Balfour Beatty plc remained a partner in the shortlisted Metronet consortium. Critics of PPP pointed out that the Hatfield crash was caused by the division of the railway into rival companies and that this remained a main feature of the PPP.

In May 2002, seven people died and 76 suffered injury when a train derailed going over a set of points and ploughed into the platform at Potters Bar station in Hertfordshire. Private contractor Jarvis plc, responsible for the points in the area, briefed journalists that the crash may have been caused by vandalism or sabotage. But it was not. Nuts were missing from the points; the Health and Safety Executive blamed management failure and logged 83 faults at the points involved. London Underground Station Supervisor Paul recalls talking to LU points engineers at Hyde Park Corner station: 'they were concerned because the same sort of problem might happen when PPP came in on London Underground, because the same bosses that had tolerated that at Potters Bar would be looking after them. I remember the looks in their eyes about it.'

A CASE FOR SAFETY? 2000-2002

These tragic national railway crashes raised concerns over the possible effects of the PPP on Tube safety. There were other causes for concern too. In August 2000, BBC TV's Newsnight received a leaked letter from the Railway Inspectorate to London Underground Ltd, warning that Shadow Running had raised 'safety issues with potentially serious consequences' and that: 'the inspectorate … does not have full confidence in London Underground systems since Shadow Running commenced.'[167] LUL reassured passengers that, 'The safety of our customers and staff was our overriding priority before Shadow Running began, continues to be our overriding priority now and will remain so in future'. John Prescott echoed this, saying: 'Should people feel concerned? No. There's proper and adequately high levels of safety.' But nonetheless, he ordered London Underground Ltd and the Health and Safety Executive to meet.[168]

The Transport Select Committee expressed concern that the PPP might cause 'blurring of lines of responsibility which could lead to reduced safety standards'. It worried that while 71 per cent of London Underground's standards were 'mandatory' and would remain in LUL control, the Infracos were not obliged to co-operate with each other over the 29 per cent under their control. Moreover, an Infraco could be temporarily exempted from mandatory standards, which the Committee feared could create the 'potential for contractual abuse'. A leaked memo from LUL's Chief Engineer to its senior managers warned of a 'deterioration in control over fire safety' unless the PPP management structure changed.[169] *Guardian* transport editor Keith Harper wrote in December 2000 that 'London Underground is becoming less safe and more secretive as it moves falteringly towards the private/public partnership that John Prescott intends unleashing on the travelling public.' Harper wrote that, 'Hardly a day goes by without incidents on the Tube, from signalling failures to escalator breakdowns and train cancellations', and predicted that an upcoming Health and Safety Executive (HSE) report 'could sound the death-knell for the [PPP] project'.[170] But Underground workers' own representatives did not share Harper's expectations of the HSE. RMT health and safety representative Brian Munro wrote in reply to Harper that the HSE's Railway Inspectorate was employed by the government that was pushing PPP and that it would 'in effect be writing the very Safety Case it is supposed to be approving'. The Railway Inspectorate had also accepted Railtrack plc's Safety Case, 'the one that was in operation during the Paddington and Hatfield rail crashes.'[171]

A Safety Case is a document that a railway company is legally required to produce to show how it will meet safety standards in any policy it is pursuing. London Underground Ltd and the Railway Inspectorate laboured for many months to draft a document that would demonstrate that the PPP would work safely. An RMT representative told me that in his view, the Safety Case consultation was 'entirely skewed and geared towards PPP coming in at any cost'. He described the process: 'During the Safety Case consultation, we saw the dividing up of the assets – a huge big job of work: who owns what bit of kit, every single bit of signal, every single bit of wiring, every single lightbulb, every single switch. It was a complete and utter waste of time and resources.'

In January 2001, HSE principal inspector Peter Horton described PPP safety plans as 'inadequate and misleading'. The HSE wrote again to LUL the next month, itemising 69 outstanding safety concerns and in March, published a report identifying 204 further pressing issues.[172] When LUL held a 'stakeholder meeting' about safety, the Capital Transport

Campaign complained that:

> the atmosphere generated by London Underground at this meeting
> was inhospitable to the expression of genuine concerns about safety
> and in some respects intimidating; this approach is hard to reconcile
> with London Underground's frequently repeated mantra that safety is
> their top priority.[173]

In May 2002, when his task was nearly complete, Martin Brown left
his post as the Health and Safety Executive official in charge of the PPP
Safety Case to become the new safety chief at Tube Lines. When the HSE
approved the Safety Case, Brown's former employer (the HSE) was giving
the go-ahead to his new one (Tube Lines) to proceed with its role in the
PPP. For critics, this reinforced suspicions that the Health and Safety
Executive and the employers were not as independent of each other as
they were supposed to be.

THE MAYOR AND THE ASSEMBLY: 2000

I have argued that London Underground's history shows that it does best
when it is under the control of an elected London body. But there had
been no elected body covering all of London since the abolition of the
Greater London Council in 1986.

In May 2000, the first elections were held for the new Greater London
Authority, which consisted of a directly-elected Mayor of London and a
25-seat Greater London Assembly (the abbreviation GLA is used for both
the Authority and the Assembly). The Labour government created the
new body under the Greater London Authority Act 1999, after a
referendum of Londoners approved the proposal. The Act gave the
Authority a lead strategic role in London's economy, housing, policing,
transport, planning, environment, culture and health improvement. The
responsibilities rested with the Mayor, and the Assembly's role was to
scrutinise and hold the Mayor to account. The Mayor would appoint
members to three bodies to run three of the key responsibilities:
transport, policing, and fire and emergency planning. The new body to
run the capital's transport was Transport for London (TfL).

Policy for London Underground was a major theme in the election.
Londoners used public transport one-third more often than people in the
rest of the country, and used trains – including the Underground – more

than twice as much.[174] An opinion poll the previous year saw 59 per cent of Londoners name transport issues as the single most important for the new Mayor to tackle, with a near-unanimous 93 per cent naming transport among the Mayor's priorities.[175] As the election approached, the BBC explained that 'The future of the capital's ailing [London Underground] network is a key issue in the race to be London mayor'.[176]

The Conservatives' original candidate for Mayor was Jeffrey Archer, who said that if elected, he would repudiate the PPP. But when he was caught lying in a libel case, the Conservatives replaced him with Steven Norris, former Transport Secretary and future Chairman of Jarvis plc, part of the Tube Lines consortium that was bidding for the PPP contracts. The Conservatives' policy remained that London Underground should be fully privatised; for this election, they added a sweetener of free shares for staff, Londoners and season ticket holders. The Liberal Democrats' candidate was banker Susan Kramer, and their policy was to retain the Tube in public hands and raise funds through a bond issue.[177] The LibDems added 'against Tube sell-off' to their party name on the ballot paper, hoping to win votes from PPP's unpopularity.

Former GLC leader Ken Livingstone wanted to be Labour's candidate, and stated that he would 'never budge' from opposing PPP.[178] Livingstone's criticisms of PPP, together with his reputation as a left-winger and a maverick, convinced Labour's leadership that it must prevent him becoming the party's candidate. Livingstone's rivals to be Labour's candidate for Mayor were Glenda Jackson and Holborn and St Pancras MP Frank Dobson. The party hierarchy went to extraordinary lengths to ensure that Dobson, the one it trusted to defend PPP, became the candidate. A selection panel interviewed the hopefuls, and demanded a 'loyalty oath' to abide by party policy in their manifestos, plus a specific pledge to not seriously depart from party transport policy. All the aspiring candidates agreed. Ken Livingstone argued that since John Prescott had pledged not to proceed with the PPP if it proved a bad deal for London, his stance fell within party policy. A more telling argument might have been that since Labour's members had never voted to endorse PPP, it was not properly party policy. Livingstone told reporters that he 'would swear an oath of loyalty on the bones of a saint or pull a sword from a stone if [he] had to.'[179]

Labour's National Executive created an 'electoral college' to decide who would be the party's candidate, with votes counted from three categories: one-third party members; one-third Labour MPs, Euro-MPs and GLA candidates; and one-third affiliated bodies, including trade unions. In practice, an MP's vote was worth more than 450 times a Labour party member's vote.[180] Party officials found pretexts to disallow the votes of RMT, ASLEF and other trade unions whose members had voted in union ballots to back Livingstone, while leaders of a few unions – such as the AEEU, which had members in the Tube's Confed – cast block votes for Dobson without balloting their members. When the result was announced, over 70,000 votes had been cast for Livingstone, around 20,000 for Dobson – but Dobson had won!

Livingstone challenged Labour to drop the PPP, but the party's leaders did not. When Dobson declared himself 'not dogmatic' about Tube funding, Labour's leadership told him that it would not let him change the PPP policy.[181] So in March, Livingstone announced that he would stand for Mayor of London as an independent candidate. Many welcomed this move, with RMT and ASLEF pledging support despite their Labour affiliation. One RMT representative explained to me that 'We saw Livingstone as somebody who campaigned against PPP. If Dobson had got elected as Mayor, he would have continued to drive the PPP process through and given it political authority as the Mayor.'

Labour Party officials filtered prospective GLA candidates through a 'loyalty commission' which weeded out 136 of the 230 who applied, including those who opposed the PPP. Some RMT members stood in the election for the Assembly under the banner of the Campaign Against Tube Privatisation; others backed the newly-formed London Socialist Alliance.

Voters went to the polls on 4 May 2000, and Ken Livingstone won the election for Mayor convincingly, with 776,427 votes in the final round to Norris' 564,137. Dobson trailed in third with 223,884 first-preference votes, Kramer fourth with 203,452. Labour and the Conservatives each won nine of the Greater London Assembly's 25 seats, the LibDems four and the Greens three. The London Socialist Alliance polled 1.6 per cent of the vote, the Campaign Against Tube Privatisation 1 per cent.

Although the Mayor and GLA were now in place, Transport for London did not yet run London Underground, as the government had ruled that it would not take over until the PPP was in place. Until then, London Transport still ran the Underground. In the arguments to come, the similar naming of these bodies could cause confusion, so for clarity: London Transport and London Underground Ltd belonged to the government and supported the PPP; and TfL belonged to Livingstone and supported his opposition to the PPP.

CRITICS AND ALTERNATIVES

The Economist contended that, 'Since the argument over the underground was central to the mayoral election, Mr Livingstone's decisive victory looked like a vote against the government's [PPP] plan.'[182] Opinion polls gave similar results. A poll in November 2000[183] suggested that most Londoners seemed concerned about their Underground system and attentive to the government's policy: 81 per cent travelled by Tube, 45 per cent doing at least once a week; and 71 per cent were aware of the PPP policy. More than twice as many Londoners (53 per cent) opposed the PPP as supported it (23 per cent). Moreover, the majority thought that key aspects of London Underground would worsen under PPP: over twice as many thought that Tube safety would deteriorate (42 per cent) rather than improve (19 per cent); more thought services would become less reliable (38 per cent) than more reliable (24 per cent); and nearly three times as many though it would provide worse value for money for passengers (47 per cent) than better value (16 per cent). Support for the PPP had fallen significantly from the 30 per cent who backed it a month after its announcement (see **TIMELINE FEBRUARY-AUGUST 1998** pages 29-30).

London public opinion was increasingly against the PPP. But who was articulating opposition, what were they doing, and what alternatives were they proposing? It is useful at this point to summarise who was saying and doing what.

The Conservative Party opposed the PPP and instead advocated the wholesale privatisation of London Underground. The Liberal Democrats opposed the PPP and stated that they wished the Underground to remain publicly-owned, proposing to issue bonds to raise funds. Both parties had seen their candidates lose the election for Mayor of London, and both would modify their policies before the next General Election in 2001, as will be seen in the section **A Resignation, a Deal and a General Election: 2001** (see page 78). On 13 November 2000, Parliament defeated a Conservative motion criticising PPP. In the debate, Labour MP Stephen Pound condemned 'the sheer brass neck and utter effrontery of the Conservative party which ... suddenly appears to be the champion of the tube passenger'; Liberal Democrat Tom Brake called PPP a 'poll tax on wheels'; and Ken Livingstone (who remained an MP as well as being Mayor) condemned the government's failure to act on Londoners' wishes.

Livingstone had previously advocated a tax on business and the City to fund Tube improvements, but by 1999, was instead proposing a bond issue, which he described as 'the internationally tried and tested method of funding capital expenditure on public transport'.[184] Chancellor Gordon Brown dismissed bonds as 'not cost effective', while Frank Dobson called the idea 'pie in the sky'.[185] London Transport Minister Keith Hill said that a bond issue would not, unlike the PPP, bring in managerial expertise.[186]

The trade union movement opposed the PPP. The Trade Union Congress passed a resolution condemning the policy in 2000. The largest union on London Underground, RMT, had taken strike action, and would go on to take further action. ASLEF opposed the PPP but had not yet taken industrial action – it would do so in 2001 (see **TALKING AND STRIKING 2001** pages 71-77). Smaller unions TSSA and the Confed/AEEU opposed the PPP but did not take industrial action against it at any stage. RMT, ASLEF and TSSA jointly formed the 'Listen to London' lobbying group. RMT's London Transport Region organised protests, and initiated the Campaign Against Tube Privatisation (CATP) in order to involve those beyond its own membership who supported its stance. The CATP told supporters that 'Unpopularity is, in itself, not enough to stop the Government's assault on the Tube. We need to mobilise and to step up the action.'[187] Protest activity brought trade unionists into contact – and thereby into alliance – with activist groups such as Reclaim The Streets (see pages 34, 36) and the Disabled People's Direct Action Network (see page 36). A further example was the campaign against the Ilisu Dam, a Turkish government project that threatened to make thousands of Kurdish people homeless and in which Balfour Beatty plc – part of the Metronet consortium bidding for the PPP contracts – was involved. Opposition to Balfour Beatty plc's activities brought campaigners on both issues onto protests together.

The unions' alternative to the PPP was that London Underground should remain publicly-owned, with public funding and public accountability. A CATP petition demanded that 'The whole of the tube service should be in public ownership and should be made democratically accountable to the workers and passengers. We call on the Government to increase investment by the amount necessary to provide an affordable, safe, good quality tube system, funded by progressive taxation on the wealthiest in society.' However, as the proposal for a bond issue gained more attention, the unions appeared willing to accept it, as at least it would keep the Tube in public ownership.

Several of the foremost transport academics and writers opposed the PPP. Christian Wolmar called the policy 'an expensive mess, a reduction in accountability, an apparent black hole for taxpayers' money and few benefits for passengers',[188] and berated the government for refusing to consider alternatives.[189] However, while Wolmar chaired a trade union rally against the PPP in 1998, he criticised strike action against it in 2001.[190] Tony Travers, Stephen Glaister and Rosemary Scanlon published a paper describing PPP as 'flawed in principle, and impracticable'[191] and argued that 'an alternative option of funding Underground investments by way of a bond issue is preferable, with project management and construction work being undertaken by the private sector'.[192]

The Transport Select Committee of MPs examined the PPP in depth at various stages of its development, and every time found fault with it. Its criticisms became more strident.

The press also had its opinions on the PPP. When Christian Wolmar looked back through his five-year file of press clippings just before PPP was introduced, he found that 'there is barely an article which supports the concept unequivocally. And even those that give qualified approval can be counted on the fingers of both hands. The PPP is a credo in which only a minority, even among its evangelists, believes.'[193]

As a daily London newspaper often read during Tube journeys, the *Evening Standard* had the most extensive – and probably the most opinionated – coverage. Its opinion changed over time, perhaps reflecting its readers' increasing opposition to the policy. In 1999, the PPP was a 'realistic funding policy'[194] that would 'improve and update London's Tube';[195] in September 2000 the terms of the PPP contracts were 'scandalous';[196] and by July 2001, the *Standard* was running an online petition against the PPP.[197]

It seemed that even some of those who helped to conceive the PPP were having doubts. Johns Hawksworth, head of the macroeconomics unit at PricewaterhouseCoopers Ltd, the professional services firm whose report had prompted the choice of the PPP policy, said in 2000 that the contracts would be difficult to enforce and risks likely to rebound on the public sector, concluding that the case for the PPP was 'more a matter of faith than science'.[198]

We can see that there was a large body of opinion doubting and opposing the PPP. We can also see that different sections of the opposition offered different alternative policies – ranging from full public ownership with public funding raised through progressive taxation, through public ownership with borrowing, through alternative schemes of private-sector involvement, to outright privatisation. There were perhaps two types of critics of the Tube PPP. The first (including the trade unions) objected on the basis that any form of private-sector involvement brought the profit motive into a public service and therefore would prioritise profit over safety and service standards. The second (including the Conservative Party and some transport experts) objected to the particular structure and detail of the government's proposed PPP for London Underground, but did not object to the principle of private sector involvement – indeed may warmly embrace it. Perhaps the latter group struggled to win support because of the ongoing opposition to privatisation; perhaps the former might have galvanised its support more effectively if it had more vigorously promoted its alternative vision alongside its rejection of the PPP.

We have tracked Ken Livingstone's opposition to the PPP up to the point of his election as mayor of London. In the section, **The New Mayor in Office** (see page 67), we will see how Livingstone pursued – and modified – his stance once he was mayor, with the help of those he appointed, in particular his Transport Commissioner Bob Kiley. We have also seen the ructions within the Labour Party around Livingstone's candidature for mayor and opposition to the PPP. We will now look at the attempts by Labour members and affiliated unions to change the government's stance and persuade their own Party leaders to abandon the PPP.

CHANGING LABOUR'S MIND? 1999-2000

In 1999, the trade unions' 'Listen to London' campaign sent a booklet outlining its objections to the PPP to every Constituency Labour Party, Labour MP and Labour councillor in London, and to Labour's National Executive Committee members. The booklet argued that the PPP would 'damage the trust Tube users have in the Labour Party to resolve the problems of the Underground', and pointed out that:

> Nowhere in the 1997 manifesto did it say that a Labour Government would withdraw public funding for the Underground, which is the

central policy intention of the PPP. On the contrary, the electorate were clearly led to believe that the debate was between the Conservatives' ideological obsession with privatisation and Labour's commitment to an integrated, publicly-funded Tube.[199]

The booklet reassured Labour Party members that their government could withdraw the PPP without Parliament having to legislate to do so and without delaying improvements to the Underground. It also warned that PPP would cause Labour to lose seats in Parliament, especially in the commuter-belt marginal constituencies. *The Economist* pointed out that 'Labour won 57 seats in London in the last [general] election, many of which are marginal. Opinion polls show that transport is by far the most important political issue for Londoners.'[200]

It seemed that Labour members of London borough councils were losing faith in their government's policy for the Tube. In early 2000, 56 per cent told a poll that London Underground should be funded through the public sector. Only 30 per cent supported PPP, and just 18 per cent believed it to be a popular policy. 77 per cent believed that the Mayor and GLA should have the deciding say on the future of the Tube.[201]

Labour Party members and affiliated trade unions raised their opposition to the PPP at Party conference, and generally met support from fellow party members but obstruction from the party machine. The rail unions' anti-privatisation fringe meeting was the best-attended at Labour's national conference in September 2000. Two months later, RMT protested outside the Labour Party's Greater London Region conference, but inside, the Standing Orders Committee disqualified its resolution opposing PPP. Conference delegates voted to overturn this ruling, insisted on debating the resolution, and carried it by a large majority.[202]

Labour MPs were opposing PPP in greater numbers. The Socialist Campaign Group of Labour MPs opposed the policy, and 21 Labour MPs met RMT representatives to discuss how they might raise their opposition in Parliament.[203] Labour members of the Transport Select Committee, chaired by Gwyneth Dunwoody, persistently scrutinised and demanded that the government rethink the policy. A dozen Labour MPs replied to RMT's Regional Political Officer, agreeing with the union's opposition, including former Transport Minister Gavin Strang. Dunwoody wrote: 'You understand the incompatibility between putting safety first and returning a profit perfectly. Naturally, this means that I find it difficult to accept that PPPs offer the best solution to the funding of transport systems.' John McDonnell MP pointed out that 'It is a pity that some of the MPs and Ministers who are in Parliament as a result of RMT support have not remained true to union policy. If they had, we would not be in this mess.'

But PPP's opponents within the Labour Party failed in their attempts to make the Labour government change its policy for London Underground. Labour Party leaders felt able to disregard dissenting views and conference decisions that they did not like. The majority of Labour MPs remained loyal to the party leadership's line and continued to support the PPP.

THE NEW MAYOR IN OFFICE: 2000

Ken Livingstone was now Mayor of London. Although he was not yet in charge of London Underground, he had a strong platform from which to pursue his avowed opposition to the PPP. How did he use it? This section will show that while Livingstone was seen as the figurehead for opposition to the PPP, he chose a strategy of tacking closer to the policy he claimed to oppose, perhaps hoping for compromise or concessions.

London's new mayor had to appoint people to various posts, including the Board of the new Transport for London (TfL). Livingstone chose a few trade union leaders, some business representatives, and his defeated mayoral opponents Steven Norris and Susan Kramer. Livingstone also announced an 'independent inquiry' into the PPP. For some, this may have seemed a chance for another propaganda blow against PPP, but others were dismayed. *Tubeworker* – an unofficial bulletin published by a group of Underground workers for their workmates – commented that:

> Ken has a massive mandate for keeping the Tube public. **There is no need for an inquiry** – Londoners have already spoken and made their views clear ... If Livingstone really wants to stop tube privatisation the way is to mobilise the support of the millions who voted for him.[204]

The mayor nominated Will Hutton – Chief Executive of the Industrial Society, former *Observer* editor and seen as 'a new Labour guru'[205] – to carry out his inquiry. Hutton's report[206] concluded that PPP was poor value for money and could jeopardise public safety. But he gave an 'amber light' to the PPP, believing that it 'offer[ed] the prospect of significant efficiency improvement'. Hutton called for: a tougher value-for-money test; the Health and Safety Executive to investigate safety aspects; and measures to prevent 'sweetheart deals' with favoured contractors. Livingstone called the report a 'damning indictment' of PPP, but also argued that it 'offer[ed] the government an honourable way out'.[207] Minister for Transport in London Keith Hill described it as 'a good report' and pledged that the government was 'responsive to all the many positive suggestions that it contains'.[208]

KEN RECRUITS KILEY: OCTOBER 2000

The Mayor 'carried out a search for the best in the world' to be his Commissioner of Transport for London, the senior official in charge of TfL. Livingstone chose former New York subway chief Bob Kiley. After an early career in the CIA and a stint as Chair of Boston's transit system in the 1970s, Kiley took over New York's Metropolitan Transportation Authority in 1983. Livingstone claimed that he 'turned New York's transport system from one of the most crisis ridden in the world into one of the best'.[209]

The *Daily Telegraph* headlined, 'Red Ken hires union buster to run Tube' and the *Evening Standard* explained that Kiley had 'earned himself a reputation in New York as a tough operator, taking on the unions in his struggle to impose modern management techniques'.[210] Steve Downs, a New York subway train operator and trade unionist, said that Kiley and the managers he appointed 'went after the workforce with a vengeance'.[211] RMT's Bob Crow 'hope[d] that [Kiley] leaves any anti-union attitudes on the other side of the Atlantic and recognises that underground workers are a vital part of any attempt to improve our tube', but nevertheless called the appointment 'an important step towards turning our tube round'.[212]

Livingstone gave Kiley a salary of £2m over four years, half dependent on performance, admitting that this made him 'the highest paid public servant in Britain by a mile'.[213] Kiley moved into a three-storey, £2.1m Georgian house in Belgravia provided by TfL. Livingstone explained that, 'His high salary is a reflection of the fact that, whether you're in the public or private sector, if you want to recruit the best person for the job, you have to provide a package that can compete internationally.'[214] John Biggs, Labour's GLA transport spokesperson, called the Mayor 'two-faced' for 'one day attack[ing] the private sector and the next outbid[ding] them'.[215] Kiley remarked, 'I keep looking for Red Ken, and I can't find him anywhere'.[216]

Kiley described Labour's PPP plan as 'a prescription for real problems'.[217] He favoured a bond issue to raise money for London Underground, having raised billions of dollars for the New York Subway through a similar scheme.

The election of a mayor on an anti-PPP platform did not, however, deter the government from pursuing the policy. On 13 November 2000, Parliament passed a motion approving the PPP, and London Transport Minister Keith Hill confidently asserted that 'The London Underground PPP is well on course and set to deliver substantial improvements to the system soon'. But the PPP's progress stumbled just a week later, as London Underground Ltd rejected the bidders' Best and Final Offers for the BCV and JNP Infracos. Their best was not good enough and their final not actually final: LUL instructed the Infracos to submit revised offers by January 2001 which cut their prices by scrapping or postponing some projects. On 6 December 2000, the Greater London Assembly passed a motion to oppose the PPP: Livingstone welcomed the vote, but the government remained unmoved.

Livingstone asked his new commissioner, Bob Kiley (see box on previous page), to produce another report on the PPP. Kiley's report concluded that 'the basic structure of the PPP is fatally flawed, that it is not an effective way to restore the London Underground to a good state of repair, and that it will not promote an improvement in the service being offered to Londoners'.[218]

Kiley's main complaint was that the PPP gave the public-sector TfL little control over the private Infracos – for example, London Underground Ltd had no right to select a new contractor in order to remedy serious mistakes, nor to order immediate changes in the work programme. This, he argued, would enable the Infracos to 'place the Underground in a "heads I win, tails you lose" situation'. Kiley seemed convinced that if he were given greater powers, then the PPP might become acceptable. His report concluded: 'Can PPP be salvaged? Of course. ... [W]e firmly believe we can work in productive partnership with the private sector.'

On the same day that he published his report, Kiley also published a document outlining TfL's alternative proposal for the Tube.[219] The document declared that TfL had concerns with the particular structure of the PPP, but 'supports wholeheartedly substantial roles for the public and private sectors in the future of the Tube.' Kiley proposed that funds come from fares, central government grant and Revenue Securitisation Obligations (bonds secured by London Underground's revenues). He also proposed that LUL award Private Performance Contracts (PPCs) to private companies for maintenance and improvement work. Kiley called his plan 'an opportunity to tap the experience and strengths of the many world class companies that have participated in the PPP contract bidding' (the same companies that Livingstone had called 'the worst scum of capitalism'; see **The Shortlisted Bidders** pages 54-56). Kiley boasted that his alternative plan would involve more private companies than PPP.[220] Livingstone described Kiley's proposals approvingly as 'son of PPP'.[221] Livingstone's stance had shifted away from opposing PPP towards demanding 'unified management'. With these two documents – the report and the alternative proposal – Ken Livingstone's TfL placed itself in the camp of that part of the opposition to the PPP which objected on technical grounds rather than objecting to any form of privatisation on principle. By his own admission, Livingstone was 'not opposed to public private partnership ... I did not vote against it in committee ... My opposition is not ideological, it is purely empirical.'[222]

TfL and the government began talks. Bob Kiley attended the first meeting with a team of his appointees. These included TfL finance chief Jay Walder, lawyer Steve Polan, and David Gunn, the man Kiley wanted to run London Underground if a deal could be made. Opposite them, the pro-PPP team comprised Adrian Montague of soon-to-be-privatised PFI quango Partnerships UK; David Rowlands, rail chief at the Department of Transport; Tony Poulter of PricewaterhouseCoopers Ltd; John Gieve, the Treasury's head of finance; Shriti Vadera, special adviser to Gordon Brown; Richard Phillips of Freshfields LLP lawyers; and London Underground Ltd's Martin Callaghan. No-one attending the meeting was an elected office-holder, and the attendees had more expertise in law and finance than in running railways. When Kiley commented that the other side of the table had 'Not an operator among them',[223] it was unclear whether he meant a railway operator or a political operator.

The *Telegraph* claimed that Prime Minister Tony Blair had ordered his Deputy John Prescott to reach a deal with Ken Livingstone. Prescott denied this, and claimed instead that Livingstone and Kiley had moved towards a compromise, which would be worked out in January.[224] Thus began months of meetings – over a hundred, according to Livingstone[225] – accompanied by claim and counterclaim, breakthroughs and false dawns, one day going brilliantly, the next on the edge of collapse.

TIMELINE: STRIKING A DEAL, 2001

25 January: RMT and ASLEF name strikes for Mondays 5, 12 and 19 February.[†]

1 February: Court grants injunction against RMT strike.

2 February: Announcement of a deal between Prescott and Kiley.

5 February: ASLEF strikes officially; RMT members join in unofficially.

29 March: International Transport Workers' Federation's worldwide railway safety day. RMT strikes officially; ASLEF members join in unofficially.

2 May: Preferred bidders announced.

8 May: RMT representatives' meeting calls for new strikes.

1 June: RMT representatives accept 'jobs for life' deal.

7 June: General Election.

TALKING AND STRIKING: 2001

As the talks began, trade union members pressed their leaders to restart industrial action. RMT and ASLEF together tabled four demands to London Underground Ltd: the establishment of a joint body of employers and unions to oversee maintenance and safety; no compulsory redundancies; staffing levels to be agreed with the unions; and employees to remain on existing terms and conditions with their existing employer unless agreed otherwise. The companies refused all four demands, and the two unions jointly held a large rally on 8 January 2001 and balloted their members for industrial action. 83 per cent voted to strike: 89 per cent of RMT members, 74 per cent of ASLEF members. The unions called strikes hitting three successive Mondays from 5 February 2001. (Leaders of the two smaller unions, TSSA and AEEU, chose not to ballot their members.) RMT and ASLEF issued a leaflet to Tube passengers:

† Technically, the strikes began on the Sunday evenings, but the intention was to stop Monday services.

Tube staff are in the best position to identify safety concerns. For months we have been saying that staff and passengers need safeguards. We have asked that a joint body is set up to enforce rigorous safety standards. We have argued that cuts in staff numbers will undermine safety.

But London Underground has refused to listen. That is why, very reluctantly, we are taking strike action as a last resort.

We are prepared to lose pay to put safety first. We are deeply sorry for any inconvenience. But we cannot allow a Hatfield on the tube.

But before the first strike was due to take place, the government announced that the disagreements about PPP were resolved. Talks that had been 'delicate' on 26 January and 'on the verge of collapse' on 29 January[226] produced a deal on 2 February. The deal was widely presented as a climb-down by Prescott,[227] and saw him allow Kiley access to all documentation and invite him to 'take the lead in working up proposals for modifying the PPP'. Kiley dropped his proposal to raise finance through bonds, saying that it was 'not an issue' any more. Livingstone declared that the PPP, a 'massively difficult, divisive issue ... has been resolved and everyone in London will be delighted ... This is an excellent deal, this is what Londoners need.' Livingstone claimed that, 'Once the unions have seen the outline of this deal they will realise their worries about safety have been resolved.' But they were not reassured, and ASLEF explained that 'Our dispute is ... about the situation as currently exists on the Tube following the separation into different sections of the Underground last year in readiness for PPP. LU has not answered our questions. The strike is still on.'[228]

RMT's strike, though, had fallen foul of the law. Legislation by the previous Conservative government had required unions to give employers the names of all members balloted for industrial action. New Labour replaced this with a requirement to provide 'such information in the union's possession as would help the employer to make plans and bring information to the attention of his employees'. The trade union movement had broadly welcomed this change, believing that it made the process simpler and less invasive of members' privacy. For this dispute, as for previous disputes, RMT notified London Underground that it was balloting its members 'in all categories and workplaces'. London Transport applied to the court for an injunction barring the strike, claiming that the union should have given it more detailed information than this. Justice Gibbs granted the injunction, ruling that RMT should have told LUL the number of its members in each of London Underground's hundreds of work locations and grades.

Mike Brown told me that the London Transport Board went to the courts because 'we were in an impossible position. If we didn't try to keep running the place, someone would say to us that all your arguments, anything they ever listened to us about, was all gone, and they would just bring someone else in.' But the union and its members saw the move as an attack on their rights. RMT General Secretary Jimmy Knapp condemned the ruling as having 'stood the law on its head and made it harder, not easier to conduct a legal ballot'.[229] One RMT activist explained how anger turned into defiance:

> We had a mandate to strike, and for the courts to say that our democratic wishes weren't valid and were illegal was a total disgrace. So we organised on the ground to keep the action on despite edicts from the courts. I remember standing on the platforms as drivers were coming through saying we were taking strike action alongside ASLEF, we're not going to be abiding by the courts, and saying the same to station staff. We went round spreading the word.

Tubeworker asked rhetorically: 'What choice have we got? If we buckle under, and call off the strikes because the courts tell us to, then we are effectively conceding that going on strike is illegal.'[230] But while the London Transport workers' representative on RMT's national Executive, John Leach, voted to press ahead with the action, all but one of the other Executive members voted to call it off. Knapp rushed a letter to members telling them to attend work as normal while ASLEF was striking. Why did Leach want to defy the law?

> Me and Bob Crow and then-President Phil Boston were in the High Court, being told we were going to be in contempt of court: it was a really highly-charged moment. In the evening I was at a mass meeting at the Hackney Empire and was called on stage to give a speech. I knew that regardless of any of these court judgments, the members were just going to walk out. I've never known a mood quite like it. So I said that the judge could stuff his injunction. I had to go back in front

of that judge the next morning!

London Transport had not applied for a similar injunction against ASLEF, so ASLEF's strike went ahead officially. Thousands of RMT members joined it unofficially, with pickets wearing the armbands of both unions. With trade union head offices feeling unable to officially endorse unofficial strikes, bulletins produced by Underground workers took on a new significance. *Tubeworker* published three issues during the week of the strike. It explained why workers felt confident enough to defy the law: 'If we have to go 'unofficial', then if thousands stay away from work, there is no way that management can victimise us all – who would run their railway?'[231] Mike Brown told me that the company's management did not even discuss taking disciplinary action against unofficial strikers, and that he and some other directors understood the workers' actions: 'I always knew there was going to be some serious dispute on this issue. I think I knew the strength of feeling about this. It was a genuinely-held, real concern for what the future of the place was going to be.'

Nine-tenths of trains were cancelled on the strike day. London Underground management confessed that 'The strike has really bitten hard'.[232] I wrote at the time that, 'All the people who came up to our station said that they fully supported us. Nobody could be found for the TV vox pop interviews or the radio phone-ins to slag off the strike.'[233] The *Evening Standard* admitted that: 'Despite the inconvenience, many commuters were broadly supportive of ASLEF's action', quoting passenger Toni Adams: 'I sympathise with the action if the drivers are thinking of public safety, so I'm prepared to put up with it.[234]

After the strike, trains resumed running and London Underground Ltd's management and unions resumed talking. A management negotiator described the unions' demands as 'completely unrealistic. We couldn't say yes to them even if we wanted to.'[235] But just three days later, LUL agreed to the first demand – the establishment of a cross-company safety body comprising unions and management – and set up working groups to discuss the others. It seemed that under pressure from effective industrial action, 'completely unrealistic' demands became rather more realistic. ASLEF suspended the strikes scheduled for 12 and 19 February. RMT lost its legal appeal against the court injunction banning its strike and balloted its members again. This time, members voted by a ratio of

11:1 in favour of strikes, greater even than the 9:1 majority in the previous vote. The union announced that it would strike on Thursday 29 March. Just as had happened in January, an approaching strike prompted an announcement from the government that talks between TfL and the government were progressing very well. A new Transport Minister, Gus Macdonald – a former journalist and now a member of the House of Lords – announced that the government was 'close to a deal' with Livingstone and that a 55-point plan drawn up by Kiley 'could be the basis for an agreement'.[236]

At this point, ASLEF reached an agreement with London Underground Ltd which ended the union's involvement in industrial action. The agreement did not fully meet the unions' demands – for example pledging only to try to avoid compulsory redundancies rather than guaranteeing that there would be none – but ASLEF's leaders felt that they had obtained sufficient concessions. Just as the calling of strikes had prompted reports of great progress in talks between the government and TfL, so ASLEF's cancellation of strikes was quickly followed by an admission that those talks had 'hit deadlock'. Bob Kiley and the government accused each other of last-minute changes to their stance. Kiley had demanded the power to: define capital investment priorities and approve Infraco workplans and budgets; directly control all maintenance activities that affect train movement; and direct changes in Infracos' work. Prescott called these demands 'wholly incompatible with the key risk transfer and performance management characteristics of the PPP.'[237] This suggests that PPP *by definition* removes LUL's control over its own maintenance and improvement. The government decided to press ahead with the PPP, which a furious Mayor Livingstone denounced as 'a show of contempt for the overwhelming views of London'.[238] Thwarted in talks, Livingstone now turned to the courts, and TfL lodged an application for a Judicial Review of the PPP.

Although ASLEF's leaders had withdrawn from industrial action, many of the union's members wanted to keep battling. RMT rejected the deal with London Underground Ltd that ASLEF had accepted, and activists from both unions held joint strike meetings. RMT's strike went ahead on 29 March, and had even more support, and an even greater impact on services, than February's strike. London Underground ran just 25 of its 500 scheduled trains. Following a members' meeting on 17 April, RMT named a further strike date: 3 May. John Monks and Brendan

Barber, current and future TUC General Secretaries, intervened at the negotiations at the Advisory, Conciliation and Arbitration Service (ACAS) and tried to persuade RMT to call off the strike. London Underground Ltd's Mike Brown remembered Brendan Barber being 'very helpful', but RMT's John Leach saw the intervention as 'strong-arm tactics'. On the eve of the strike, LUL proposed wording which did not meet the union's demands but did prompt Monks to write to RMT formally requesting it to suspend the strike.[239] Just four hours before the strike was due to start, RMT's Executive voted to call it off and name a further strike on 14-15 May instead. Leach explained why he and two others dissented: 'I wouldn't accept it because I knew we could get more out of them and we were in a really strong position.' A few days later, RMT workplace representatives met with the union's leaders and told them that they should not have cancelled the earlier strike and to reject LUL's offer. The union accepted its reps' view and kept the union in dispute, but called off the May strike. RMT instead called two 24-hour strikes on Monday 4 and Wednesday 6 June, immediately before the General Election on 7 June.

As RMT's strikes continued, the *Evening Standard*'s denunciation of the union grew more shrill. On 29 March, it carried the headline: 'RAGE AGAINST TUBE STRIKERS', although in the accompanying article, commuter Christine Davis blamed the government rather than the strikers: 'John Prescott and Gordon Brown have got a lot to answer for.' In April, the *Standard* called RMT 'vandals' and 'neanderthals', advocating a 'showdown' with RMT and ASLEF involving 'mass sackings'.[240] On 16 May, it published a double-page spread profiling 'The men who are wrecking the lives of London's commuters', including RMT Assistant General Secretary Bob Crow and Executive members John Leach, Alex Gordon and Greg Tucker. The *Standard* headlined 'Hardliners on the RMT' and called them 'wretched men'.

The *Evening Standard* repeatedly argued that RMT's strikes were not about safety but rather about 'jobs for life' – the term it used to describe the union's demand for a guarantee that no workers would be made compulsorily redundant. The union replied that this demand was as much a safety issue as its other demands: Underground safety standards would suffer if skilled, experienced, safety-conscious workers were forced out of their jobs as they had been on the former British Rail. Driver Jock put the workers' point of view in rhetorical questions:

Why can't people have a job for life? Why do people have to have an expectation that they can be thrown on the dole for whatever reason? To say that the workers in Britain should be in constant anxiety and fear of unemployment or constant anxiety about their ability to raise their children, pay their bills, pay their mortgage is wrong. It should be a positive thing to have a job for life.

PREFERRED BIDDERS: 2001

We have reached May 2001. Trade unions and others continued to oppose the PPP, and talks between the government and Transport for London on a possible compromise structure for the PPP had broken down. Determined to proceed with the PPP, on 2 May – the month before the General Election – London Underground Ltd named its preferred bidders for the BCV and JNP Infraco contracts: Metronet and Tube Lines respectively.

Metronet – a consortium whose equal partners were Bombardier Transportation Ltd (following Bombardier Inc's purchase of Adtranz), SEEBOARD plc, Balfour Beatty plc, Thames Water plc and Atkins plc – claimed that it had 'the skills, the knowledge and the ability along with sound financial backing to help turn London Underground into a system fit for the 21st century'.[241] Its Chief Executive was Rod Hoare, a former British Airports Authority executive who had a 'tough management style' and would enjoy a 'highly lucrative package'.[242]

The Tube Lines consortium was formed by subsidiaries of Amey plc, Bechtel Corp. and Jarvis plc, who described themselves as 'three of the most highly regarded operational and project management organisations in the world'. Tube Lines said that it would 'add value to the vital public service provided by LUL by delivering on time and to budget'.[243] Its Chief Executive, Iain Coucher, came from TranSys and later went to Network Rail Ltd.

Critics argued that it was a mistake to name the preferred bidders at this stage of the process, while the exact content of the contracts was still being discussed. The bidders would now have huge influence over how the contracts would develop: if the government refused the contract terms that the preferred bidders wanted, those bidders could walk away and make the process start again. The cost to the government in time, money and credibility would be prohibitive, so the government would find it easier to give the bidders what they wanted. We will see below how the bidders were able to use their position to the benefit of themselves and to the detriment of London Underground and its passengers.

Journalist Simon Jenkins saw the naming of the preferred bidders as 'a victory for the Treasury, after months in which insiders were predicting its defeat ... A Government department that loathes the public sector and is besotted with private money has got its way.' Jenkins poured scorn on Treasury official Steve Robson, the 'long-term architect of transport "fragmentation"' who had 'already fled to the City he so enriched'. He similarly denounced Robson's successor Shriti Vadera, a former merchant banker who 'will doubtless return to the same lucrative haunt. If they ever use a train, they had better go incognito.'[244]

Bob Kiley called for the selection to be delayed, calling its methods 'highly questionable' and 'illogical'.[245] But Kiley's bitter pill was sweetened by the government appointing him Chair of London Transport, putting him in charge of negotiating the contracts with the bidders. Livingstone later confessed that 'Bob was suspicious it was a gimmick to get past the [general] election, but he did his best to make it work.'[246] The Mayor who had previously talked of opposing the PPP was now talking of helping it along. The unsuccessful LINC consortium later revealed that Kiley's appointment was 'greeted with incredulity on the part of the bidders because of the conflict of duty between having to comply with the statutory requirements to implement the PPP and his political stance on behalf of TfL which was to destroy it'.[247] Simon Jenkins railed that the deal 'would make a Paraguayan junta hold its nose'. A government adviser admitted that, 'No.10 has got the heebie-jeebies over the political position and wants to sort it out'.[248] It looked like a fragile settlement designed to show the government and TfL singing from the same hymn sheet and so stop the PPP being a general election issue in London. But if Tony Blair and Ken Livingstone wanted to keep PPP off the agenda, RMT's planned strikes in election week seemed likely to keep it fully in view.

A RESIGNATION, A DEAL AND A GENERAL ELECTION: 2001

In the months before the general election, Mayor Livingstone used strong language to denounce London Underground Ltd's senior managers, calling them 'knuckleheads' and 'dullards'. LUL's Managing Director Derek Smith asked him to stop making 'unwarranted, abusive' attacks which, Smith claimed, were having 'a disruptive and unsettling effect on morale in the company'.[249] A future Managing Director, Mike Brown, recalled a graphic on the BBC of all the LUL Directors being flushed down the toilet! Livingstone declared his intention to sack many managers when he took charge, but Derek Smith was not going to wait for that: he resigned. Smith departed later that year to be replaced by Paul Godier, LUL's Director of Train Services. Other top managers left at the same time as Smith, some to work for the Infracos.[250]

LUL and the government were keen to persuade RMT to call off its planned strikes, and began to seriously consider the union's demands, despite having previously described them as 'impossible'. LUL negotiators had previously held the view (in Mike Brown's words) that 'it was quite difficult to make a commitment on behalf of a future employer'. Now, they began to accept that RMT's demands were for 'very reasonable guarantees'. While talks took place between LUL and the union, LUL's negotiators had to check what they said with the government. Mike Brown told me that 'We would draw up some ideas, framed in words, and government officials would look at it, then say that was fine, or not. We eased our way forward on that basis. They were strange negotiations because of that political involvement.'

According to Livingstone, 'transport minister, Gus Macdonald, ordered tube officials to concede the jobs-for-life guarantee to avoid a strike the week before the election.'[251] Brown did not remember a direct instruction, but admitted that 'the government moves in mysterious ways: the Managing Director could well have had a phone call saying you've got to sort something out here.' Whether directly ordered to or not, the pressure of the impending strike made London Underground Ltd offer not just 'jobs for life' but also: negotiation of staffing levels between employers and unions; protection of workers' terms and conditions; and no staff to transfer to the new, private employers while the Mayor and the government were still discussing the PPP. RMT's leaders – this time including John Leach – recommended the offer to a meeting of the union's workplace representatives. The majority agreed to accept it, one explaining why: 'They were trying to draw up our protections. When we knew PPP was going to happen, really going to happen, it became about making a good deal for people.' A minority of reps disagreed, arguing that there were 'holes' in the offer which would let the employers back out of their commitments; that it offered little protection to future workers; and that if it called off its strikes, RMT would in effect call off its chances of stopping the PPP. The union cancelled the strikes, declared that the settlement 'probably represents the best deal any union has ever won for its members',[252] and pledged that its campaign against PPP would go on.

The unions had decided at an early stage to take industrial action on employment demands only. They believed that the courts would declare a strike explicitly against the PPP illegal under laws that allow unions to strike only about 'trade disputes' not political issues. The fruit of this decision was that when those demands appeared to be met, the union settled its dispute, even though most people understood the strikes as being against PPP itself. In April 2001, the Employment Appeals Tribunal had ruled in a separate case[253] that industrial action directly against privatisation could in fact constitute a legitimate trade dispute. But news of this case did not spread around the trade union movement, so London Underground workers remained unaware that they could perhaps have taken industrial action directly against PPP after all.

With the dispute with the unions settled, the Labour government avoided the embarrassment of strikes during the same week as the 2001 General Election. Labour's manifesto told voters that, 'Our agreement with the London Mayor and Transport Commissioner offers the best chance in a generation to upgrade the Tube.' The Conservatives promised that, 'Subject to a "no strike" deal we will work with Bob Kiley ... and support his ambitions to create a world class London Underground.' The Liberal Democrats argued that, 'the best way to modernise the Underground, without compromising safety, is through a not-for-profit, public interest company funded through bonds.' The LibDems sought London Underground staff's votes, and delivered a publicity pack to each station presenting themselves as the anti-PPP party. The Tube unions continued to support the Labour Party, but while many members voted Labour, others rejected it because of PPP, some voting Socialist Alliance, some for other parties, some not voting at all. The 59 per cent turnout for the General Election was the lowest since 1918, before which not all adults had the right to vote. Labour won a second successive landslide, down only six seats to 413. Two of those lost seats (Romford and Upminster) were in London; Labour lost both to the Conservatives. PPP's unpopularity may have helped the LibDems increase their share of the London vote by 2.9 per cent, nearly double their 1.5 per cent increase across the country. The Socialist Alliance's 24 candidates in London constituencies polled between 0.9 per cent and 4.6 per cent of the vote.

TIMELINE: COURT CASES AND CONTRACTS, 2001-2002

2001

April: TfL lodges papers for a Judicial Review of the PPP.

3 July: Bob Kiley unable to agree terms with the bidders.

5 July: Secretary of State Stephen Byers announces he will impose PPP.

17 July: Byers sacks Kiley as Chair of London Transport.

23-30 July: Ken Livingstone's legal challenge to PPP heard in court; fails.

19 September: Metronet named as preferred bidder for Sub-Surface Lines Infraco.

19 September: LUL holds a 'stakeholder meeting' to discuss safety.

15 October: Byers announces withdrawal of government support for Railtrack plc.

15 November: Draft PPP contracts released.

2002

7 February: Publication of Ernst and Young LLP report.

13 February: Bob Crow elected RMT General Secretary.

6 March: Transport Select Committee report urges government to drop PPP.

8 May: Infracos sign the PPP contracts, subject to final details and financial backing.

19 July: Advertising Standards Authority rules that LUL misled the public with two adverts that it placed in newspapers in February and March in support of the PPP.

27 July: Livingstone and Kiley's Judicial Review application fails.

2 October: European Commission rules that the PPP does not breach State Aid rules.

AFTER THE 2001 GENERAL ELECTION

As Labour resumed government following its June 2001 General Election win, let us recap the situation with the London Underground PPP. The 'new Labour' government first elected in 1997 was preparing to bring in new investment and improvements to London Underground with its 'Public-Private Partnership'. Improvement was certainly very much needed. The PPP was supposed to have been in place by 2000, but it had encountered obstacles and criticisms that had delayed its implementation. London Underground was operating 'Shadow Running', having reorganised into the structure it would have under the PPP – one operating company (Opsco) and three infrastructure companies (Infracos) which would be taken over by private consortia for the duration of the PPP's 30-year contracts.

The Labour government had also created a new London-wide elected authority – the Mayor and Greater London Assembly – and along with it, a new body to run the Tube and other transport services in the capital, Transport for London. But the Labour Party had lost the election for Mayor to a renegade member of its own, Ken Livingstone, elected on a platform of opposing the PPP. Livingstone had appointed a TfL Commissioner, Bob Kiley, who shared his opposition to the PPP, and had initiated legal action to block the policy. Strikes by Tube staff had forced London Underground Ltd and the government to guarantee protections for Underground workers, and had increased the profile of opposition to the PPP. Opinion polls showed increasing public antipathy to the PPP policy. A range of groups and individuals opposed the PPP, including from within Labour's own ranks, but proposed a range of alternative policies.

Following a bidding competition and a shortlisting process, London Underground Ltd had announced its preferred bidders for two of the three Infracos – Metronet and Tube Lines. Following months of volatile talks between Transport for London and the government, Commissioner Kiley was now in talks with the preferred bidders about the detailed terms of the PPP contracts. This arrangement had given the appearance of co-operation rather than conflict while the 2001 General Election took place. Now the election was over and Labour had been re-elected. The government had further hurdles to jump before introducing its PPP policy: securing the approval of the Health and Safety Executive; surviving the legal challenges; selecting the preferred bidder for the third (Sub-Surface Lines) Infraco; and finalising the content of the contracts so that both London Underground Ltd and the private bidders would sign them. It would also need to mollify critics and disregard outright opposition; and to sail through choppy political and economic waters.

Immediately after the General Election, Prime Minister Tony Blair reshuffled his Cabinet. John Prescott remained Deputy Prime Minister, but his Department of the Environment, Transport and the Regions was replaced by the new Department for Transport, Local Government and the Regions. Former Trade and Industry Secretary Stephen Byers became its Secretary of State. Within a month of the election being over, the PPP truce ended too. On 3 July, Kiley told Byers that he could not agree the contractual terms with the bidders, because 'there is a yawning chasm between this convoluted 30-year privatisation and the single-point accountability for investment and service delivery the Underground's passengers deserve. No amount of contractual changes to the PPP will bridge the divide.'[254] Two days later, Byers told Parliament that he would now impose the PPP, and the following day, the Health and Safety Executive endorsed the PPP Safety Case (although there were further stages to the Safety Case process still to come). The bidders were delighted, Metronet's Rod Hoare declaring that, 'It is time the talking stopped and the pounds were put into the ground.'[255] But others were not so pleased. Hendon Labour MP Andrew Dismore said, 'Before I was an MP I was a personal injury lawyer. I sat through over 100 days of the inquiry into the 1987 King's Cross fire. Nobody needs to tell me about tube safety, and I don't believe the people of London can be reassured by this proposal.'[256]

With Kiley's job done – or rather, not done – Byers sacked him as London Transport Chair on 17 July. Byers reported receiving 'a letter signed on behalf of a majority of the London Transport Board saying that they cannot work with Bob Kiley and thus it is impossible for the London Transport Board to function effectively. In light of this, I have decided to end his appointment.' He also said that Kiley had been trying 'to use his Board position to block negotiations with the bidders since I announced the government's decision [to proceed with the PPP] ... This is unacceptable.'[257] Byers replaced Kiley with Malcolm Bates, the man Kiley himself had replaced, and who had helped to set up the PPP.

On 4 September 2001, soon-to-depart London Underground Ltd Managing Director Derek Smith announced the resumption of 'detailed negotiations' with Metronet and Tube Lines. Fifteen day later, Metronet was named preferred bidder for the Sub-Surface Lines Infraco contract, covering the Circle, District, Hammersmith & City, Metropolitan and East London lines. Smith said that 'with the selection of the third and final consortium for the SSL, we are making real progress', but Bob Kiley condemned the announcement as 'rushed, premature and taken without meaningful consultation with Transport for London'.[258]

Ken Livingstone took his opposition to the PPP into the courts, but met with little success. In July 2001, his legal challenge to the PPP was heard in the High Court, while supporters of his action demonstrated outside. TfL's barrister argued that the PPP breached the 1999 Greater London Authority Act because it stopped the Mayor meeting that law's requirement that he 'develop and implement policies for the promotion of safe, integrated, efficient and economic transport facilities and services'. But Justice Sullivan – the same judge who had banned RMT's strike – upheld the government's case that its authority was superior because it derived from Parliament, and ruled that PPP could go ahead.

Livingstone and Kiley returned to court in July 2002, seeking a Judicial Review. They argued that the PPP's procurement had broken European and UK rules, as the contracts had changed significantly since the preferred bidders had been named. They also challenged a funding gap of nearly £1.5bn between the cost of PPP to TfL and the grant given to it by the government over the first 7½-year Review Period. However, it soon became clear that the case was unlikely to succeed, and Livingstone withdrew it. The failure of the legal challenges should not have come as a surprise, as it has never been illegal for a government to impose private-sector involvement in public services. As Nick Cohen wrote: 'Many of the most dangerous policies and disastrous initiatives are completely lawful, but their legality doesn't make them less disastrous ... the biggest crooks aren't crooks in the eyes of the law'.[259]

VALUE FOR MONEY? 2000-2002

Stephen Byers had said that he would proceed with the PPP, but he assured the Transport Select Committee that the policy would need to pass tests for safety and value for money first; that it would not proceed just 'for dogmatic reasons'; and that scrapping PPP and keeping the whole of London Underground in the public sector was still an option.[260] However, he and his government ensured that PPP would overcome these obstacles by fair means or foul. They fiddled the figures.

PPP's value for money was tested by comparing its cost to a public sector comparator (PSC), an estimate of how much it would cost a public-sector London Underground to carry out the same work that the Infracos were to do. The PPP would be judged to provide value for money only if its cost were lower than the PSC. LUL calculated a figure for the PSC, but in 2000, the government's own spending watchdog, the National Audit Office, found flaws in LUL's calculation and described the company's financial analysis as 'useful but incomplete'. The National Audit Office reported that the case for the PPP was 'clearly not proved'.[261] Assistant auditor general Jeremy Colman said, 'We are not saying think again. We are saying think.'

In 2001, Transport for London commissioned accountants Deloitte and Touche plc to report on how London Underground had assessed the PPP's value for money. London Underground Ltd obtained a court injunction preventing the publication of the report, but Livingstone and Kiley successfully applied to the court to overturn this injunction and published it.[262] Deloitte and Touche plc found that:

- the comparisons between the PPP and the public sector comparator did not provide a satisfactory basis for establishing value for money, either over the thirty years of the contracts or the 7½-year Review Periods;
- LUL's adjustments to the public sector comparator were 'judgmental, volatile or statistically simplistic';
- there was probably some double-counting in LUL's calculations;
- some statistical analysis was arbitrary and open to misinterpretation;
- LUL selected bidders too early.

In short, London Underground Ltd had manipulated the process to make PPP look like it offered value for money even if it did not, mainly by inflating the cost of the public sector comparator (PSC) to make it seem as expensive as possible. LUL's adjustments to the 'base costs' of the PSC increased it by around £2.5bn, including over £1bn based on the 'expected failure' of LUL to meet requirements. London Underground Ltd's calculations assumed that it would fail to do its own job! The PSC still threatened to come in cheaper than the PPP, and LUL introduced the concept of 'reputational externality' to its calculations. This seemed to mean that a PSC would cost around £700m more simply because outsiders did not have a very high opinion of London Underground Ltd. London Underground Ltd and the government would not accept Deloitte and Touche plc's findings. LUL Managing Director Derek Smith dismissed the report as 'rushed, wrong and riddled with mistakes'.[263] Stephen Byers responded to it by commissioning professional services firm Ernst and Young LLP to produce another report.[264] Ernst and Young LLP concluded that LUL's methodology had overall been 'robust and appropriate' and had used 'a blend of subjective judgements and fact-based analysis'. It revealed that LUL had used 'social cost adjustments' to increase its estimate of the cost of the public sector comparator by 9 per cent and decrease its estimate of the PPP's cost by 5 per cent, a net money movement of £2.1bn. It seemed that where the 'fact-based analysis' gave the wrong answer, LUL used the 'subjective judgements' to get the result it wanted. Following the publication of the Ernst and Young LLP report in February 2002, Byers announced to Parliament that the London Transport Board was 'minded to proceed' with the PPP.

The Transport Select Committee described the Ernst and Young LLP report's conclusion as 'vapid', and expressed great concern that 'after four years [and] £100 million of costs, this pivotal decision for London is "subjective".'[265] Gwyneth Dunwoody denounced the decision to proceed with a PPP scheme which she called 'manifestly unworkable', 'not value for money', and which opened up 'the viper's nest of exactly the contractual problems that destroyed Railtrack'. Of 21 Labour MPs who spoke on Byers' statement to Parliament, only five supported PPP. Byers relied on two arguments to defend his decision to proceed with the PPP. The first was that the only options were to 'get on with the job' or to 'continue with constant political bickering'. The second was his claim that under PPP, London Underground would save £2bn over the first 15 years and that faster, more reliable Tube journeys would benefit passengers to the tune of a further £2bn. The Transport Select Committee disagreed and concluded that the government should drop PPP and find an alternative.[266]

While the public sector seemed uncertain that it would get value for money from the PPP, the private sector seemed confident that it would. The *Evening Standard* headlined on 21 March 2002, 'TUBE FIRMS TO MAKE BILLIONS', claiming that Metronet and Tube Lines expected to make £2.7bn on direct investments of £530m over the life of the PPP contracts. Amey plc Chief Executive Brian Staples told shareholders that he expected the company to make around £10m per year on its £60m investment. Apply that to all three Tube Lines investors and the thirty years of the contract and the companies would put £180m in and get £900m out.

The private consortia bidding for the PPP contracts were in a position to influence the development of the PPP's structure, and worked to influence matters in their own interest: they demanded reimbursement of bidding costs; they blocked Bob Kiley's demands for 'unified management'; they worked to cut and reduce the level of any improvements that they would be expected to deliver and they responded to Railtrack plc being placed in administration by insisting that the government should underwrite the debts they would incur with their lenders under the Tube PPP.

After the Paddington crash in 1999, the bidders claimed that market interest in the PPP was fading. They argued that if it became very expensive to bid, they would have little money left for other business opportunities, and and so exerted 'sustained pressure' on London Underground Ltd, which agreed to reimburse their bidding costs. Initially, LUL offered each runner-up 75 per cent of its 'reasonable and audited' bid costs, plus a 'pool' of £4m for each bidding competition, to be shared between the continuing bidders. This figure later rose to £19m per Infraco, a total of £57m.[267] That was just for the failed bidders: the total reimbursed to all bidders was £275m. This was public money paid to private companies to draw up plans to obtain more public money. Transport Minister David Jamieson described reimbursement of bidding costs as 'perfectly normal commercial practice'. The National Audit Office admitted that it was 'unusual but not unprecedented'.[268]

When in the run-up to the 2001 General Election, Bob Kiley appeared to be making ground in his demands, the bidders were, apparently, 'fuming'. A Balfour Beatty plc director insisted that there was 'no question' of the private sector putting up the money if Kiley's 'unified management' meant that the Commissioner, rather than the Infracos, would decide how it would be spent.[269] But industry journal *Building* assured readers that 'The Treasury will not permit any changes to the contractual structure of PPP that might make banks reluctant to take equity stakes.'[270] As we have seen, Kiley did not get his way.

In October 2001, Stephen Byers withdrew government financial support from a failing Railtrack plc, placing it in administration. Many people found it hard to understand why he was calling time on one part of rail privatisation while pressing ahead with another, the Tube PPP. But the PPP bidders smelt an opportunity. As Railtrack plc's fate had 'an impact on market sentiment', they persuaded London Underground that the Infracos should be liable for just 5 per cent of their own debts should things go wrong. Byers sent a 'comfort letter' to the Infracos, pledging that the government would underwrite 95 per cent of their bank loans and guaranteeing up to £33.7bn.[271] Suitably comforted, the Infracos signed the PPP contracts on 8 May 2002, subject to final details and financial backing.

Expectations of improvements to London Underground had tumbled by the time contracts were signed. The Infracos would modernise just 61 stations during the first 7½-year Review Period, 135 fewer than first promised; 318 years had been added to the station modernisation programme. London Underground Ltd had previously asked the Infracos to ensure that 100 per cent of track drainage was in a satisfactory condition by the end of the first Review Period, but it now asked for less than 85 per cent. Similar requirements for embankments dropped from 100 per cent to around 92 per cent; for bridges and structures from 95 per cent to 90 per cent; and for ballast in sub-surface sections from over half to just over one-third.[272] As well as lower standards, the bidders also wanted more money: the consortia called their higher charges 'protection from the consequences of adverse conditions exceeding prudent levels of contingency'.[273]

It seemed that the bidding consortia used whatever problem arose as a pretext to demand more money, and that the government, rather than recognise these problems as reasons to abandon PPP, conceded the Infracos' demands. Uncertain condition of the Underground's assets – more money; the expenses of bidding – more money; possibility of being accountable to public officials – more money; loss of opportunity to make money elsewhere – more money; lack of public support for PPP – more money for the private companies.

TIMELINE: RESIGNATIONS AND RESOLUTIONS, 2002

10 May 2002: Potters Bar crash.

28 May: Stephen Byers resigns as Transport Secretary.

1 June: Ken Livingstone appoints Bob Crow to the TfL Board.

27 June: John Prescott resigns his RMT membership.

10 July: Health and Safety Executive approves the PPP Safety Case.

17-18 July: RMT 24-hour strike.

30 September: Labour Party conference passes a resolution opposing PPP and PFI.

OPPONENTS' LAST STAND: 2002

Numerous reports criticised the London Underground PPP. But the *Tubeworker* bulletin warned that 'Reports won't save us. A rainforest of paperwork has condemned privatisation, yet the 'Labour' government presses ahead. We need to go back on strike to stop PPP as soon as possible.'[274]

Following the death from cancer of Jimmy Knapp, RMT members elected Bob Crow as General Secretary in February 2002. This was widely seen as a vote for a more militant stance against privatisation and PPP, and the *Guardian* reported that, 'His victory was greeted with dismay in Millbank [Labour Party HQ] and at the transport department, as well as in train operating company boardrooms.'[275] Soon after Crow's election, RMT reorganised its Parliamentary group, to include only those Labour MPs who opposed privatisation and PPP. RMT's Annual General Meeting voted to endorse this policy, and John Prescott resigned his RMT membership, to little protest from the union.

Stephen Byers had been under fire for defending 'spin doctor' Jo Moore's email suggesting that 9/11 was 'a good day to bury bad news', and was resented by the City for allowing Railtrack plc to collapse. In May 2002, after the Potters Bar crash and a Transport Select Committee report describing his ten-year transport plan as 'incomprehensible', Byers resigned. Alistair Darling replaced him as Secretary of State for Transport, and the Department of Transport, Local Government and the Regions was no more.

Jackie Darby, a Tube engineer who had heard Labour GLA Transport spokesperson John Biggs address a TSSA trade union event, wrote to Biggs to passionately argue for a rethink:

> The decision to split up the engineering arm of London Underground Ltd into three has been the most destructive and negative aspect of the PPP process so far. In forming the new companies the very specialist engineering skills have had to be divided between them. As a result each Infraco is minus sufficient experienced engineers in some of the disciplines. This has been exacerbated by the need to retain the most senior engineers in LUL in order to oversee the Infracos' work. We have had to recruit people with no railway background ...
>
> [W]e and our operating colleagues were proud to work together to provide a service to the public. Separating us like this is an act of

wanton destruction. ... And what are the public getting for it? A less good service than at present, according to the contract – and a more expensive method of funding it, to which we will all have to contribute. ...

It is a scandal.[276]

By spring 2002, many Underground workers wanted their unions to strike against PPP again. One driver wrote that, 'Since our strikes were called off last June, too many people have been relying on outside factors to stop PPP for us – Ken Livingstone's doomed court cases, the 'Value for Money' test, occasional protest events.'[277] RMT balloted members for industrial action demanding action over safety fears, and following a 9:1 majority vote, the union called a 24-hour strike starting on 17 June 2002, which was joined by many ASLEF members refusing to cross RMT picket lines. That autumn, the two unions did strike together, over pay. Some union representatives felt that the strikes should have been about both pay and PPP, seeing a link between the two: 'the reason that management have refused us a reasonable [pay] offer is because the Treasury are holding the purse strings in preparation for PPP'.[278]After two strikes, the pay dispute was settled when Ken Livingstone promised to abide by mediation once he took over London Underground Ltd the following year.

Shortly after this, another dispute flared over safety cover. In November, firefighters took strike action to demand an increase in their wages to £30,000, and no other reliable fire services were available. Over 300 Underground workers – mainly drivers – refused to work their normal duties without adequate fire cover.

The signing of the final PPP contracts was approaching. Several Tube trade union branches asked their unions to call further industrial action, confident that members would have supported more strikes against the PPP – but the unions did not do so.

However, there were signs that the London Underground PPP might yet fall at the final hurdle: Ken Livingstone was pursuing legal action again; and the private finance policy was in crisis. Livingstone threatened an appeal to the European Court against the European Commission's decision that the PPP did not breach state aid rules. Global share prices were collapsing, leaving a shortage of the upfront capital that PFI relies on. The Tube bidders were in the thick of the trouble: Balfour Beatty plc's

market capitalisation slumped by 45 per cent; Jarvis plc's fell 65 per cent;
Atkins plc's collapsed by 90 per cent; and Amey plc's by a catastrophic 94
per cent. Amey plc's Finance Director resigned in September, and his
replacement resigned just five weeks later. Atkins plc issued a profit
warning, and its Chief Executive and Finance Director both resigned. One
chief executive was heard to say that 'The private finance idea is dead',
and the banks which planned to lend to the PPP Infracos were apparently
'thinking again'.[279]

But the government and the companies came to PPP's rescue. Amey
plc was bailed out by its Tube Lines consortium partners Bechtel Corp
and Jarvis plc (the other consortium member, Hyder plc, had broken up
in 2000), although Gwyneth Dunwoody MP warned that 'three legged
stools have a nasty habit of falling over if one leg is cut'. Alistair Darling
reassured MPs that, 'the prospects of insolvency are remote'.[280] Darling
helped the Infracos' beleaguered finances by 'reprofiling' the first year of
the JNP contract so that the government would pay its share of the
financing first and the Tube Lines consortim would not start 'drawing
down' on its debt until October 2003, saving it £25m in charges. He
neutralised Livingstone's legal threat by promising to pay the Infracos
the losses they would incur from any delay it caused. Then on New Year's
Eve, during the holiday period and a week earlier than expected, the
government and Tube Lines signed the contract to transfer the JNP
Infraco. This meant that Tube Lines – a consortium of private companies
– now held the 30-year lease for work on London Underground's Jubilee,
Northern and Piccadilly lines. One-third of the PPP was now in place.
On 5 April 2003, Metronet signed the contracts for the two other Infracos
– the Bakerloo, Central and Victoria lines, and the Sub-Surface lines. The
five years of development, argument and protest were over. Despite all
the difficulties and criticisms, London Underground was now operating
under the controversial Public-Private Partnership: LUL no longer
maintained or improved its own infrastructure, but paid fees to private
consortia to do so.

Once the JNP contract was signed, Ken Livingstone withdrew his legal
action and gave up his battle against PPP. He wrote to Alistair Darling,
'An orderly and rapid transfer of the Tube is critical for the management
of these complex contracts and to improve the transport services we are
providing to the millions of people who use the Tube each day.'[281] Perhaps
this vindicated the 'consortium source' who had said in 2001 that

'Livingstone was always resigned to making PPP work ... his all-out opposition was a front designed to wring sufficient concessions from the government.'[282]

WERE THEY GOOD DEALS?

After the PPP contracts were signed, the National Audit Office (NAO) asked, 'Were they good deals?'.[283] The NAO reported that the *net present value* of the PPP was £15.7bn over the full thirty years, £9.7bn over the first 7½ years. The private sector would pay 25 per cent towards the work to be done, government grants 60 per cent and fares 15 per cent[284] – although even that 25 per cent would actually come from taxpayers and fare-payers, via the Infrastructure Service Charge.

The process of procuring and negotiating the PPP contracts had cost the public sector £180m and the bidders £275m. The public sector paid for the bidders' costs as well as its own, so the total public spend was £455m, 2.8 per cent of the value of the PPP.

Of the £180m, £109m went to advisers:

Freshfields LLP, legal: £29.2m

PricewaterhouseCoopers Ltd, commercial: £21.4m

Arthur Anderson Ltd, reorganising operations: £13.8m

PA Consulting Group Ltd, reorganising engineering: £12.5m

Ove Arup Ltd, engineering: £6m

Hornagold and Hills Ltd, KPMG and 25+ other firms: £26.5m

The initial budgets for Freshfields LLP and PricewaterhouseCoopers Ltd were £4m each, but rose exponentially as the process went on. Freshfields LLP 'found that more partner time was required on an ongoing basis than it had estimated', so it renegotiated and charged more. Asked by the Transport Select Committee whether the amount spent on consultants represented value for money, Stephen Byers admitted that, 'It certainly has been best value for them'.[285]

The NAO concluded that there was 'only limited assurance' that the price paid to the private sector would be reasonable, and recognised that terms had 'changed markedly' during the prolonged negotiations with the bidders. The terms had in fact changed markedly *in favour of the bidders*, so much so that for them, the deal was almost risk-free.

CHAPTER 3 – PPP IN PRACTICE

After five years of argument and preparation, the London Underground Public-Private Partnership (PPP) was now in place. Under the new structure, London Underground Ltd now operated the Tube's services – running stations, trains and signalling – and three consortia of private companies had responsibility for the Tube's infrastructure: the Tube Lines consortium for the Jubilee, Northern and Piccadilly lines; Metronet Rail BCV Ltd for the Bakerloo, Central and Victoria lines; and Metronet Rail SSL Ltd for the remaining, 'Sub-Surface' lines. Each of these three 'Infracos' (infrastructure companies) had a contract with London Underground Ltd for thirty years, during which time the Infraco was expected to maintain and improve the infrastructure in its area. The thirty-year contract term was divided into four Review Periods of 7½ years each. For its work, each Infraco would be paid a fee (the Infrastructure Service Charge: ISC) by London Underground Ltd, with bonuses added for exceeding 'benchmark' standards for factors including Availability, Capability and Ambience, and 'abatements' deducted for falling short of those standards. Tube Lines signed its contract with London Underground Ltd on 31 December 2002. The two Metronet Infracos signed their contracts with London Underground Ltd on 5 April 2003.

Londoners would now be able to find out whether the PPP's supporters or its opponents were right in their assessment of the policy. The government had promised that the PPP would bring efficient maintenance and big improvements to London Underground; that opponents' safety fears were unfounded; and that Infracos' profits would be just rewards for their work. This chapter examines how well the PPP measured up to these promises in practice. I suggest that the evidence shows that it failed. Moreover, the Private Finance Initiative schemes that preceded PPP continued to cause problems, and Mayor of London Ken Livingstone shifted steadily away from opposing privatisation towards embracing it. Powerless to prevent PPP's failings, London Underground Ltd suffered financial difficulties and addressed them by cutting standards further.

ARBITER APPOINTED

Secretary of State for Transport Alistair Darling appointed former stand-in Rail Regulator Chris Bolt to the new post of PPP Arbiter.

The Arbiter's remit was set out in the Greater London Authority Act and the PPP Agreements. Bolt described it as 'principally to ensure that any differences between London Underground and the relevant Infraco or about efficiency and economy can be resolved independently, swiftly and with certainty'; it was a role that had 'no close parallel'.[286] He was 'optimistic about the prospects for the PPP and for the role of Arbiter', believing that 'the structures of the PPP arrangements seem more robust than those for the national rail network'.[287]

The Arbiter's office had six permanent staff. It was funded by a grant from the Department of Transport: £1.1m in 2003/04, rising to £4.25m in 2009/10.[288] In October 2003, Bolt appointed an Advisory Board. All were, like him, experts in privatised public services:

Peter Gray, a partner in law firm Linklaters LLP, who had 'advised on a wide range of international, UK domestic project finance and PFI transactions';

Keith Lloyd, who had just retired as Vice President of Alstom Transport UK plc, where he had 'devoted most of his time to privately financed rail projects'; and

John O'Brien, former Railtrack plc Commercial Director and Franchising Director at the Office of Passenger Rail Franchising (OPRAF).

In May 2006, these three were joined by **John Thomas**, Director of Competition and Regulatory Economics at the Office of Rail Regulation; and in July 2007 by **Andrew Géczy** of Lloyds Banking Group.[289]

PROMISES AND END-OF-YEAR REPORTS: 2003-2005

What did the Infacos promise, and what did they deliver? How did their performance measure up to their targets? And how did they improve access for disabled passengers?

Tube Lines ran the JNP Infraco from the start of 2003. It announced plans to spend £4.4bn upgrading the Jubilee, Northern and Piccadilly lines over the first 7½-year review period. Its top priority would be to improve the reliability of the train service, aiming to cut delays by 10 per cent within twelve months. It also pledged to improve 97 stations. Terry Morgan,[290] the new Managing Director of the Tube Lines consortium, saw a bright new dawn: 'For the first time London Underground can think about a sustainable improvement in performance.'[291] Tube Lines' shareholder Amey plc parted company with its Chief Executive in January 2003. It escaped its financial straits in April, when it was acquired by Ferrovial S.A., Spain's biggest construction company, for £81m.

Tube Lines awarded several contracts, the first to Marconi Company Ltd to maintain communication systems on the Jubilee line.[292] The Infraco awarded Alstom plc a £101m contract to supply four new full trains and 59 new carriages to facilitate lengthening Jubilee line trains from six carriages to seven.[293] But Tube Lines' own consortium member Jarvis plc lost out on a £150m contract to replace or refurbish 150km of track, awarded instead to a joint bid from GrantRail Ltd (now Volkerrail) and Trackwork Ltd.[294]

Metronet signed the final contracts for Infracos BCV and SSL in April 2003. It promised to spend £17bn improving its lines over the thirty-year contracts, with £4.4bn in the first 7½-year Review Period. It pledged to deep clean all stations and trains in the first year, and to install new closed-circuit television (CCTV), public address systems, help points and destination indicators at all its 150 stations. Metronet said that within three years it would improve over fifty stations, 25 miles of track and 27 District line trains. It set targets to cut delays on the Bakerloo, Central and Victoria lines, and announced that the Victoria line would get new state-of-the-art trains by 2008.[295]

The Infracos took charge of day-to-day maintenance and went to work. Were London Underground's managers and workers impressed with that work? London Underground manager Howard Collins told me that the Infracos started by 'painting the lamp-posts rather than tackling the big issues. Some of those station modernisations were very thorough, but it was like decorating your house rather than dealing with the foundations.' Bakerloo driver Jock observed that 'The main change was about reporting faults and getting them fixed. The whole maintenance regime got bogged down in bureaucracy, people passing the buck, trying to chase down who was responsible, trying to get things done. Whereas previously faults would get fixed relatively quickly, now you'd get bogged down in some bureaucratic quagmire.'

Tube Lines' end-of-first-year report was one that any schoolchild would be nervous about taking home. The year was divided into 13 four-week periods, and as Tube Lines had responsibility for three lines, it had 39 benchmark targets for availability, measured in 'lost customer hours'. It missed 22 of them, and had not a single day without delays in its first six months.[296] The Infraco pointed out that it had beaten targets on other performance measures, for example ensuring that dot-matrix destination indicator signs were working properly and that trains were cleaner and had less graffiti.

In 2003, the Infracos presided over a surge in the number of breakdowns, points failures and track problems, and missed reliability targets on six lines. 'Track safety compromised' incidents[†] more than doubled from 69 in 2001/02 to 149 in 2003/04. Broken rails rose from 25 to 33 in the same period. The House of Commons Transport Committee examined the Infracos' performance. It recalled that the benchmarks were set at a level 5 per cent below the performance levels that London Underground Ltd had achieved during Shadow Running, even though their performance then was 'abysmal'. The Committee reported that 'all the Infracos needed to do to meet their availability targets was to perform only a little worse than in the past. On most lines they did not even manage that.'

The Committee had 'no confidence' that the Infracos would meet future targets, noted that many improvements had been deferred until after the first 7½-year Review Period, and concluded that, 'improvements in facilities and performance are not in proportion to the huge sums of money flowing through the PPP'.[297] London Underground rejected Tube Lines' plans for station enhancements as 'inadequate', and Transport for London complained that the Infracos were failing to invest in new equipment. New London Underground Ltd Managing Director Tim O'Toole complained that he had very little power to do anything about this.[298] Mayor Ken Livingstone appointed O'Toole in February 2003, to take over from Paul Godier as Managing Director when TfL took control of London Underground on 15 July 2003. O'Toole was the former Chief Executive of US rail freight company Consolidated Rail Corporation, Conrail. Christian Wolmar explained that, 'cows were the only living things he carried on his previous railways and he did not take kindly to the frequent reference to cattle trucks by [the] *Evening Standard*'s veteran transport correspondent Dick Murray.[299]

† Incidents when work is undertaken in such a way as to compromise the safety of the whole working environment – does not refer to track condition.

TABLE 4: LOST CUSTOMER HOURS: PERFORMANCE AGAINST BENCHMARKS, APRIL 2003 – MARCH 2004

Line	No. of periods performance was below benchmark (out of 13)	No. of periods performance was 'unacceptable'
Bakerloo	4	2
Central	8	5
Victoria	9	5
Waterloo & City	9	6
Metropolitan, Circle and Hammersmith & City	1	0
District	0	0
East London	6	3
Jubilee	8	5
Northern	7	6
Piccadilly	7	2

In January 2004, snowfall brought severe disruption to Tube services. London Underground Ltd deployed dozens of extra drivers to run de-icing trains, only to find that the Infracos had not cleared snow from the tracks in the trains' depots, leaving the trains unable to move out of the depots and into passenger service.[300] By late 2004, a London Underground Ltd report stated that key parts of the Tube's service had not improved under PPP, and that existing assets would not be in a good state until 2025. LUL accused Metronet and Tube Lines of producing 'non-existent, incompetent or inconsistent' work plans.[301] The National Audit Office also produced a report,[302] which questioned whether the various parties were clear about their responsibilities under PPP, citing as an example a row about who should pay for repairs to bearing faults on Piccadilly line trains' axle boxes. The report also complained of 'low productivity' by Infracos during weekend closures.

Into PPP's second year, the situation was not improving. Transport for London's report on PPP's second year revealed the extent of TfL's concerns, as outlined below.[303]

Only ten of the 18 station refurbishments due by March 2005 were completed on time. Work to upgrade London Underground's lines had only just started, and LUL was unhappy with the paucity of information from the Infracos about their plans. The Tube Lines consortium had completed only 17 projects to refurbish or replace escalators, far fewer than its bid promised. Metronet's escalator work was running slightly ahead of schedule, but the schedule on BCV was 21 per cent less than its bid. On SSL, Metronet had spent 50 per cent of its expected costs for just 25 per cent of the completed work. In a portent of the poor financial practices that would eventually bring it down, Metronet was paying its contractors for work before they actually did it.

Overall, the trains were getting better and track problems were decreasing. However, London Underground had to issue two **Corrective Action Notices**: one to Metronet BCV for failure in track maintenance processes; and one to Metronet SSL for poorly-managed and unsafe track renewal work. The programme to extend the life of the 26-year-old District line train fleet by eight years was running over a year late. By the end of Year Two, 42.3 km of track had been replaced, just 69 per cent of the 61 km promised in the bids.

Signalling was in trouble. In 2004/05, Metronet BCV averaged around 70 failures per period; Metronet SSL had a 7 per cent reduction in the number of failures but a 10 per cent increase in their duration; and Tube Lines suffered an average 82.8 failures per period, a 10 per cent worsening on 2003/04. 'Signals Passed At Danger' (SPADs) were 2.8 per cent down on 2003/04, but while those caused by drivers fell by 10 per cent, those caused by technical problems leapt by 30 per cent. In other words, the efforts of train drivers to reduce SPADs were cancelled out three times over by the Infracos' failure to maintain signalling equipment.

Excluding the Bakerloo line, Infraco BCV's 'Availability' performance fell 30 per cent below Metronet's bid. London Underground said that 'this raises concerns about whether Metronet is addressing asset performance issues as successfully as it hoped'. It should also have raised concerns about how honest the bid was. Metronet SSL's performance was the partial exception to the poor Availability scores, exceeding both benchmark and bid. But this exception also had an exception: the East London line, whose Year Two performance was 3 per cent below Year One and 4 per cent below Metronet's bid.

Scores for Ambience – the quality of the customer environment – fell short of the bids, as a rise in graffiti-removal scores was dragged down by poor station décor. The Infracos received frequent abatements for faults in facilities such as CCTV, public address systems and help points. Despite the generous allowance of 'Service Points' they could incur before being abated, Metronet BCV and Tube Lines exceeded the threshold in all thirteen four-week periods of the year and Metronet SSL exceeded the threshold in four periods. Tube Lines also suffered two abatements for (shortcomings in) 'fault rectification'. While Metronet avoided abatements in this area, it showed 'no evidence' of an improving trend. With no abatement, why would it?

The latest Transport Minister, Tony McNulty, admitted that PPP was having 'teething problems', but the situation was beginning to look more like serious dental rot. In July 2004, London Underground put up posters apologising for 'horrible' delays caused by signalling problems affecting seven lines on just one day. One October morning, Manor House station closed shortly after it opened, when plaster applied to the ceiling overnight collapsed over the westbound platform, dislodged by the vibration of the first train.[304] An embarrassing year reached an almost comical climax when it emerged that Tube Lines was buying spare parts on eBay.[305]

London Underground Ltd was 'far from impressed' with Metronet's performance in January 2005, when the Infraco's failure to complete night engineering work left 100,000 Central line passengers stranded and disrupted other lines too. LUL Managing Director Tim O'Toole castigated the Infracos: 'these guys are supposed to be the cavalry, but so far they're the same world-weary infantry we saw under London Underground'.[306]

When the Infracos finished their overnight maintenance work late, the train service started late. This delayed early morning passengers, often causing waves of delay into and beyond the morning peak period, inconveniencing and frustrating untold thousands. These 'engineering overruns' blighted morning passengers' journeys. Bakerloo driver Jock told me that 'once the service did start, the platforms would be heaving, the trains would be maxed out, and as a driver, you would get the brunt of it, passengers coming up and complaining, saying this is a disgrace'. Year Two saw 35 per cent more engineering overruns than Year One. In Year Three, overruns were up again, disrupting early-morning journeys 207 times during the year, or four times a week on average. Many were caused by avoidable failures such as the Infracos not checking that their people had the right tools or not telling the control centre when they had finished their work. But the 278 engineering overruns from the start of PPP to the beginning of 2005 attracted just £1.2m in penalty payments, only a little more than the profit made by each Infraco each week. Mike Brown told me that:

> Penalties for overruns were very low – they gave a penalty for the initial overruns, but nothing in terms of the knock-on effect. I was London Underground's Chief Operating Officer, so the issue of late starts in the morning was in my face. There were some very blunt discussions. We put in an 8 o'clock conference call every morning. [The Infracos] had their bigwigs on, we had ours, and we'd go through all the items on the sheets from the previous day, whether that was an engineering overrun or an asset failure or whatever it was. There was also a series of more formal monthly reviews.

Not only were the Infracos falling short; the companies to which they contracted much of their work were also causing problems. In one example, contractors fitted large makeshift brackets to tunnel walls between Farringdon and Barbican stations during the night of 10-11 February 2004. The brackets protruded too far, but the contractors did not check or correct this. When the morning's trains drove through, their windows shattered, with ten trains sustaining damage.[307] The RMT trade union's Regional Organiser Bobby Law blamed the 'complex web' of subcontracting under PPP.[308] Tim O'Toole declared that, 'The performance of the Underground defies any defence through this period'. Transport for London Commissioner Bob Kiley told the TfL Board that, 'If we don't see improvements ... we may be at a point where we will have to revisit these contracts in a pretty vigorous way.'[309]

Another example of mistakes by contractors occurred when Metronet wanted to help speed up the train service by reducing the time it took train doors to close. The Infraco subcontracted the work to RPL, which the RMT union claimed used agency workers without the right qualifications. Their substandard work led to increased air pressure damaging door guides. On 20 October 2005 at around 7pm, a Victoria line train travelled between stations with a door nearly 40cm open. After the incident, fully-qualified Metronet staff found numerous other faults.[310] Agencies also supplied staff for other work, such as cleaning escalators. Sometimes the agencies did not even employ the staff, but defined them as self-employed, paid them by the hour, and gave them no sick pay and no paid holidays.[311] Even Protection Masters, who ensure the safety of people working on the track, were contracted out.

In a 2005 report, the Greater London Assembly's Transport Committee described passengers' distressing experience when travelling on London Underground:

> Message boards on each and every station across the Tube network regularly list 'severe delays'; posters on stations offer apologies from London Underground about why a line wasn't operating the previous day, and every morning passengers whose tube lines are being worked on the night before wince in anticipation of a fresh delay.[312]

DISABLED ACCESS?[313]

London Underground was (and still is) beyond use for many disabled people. Its obstacle course of steps, gaps and obstructions kept many people out. At the start of the PPP, only 43 – around one in seven – London Underground stations were 'step-free', allowing people to journey from the street to the ticket hall to the platform and onto the train without encountering a step, which may be an insurmountable obstacle to a wheelchair user. People with visual and other sensory impairments did not have guidance in the formats they needed, and short-staffing left passengers with disabilities often unable to find assistance.

London Underground was public transport that did not provide transport for a section of the public. Disabled people had long been campaigning for access, and Transport Minister David Jamieson assured MPs that 'The PPP will result in real improvements to the accessibility of the Underground'.[314] But would the PPP really unlock the Tube?

PPP's contracts required the Infracos to comply with the Rail Vehicle Accessibility Regulations. The stations enhancement programme included accessibility improvements such as tactile guidance systems, colour contrasts on steps and stairs, induction loops to assist hearing-impaired passengers using ticket offices and help points, and better audio and visual information. New and refurbished trains would be similarly enhanced. When the section of the Disability Discrimination

Act governing transport came into force in October 2004, it raised the prospect of disabled passengers suing London Underground for its inaccessibility. But the Infracos had ensured that they were protected: they successfully demanded that a clause was inserted into the PPP contracts giving them the right to challenge LUL's plans for improving access if they thought those plans were greater than the bare legal minimum. TfL wrote that, 'In effect, this means that the LUL accessibility plan can no longer go forward based solely on LUL's view that it should.'[315]

Moreover, the core PPP contracts did not require the Infracos to make stations accessible without steps, as this was explicitly removed.[316] The government claimed that sixteen stations would be made step-free by 2009 under PPP, but even this small figure was above the mere thirteen stated in the contracts.[317] Any work to improve access beyond this would have to be done outside the contract. In 2004, TfL announced a five-year plan that included a target of making London Underground 25 per cent step-free by 2010 and 50 per cent thereafter. But within a year, LUL was complaining that the Infracos were 'slow' to address work it requested on step-free access. It set up an 'alternative supplier framework' to get someone else to do the job. Tim O'Toole blamed the PPP's output-based contracts: 'This contractual situation means that if LU wishes to specify something, especially on maintenance issues, we are not in a strong position. If we wish for specific works to be undertaken, we can request this but it is ultimately at the Infracos' discretion whether or not to do it.'[318]

Perhaps disabled passengers might benefit from the renewal of the existing lifts that facilitated step-free access? Progress with the maintenance of these particular lifts is monitored separately from lifts in general, and this revealed 'an unacceptable level of failures' in the first three years of PPP.

Metronet and Tube Lines both promised in their bids to refurbish or replace all the lifts in their charge, most during the first 7½-year review period. But both Infracos backpedalled on their bid commitment. Metronet BCV managed 18 lifts, promised in its bid to renew 17 of them during Review Period One (RP1), and reduced this in its 'asset management plan' to just eleven. It renewed two in Year One, and none in Years Two and Three. Metronet SSL had few lifts, but had not renewed any of them by the end of Year Three. By Year Two, it had scaled down its plans to renew just eight lifts in RP1. The following year, it halved this unambitious plan to just four. Tube Lines promised in its bid to refurbish or replace thirty lifts by the end of Year Three, but only completed its first two in the third year. Its explanation was that it had adopted an alternative approach: 'incremental component replacement'. Instead of revamping lifts, Tube Lines would just take out broken parts and put new parts in.[319]

Passengers using Queensway station rely on its two lifts for access between the street and the platforms. By 2006, the station had been closed for over a year for a refurbishment that Metronet had still not finished. The Infraco apologised, explaining that replacing the lifts was 'extremely complex'. A progress inspection in February 2006 reported 'little work being done', a 'complete lack of drive' and weekends being 'totally wasted'. When Metronet declared the Queensway refurbishment project 'finished' in June 2006 (six weeks late), an inspection found 346 electrical faults, 214 faulty fixtures and fittings, 125 communications equipment faults and 42 fire alarm faults. Despite this, Metronet managers invited 78 guests to a drink and dinner in a private room at the Lord Raglan pub in the City of London, paid for by the company, to 'celebrate our success'.[320] Problems continued, with the lifts failing on occasion, and an incident in which the eastbound platform closed as its 'Way Out' sign dangled in mid-air.[321]

DERAILED: 2003-2004

To scrutinise how PPP's safety claims worked out in practice, we will consider two major risks for underground railways: derailments and fire. The first of these crashed into the headlines in the PPP's earliest days.

Just before 2pm on Saturday 25 January 2003, a westbound Central line train entered Chancery Lane station. The rear of its fifth carriage came off the tracks, pulling the three carriages behind it off the tracks too, smashing them along the tunnel walls. The windows caved in and passengers were thrown from their seats. Passenger Allan Moore told the BBC:

There was a tremendous bang, the glass shattered and flowed like a river of glass. People were screaming. There was smoke and there was the smell of burning. There was blood on the floor. At one point the lights on the train failed and people moved forward in the dark. One of the doors had been ripped off and was laying on the platform.[322]

Medics took over thirty people to hospital, and treated the train's driver for smoke inhalation. Mike Brown – who became London Underground's Chief Operating Officer in 2003 – turned up at the scene of the derailment, to face 'a huge mass of media'. It was LU's worst incident for years, but as Brown admitted, 'It could have been so much worse. These things are very sobering.'

What had happened? At around 1.30pm, the driver of an eastbound Central line train reported hearing a noise from the westbound train as he drove past it. Station staff confirmed that there was an 'unusual noise', but the Central line control room instructed the driver to continue to Holborn, to empty his train of passengers and drive it into the sidings there. But as the train approached Chancery Lane – the stop before Holborn – a traction motor weighing nearly half a tonne broke free from its mountings, causing the crash. Within days, the BBC was linking the Chancery Lane crash to Shadow Running and PPP, noting that: 'the Central Line and its trains are already being managed in the same way they will be under their new private owners.'[323] For Mike Brown, 'Whether it was a direct cause or not, when you get a management team distracted from day to day delivery by other political machinations and a legal war over the future between the current and future owners, there will be less than 100 per cent focus on the job in hand'.

London Underground Ltd's report into the Chancery Lane derailment blamed confusion, communication breakdown and an institutionalised buck-passing blame culture. But it concluded that the main underlying cause was that the lessons of earlier incidents had not been learned. The previous September, a Central line train had derailed in the sidings at Loughton, a motor shearing off its mountings; in another incident, a brake fluid tank fell off a Central line train near Shepherd's Bush. Infraco BCV (as it was called under Shadow Running before its transfer to Metronet) had issued a safety alert after the Loughton derailment, but had not communicated adequately to LUL or to its own staff.[324] Infraco BCV and London Underground Ltd both knew that there was a serious problem with motor bolts, safety brackets and gearboxes, but failed to act because of cost and complacency.

Central line maintenance staff suggested other factors that may have been undermining safety standards. They had been working overtime just to cover basic duties; agencies were being used to carry out safety-critical work including the five-day inspections on motor bolts; some agency staff checking bolts were not formally trained; and tools supplied did not fit over the bolts.[325] One agency worker said that he had been required to check ten trains in one shift by himself, when the quality plan said he should check three. RMT alleged that London Underground managers were putting 'intolerable pressure on Tube workers to run suspected faulty trains in order to meet the targets'. Just a week before the Chancery Lane derailment, a union member had lodged a grievance about bullying and threats when he had refused to drive a train having reported banging noises.'[326] London Underground workers' bulletin *Tubeworker* asked: 'What kind of regime keeps a train running when it is at risk? ... the business ethos world of LUL under Shadow Running, where delays incur penalties and checks are made less often than they need to be.'[327]

Drivers felt insecure. Jock told me that they wondered:

Are our trains and tracks being properly maintained? You were going to work with a general feeling that things weren't as safe as they used to be. Trains would not be taken out of service unless they were on fire or the motors dropped off! The private companies' motivation was to keep trains in service regardless so their payments were not affected. Previously you would say 'there's an issue with the train' and the train maintainer would say 'let's get this into the depot and get it looked at'. Now their reply would be 'this can be kept in service'. You'd get sympathy from the train maintainers – 'sorry, we've been told we can't do anything about it, we have to keep this in service, my job's on the line' – but nothing would be done about the defects.

The derailment cost around £40m, with Infraco BCV liable for just £100,000, the public sector for the rest.[328] Two years later, Metronet happily reported that, 'good progress has been made with London Underground in agreeing cost recovery from the events which followed the Chancery Lane incident and for which Metronet Rail BCV had an indemnity at the point of transfer'.[329]

The government rejected calls to suspend PPP's implementation. But London Underground Ltd did suspend the Central line – at 74km, the

Tube's longest line, carrying half-a-million passengers each day – and the Waterloo and City line, which uses the same type of train. When the Waterloo and City line reopened in February, it closed just hours later when bolts came loose. When Central line services resumed through central London in April, they were promptly suspended. Dust from tunnel walls had stuck to glue left on the tracks during night work at Tottenham Court Road station, and the first trains heated the glue, creating smoke.[330] The PPP's structure required blame to be allocated. LUL said that it was not to blame, because Metronet BCV was responsible for the track; Metronet said it was not to blame, because LUL should keep the track clean and because its poster-pasting contractor, Viacom Ltd, spilt the glue on the track. Metronet added that it could not be fined because the final PPP contracts would not be signed until the next day. In September 2003, routine checks found cracks on Central line trains' motor brackets, despite over 11,000 brackets on 2,800 motors being replaced after the Chancery Lane crash. Metronet did not tell LUL about the problem for several days.[331]

Later in 2003, Tube Lines shareholder company Jarvis plc faced a court case and an investigation for two mainline derailments.[332] It pulled out of its mainline track repair business, and Railtrack plc's successor, Network Rail Ltd announced that it was to stop using private contractors for maintenance altogether. An opinion poll found that 65 per cent of respondents thought that firms which had lost contracts on the mainline railway should not be allowed to maintain London Underground.[333] But these same firms continued to maintain the Underground under the PPP. And the PPP was soon in the headlines again.

At 9.25pm on Friday 17 October 2003, the last carriage of a Piccadilly line train came off the track as it travelled eastwards from Hammersmith, dragging the train to a halt 200m short of Barons Court station. Passenger Samantha Ceranha described how, 'Sparks lit up the whole carriage, the lights went out for a bit and there was loads of smoke everywhere. It was very scary.' The BBC reported that the rail had rusted nearly three-quarters of the way through. Previously, workers had inspected the track, looking for faults like this, every 24 hours. These inspections had been cut to 72-hourly just before the PPP contract was signed.[334]

Less than two days later, another train derailed. On Sunday 19 October at 10:01, the last carriage of a Northern line train travelling northbound came off the rails, hit the wall and uncoupled from the train at Camden Town station. A witness told the BBC: 'There was a lot of blackened faces and there was one man with bandages on his face and blood streaming down. They had lined up some chairs at the top of the escalators and were sitting people down with blankets around them.'

Seven people went to hospital, one with a broken femur and another with head injuries. Tube Lines emergency response worker Tom told me that, 'It was an absolute mess down there, it was a nightmare to repair, it just seemed to take forever.' The Northern line could not operate through Camden Town for ten days. When it reopened, the junction where the two branches of the line meet was locked into two separate routes, forcing many more people than usual to change trains. The line did not return to normal until March 2004. The trade unions led calls for the PPP contracts to be suspended. But excuses for not doing so came quickly, Liberal Democrat MP Simon Hughes claiming that 'legally it would be difficult'.[335]

What had caused these two derailments? London Underground Ltd initially claimed that the Hammersmith derailment was 'unavoidable', its safety chief claiming that government inspectors gave LUL a clean bill of health after the incident. But the Railway Inspectorate complained that this claim misled staff and passengers, and LUL's safety chief had to apologise.[336] London Underground Ltd's official report blamed the derailment on job cuts and the use of subcontractors. It revealed that on that night, there were twice as many subcontractors as Metronet track staff working in the incident area, and that the on-call senior contract manager was a consultant for a third party, whom LUL had difficulty locating. Track workers did not have adequate lighting to spot defects as they inspected rails.

The Northern line train had come off the track at Camden because 'the balance between the downward force and the outward force on the left wheel of the set went outside of the tolerable range', according to London Underground Ltd's initial report. This happened because of a design weakness in the switchblade used on the points, coinciding with a rare combination of other factors.[337] But both ASLEF and RMT trade unions said that drivers had complained of track problems in the area.[338] One driver told of the convoluted process for reporting such concerns under the PPP: 'The driver gets off his train, tells his line manager, who tells his manager, who tells the fault reporting centre, where somebody passes the complaint to their manager, who sends somebody to check it out – there's so much red tape.'[339]

There had now been three derailments of trains in passenger service in the last ten months, the two most recent within just 37 hours of each other. Derailments in depots had also become more common. LUL's Chief Operating Officer Mike Brown was 'very shocked' by TfL Commissioner Bob Kiley's response: 'He said to me "Oh, we had about twelve derailments in my first two months in Boston – this is quite normal for subways."'

Was this 'normal', or had PPP contributed to the worrying number of derailments? The evidence suggests that under Shadow Running and now PPP, the regime for inspecting and maintaining track and trains had slipped dramatically. After the Hammersmith derailment, a track manager in the area said that maintenance had become 'not preventative but reactive'. Trackworkers had insufficient resources, working without the new technology which could identify cracks on the underside of rails. The west end of the Central line used to have an inspection team of 26 people. Shadow Running saw this cut to twelve, and PPP to just six. Some inspections were now carried out from a moving train rather than on foot.[340] The Health and Safety Executive reported thousands of examples of 'substantial non-compliance' with standards, most concerning track condition. London Underground Ltd confessed that, 'Manual track assessment is not being done at the required frequency due to lack of competent staff'.[341] RMT compared how workers corrected wrongly-aligned track before PPP with how they did it under PPP. Before PPP, experienced maintenance workers would reset the distance between rails to their precise alignment, one worker describing that, 'If you were just a few millimetres off, the chargehand [supervisor] would put a flea in your ear.' But under PPP, transferred staff and agency workers were expected instead to 'finish the job within the wider tolerance framework permitted by the standard'. Before PPP, if a gang sent to correct a section of rail that was wrongly aligned laterally found it was also wrongly aligned vertically, they would fix both. Under PPP, gangs were encouraged to only complete the task that was on the job ticket, not to use their initiative to do any more.[342]

In late October 2003, RMT held a meeting of its workplace representatives to discuss the derailments. The union demanded assurances on safety from London Underground Ltd and the Infracos, including the restoration of 24-hourly track inspections and the suspension of the PPP contracts pending investigations into the derailments. Union protesters sporting bowler hats and cigars demonstrated outside Metronet's Templar House office, while RMT members voted in a ballot to take industrial action. Bob Kiley tried to dissuade the union, issuing 'a call to close ranks, all of us, including the infrastructure companies and the union leadership and to focus on the job in hand'.[343] But RMT called a 'go-slow' for 9 and 10 December and for a week starting on 17 December. On 3 December, RMT General Secretary Bob Crow took London Underground Managing Director Tim O'Toole for a late-night track walk around the site of the Hammersmith derailment. As they set off down the track, a Metronet maintenance gang appeared, without hard hats, trolley lights or flashing lights – all essential safety equipment.[344]

An RMT representative recalled that:

> We had a head of steam behind us and we went into talks which management wanted to divert down the road of setting up a working party to look at patrolling frequencies. We went in there with the position that we're here to talk to you about making the patrols 24 hours, nothing else. Everyone was behind this dispute, but then a union official got involved and instead of sticking to that line, he agreed to the working party being set up, which went on for about three months, all the steam went out of the issue, then management started cutting the patrolling.

RMT called off its industrial action as the employers agreed to an emergency review of track patrolling, fault reporting and fixing, and to double-staff night-time track inspections in open (non-tunnel) sections. The derailments contributed to a £55m shortfall in TfL's budget. 50,000 Tube journeys per day moved to London's buses.[345] Passengers' fear of PPP's impact on their safety was driving them away from the Tube, with the public TfL rather than the private Infracos picking up the bill.

The next year saw another derailment. At 12.27pm on 11 May 2004, a westbound Central line train came off the track near White City. The 150 passengers escaped injury and walked to safety, but it soon became clear that there were serious issues involved. The train derailed at points in an area of such poor track quality that it was subject to a 20 mph speed limit. The points were among 42 sets identified as potentially dangerous after the Camden Town derailment. A Chief Engineer's Regulatory Notice had set out remedial work required: LUL told the Infracos, but Metronet did not tell its own Central line track team.[346] When the PPP came in, there were 15,000 known track-related items that were below the required engineering standards. The PPP contracts exempted the Infracos from fines when these caused problems, so there was no incentive for them to fix them.

The Health and Safety Executive decided not to prosecute Metronet for causing a train loaded with passengers to come off its tracks, claiming that 'an unforeseeable result of automatic train operation' had also contributed to the derailment.[347] Many people thought that the Infraco had caused a serious incident but had got away with it, and that the PPP was once again at fault. RMT General Secretary Bob Crow argued that, 'A company that fails to comply with explicit safety instructions put in place after one derailment and as a result causes another should not be allowed to continue operation on the network'.[348] New ASLEF General Secretary Keith Norman said, 'The lesson of White City is that there is no place for private ownership and profit seeking on the Underground'.[349] Norman had replaced Shaun Brady, who had replaced Mick Rix as ASLEF General Secretary. Brady's victory was widely seen as a move away from industrial militancy, political campaigning and the close relationship that Rix had forged with Bob Crow and RMT.

FIRE RISKS: 2003-2007
How did the PPP help London Underground protect itself against its greatest risk – fire? Let us look at some relevant incidents.

For six weeks as 2003 turned into 2004, Knightsbridge station had no working fire protection system. During improvement works, 'Loop Outputs' (the messages automatically relayed from the station's fire detection devices to the central hub that operated fire-fighting measures when needed) were deleted. This left the system unable to open ticket gates to allow people to escape from fire, and unable to operate smoke dampers – mechanisms which shut off ventilation when smoke is detected in order to isolate any fire. A Chief Engineer's Regulatory Notice, issued for 'non-compliance with fire standards', itemised that Tube Lines and its contractors had: failed to meet standards; failed to ensure that only demonstrably competent engineers were working on London

Underground's fire detection and alarm system; and failed to test and commission fire safety equipment before offering it to LUL.[350]

In March 2005, contractors built a timber bridge and hoist in a disused lift shaft at Oxford Circus station using wood of the lowest grade. London Underground Ltd's Fire Engineer recorded the incident as 'serious' because of the risk of the material catching fire.[351] In January 2006, a cable lost its insulation and caused a fire in a Northern line tunnel between Bank and London Bridge. Two staff and twenty passengers suffered the effects of smoke inhalation. In April 2006, Tube Lines' sub-contractors told the Charing Cross Station Supervisor that they were going to carry out a 'non-intrusive' survey. But instead, they carried out welding on the platform without a licence and without the required 'fire watchperson', then left. A fire began to smoulder, and the station had to be evacuated. The incident report concluded that there had been no safe system of working; no safety checks of the site when the work finished; no competent 'site person in charge'; a lack of competent planning; and no proper risk assessment.[352] A few months later, a Metronet project manager authorised contractor Dalkia to isolate fire detection equipment at Finsbury Park station despite knowing that this was against the rules because it effectively switched off the station's ability to notice smoke or fire. The station closed while the problem was resolved. But when it reopened, London Underground Ltd managers allowed the Metronet project manager to remain in charge of the work. The London Underground Ltd station staff refused to work with the Metronet manager because they considered him to be reckless with fire safety, and the station closed again.[353]

As well as dealing with individual incidents, London Underground faced possible changes to the rules governing how it dealt with fire risks. What were the proposed changes, and what did they have to do with the PPP?

Below-ground railway stations must abide by minimum standards set out in the Fire Precautions (Sub-Surface Railway Stations) Regulations 1989. The Secretary of State introduced these Regulations in the wake of the 1987 King's Cross fire using the provisions of Section 12 of the Fire Precautions Act 1971. Hence, the Regulations and the stations they apply to go by the name 'Section 12'. London Underground had 115 Section 12 stations, with others in Glasgow, Tyne and Wear, Liverpool and Birmingham. By law, each of these stations must meet standards of fire-resistant construction, and must have: a minimum number of staff on duty with the right equipment and trained to a set standard; means of raising the alarm, fire-fighting and escape; and means of detecting, containing and suppressing fire. But the government decided that this was 'highly prescriptive'.[354] It drafted a replacement Regulatory Reform (Fire Safety) Order in May 2004, proposing to shift fire safety policy towards an approach where the companies that owned sub-surface stations would assess the risks and regulate themselves. London Underground Ltd would be free to consider each of its stations individually and conclude that perhaps a station did not need two staff on duty at all times, or could operate without the fire protection systems previously required or maybe stay open when they broke. Legally-compulsory fire certification would give way to a 'general duty' to ensure safety.

The government claimed that, 'The proposed changes will ensure fire safety standards are maintained', and London Underground Ltd pointed out that there had been no major incidents involving fire and passengers since the King's Cross fire[355] – a fact that suggested that the Section 12 regulations were working and should be left alone. So why replace them with a new system that appeared to be weaker? The answer lay with the PPP, as RMT activist Unjum Mirza explained in his 2007 pamphlet, *I Do Mind Dying*:

> the PPP contracts have placed greater pressure on management to cut costs. The complexity of the system of fines and abatement means the closure of stations and delays to the service cost a huge amount. 'Watering down' health and safety is a means for LUL to avoid such costs ...
>
> the part-privatisation of the tube has led to a deterioration of a safe system of work as the inability to manage the increasingly complex arrangements between LUL, contractors and sub-contractors has created a situation where the left hand simply doesn't know what the right hand is doing. This in itself has led to an increase in fire risk.

The Regulatory Reform Committee of MPs examined the proposed changes and recommended that the 1989 Regulations – 'Section 12' – should remain. The government relented, although it ominously promised to 'return after consultation and guidance'.[356] It returned in

2005, this time planning to operate the Fire Safety Order alongside Section 12 in preparation for replacing it. Campaigners again objected, hundreds joining a union-organised protest at King's Cross station. The new Fire Brigades Union General Secretary, Matt Wrack, warned that the plan would be 'a serious blow to public safety'.[357] Labour MP Andrew Dismore told Parliament that he had visited King's Cross after the fire: 'the sights that I saw then will haunt me forever ... I never thought that I would see the day when my government would consider watering down fire safety protection.'[358]

At a 'working group' set up to discuss the issue, trade union representatives demonstrated that the proposed Fire Safety Order did not provide safety standards as good as the 1989 Regulations, and in early 2007 the government backed down again.[359]

THE MONEY-GO-ROUND: 2003-2005 [360]

We have seen that the PPP was not delivering the level of improvements to London Underground that it promised. Despite this, the Infracos and their shareholders seemed to be making considerable sums of money. How did the PPP's financial systems work in practice?

Metronet had agreed to give the government information about its financial plans. But in February 2003 – before it had even signed the final contracts – Metronet decided to keep secret the fees it paid to financial advisers and the returns it promised to investors, in breach of this agreement. A spokesperson boldly declared that Metronet had no intention of ever revealing these figures for fees and promised returns: 'we didn't have to, and we didn't want to'.[361]

Once it had signed the PPP contracts and taken charge of the maintenance and improvement work, Metronet adjusted the organisation of work in order to direct money to its shareholder companies. Sam, a trackworker, told me that:

> When it came to procurement of tools and materials, they cancelled the accounts we already had and opened up new arrangements through their parent companies at a higher cost. There was no need to change: it was just another way of rinsing more money from the PPP.

The Infracos' £32.3m abatements for substandard performance in PPP's first year were nearly treble their £12.1m bonuses for exceeding expectations.[362] Tube Lines Chief Executive Terry Morgan claimed that the consortium was 'in the business to make profit by good performance',[363] but the facts suggested that PPP furnished the Infracos with substantial profits despite poor performance. In their first year, the Infracos made nearly £100m profit, a margin of 13 per cent. Morgan pocketed a pay package of £552,000, while Metronet's Chief Executive John Weight received £325,000. Having already received 'success fees' for winning the contract, Tube Lines' shareholders received further pay-outs during the PPP's first two years: a 'special distribution' of £20.2m arising from Tube Lines' capital structure refinancing (taking out a new loan to pay off an old loan), plus £7.1m in dividends. But during those two years, these shareholders provided just £45m equity towards Tube Lines' work. RMT marked the start of PPP's second full year with an ironic April Fool's Day celebration outside Westminster station. Union members dressed as 'Mr Jarvis' and 'Mr Balfour-Beatty', wearing bowler hats and smoking cigars, handed out thank-yous to taxpayers for the £1.2bn of public money received so far.[364]

Despite the early claims that PPP could make London Underground self-financing, the Tube was now drawing more public subsidy than ever. Central government's grant rose from £44.1m in 1997/98 to £1,218m in 2003/04: a 27-fold increase from PPP's conception to its birth. By 31 March 2005, LUL had paid £2,220.2m Infrastructure Service Charge (ISC) to the Infracos. 66 per cent of Metronet's income was ISC, 31 per cent borrowing, and the shareholders' own money just 3 per cent. Tube Lines' figures were 51 per cent ISC, 42 per cent borrowing and 7 per cent from shareholders. So the massive injection of private funds promised by PPP turned out to be just a single-figure percentage. For a policy designed to 'lever in' private money, PPP had certainly levered in a lot of public money. The Transport Select Committee concluded that: '[PPP's] major achievement has been to ensure that the government commits itself to providing sustained funding for London Underground; a commitment which, given the political will, could have been made without any PPP'.[365]

Metronet had spent £825.6m by 31 March 2005, considerably less than the £923.5m it said it expected to invest when it took over the contracts. The actual investment may have been even less, due to Metronet's practice of paying its contractors before they did the work. Most of these contractors were its owner companies, to which it paid over

£500m in the first 18 months of PPP. Labour MP Brian Donohue accused the Infracos of 'milking it for all they are worth, for no significant improvement'.[366]

Tube Lines more often awarded contracts to outside companies, but nonetheless paid its owner companies an estimated £135m by 31 March 2005, mainly for project managers. It now had just two owners, as Ferrovial S.A., which already owned Amey plc, bought Jarvis plc's share of Tube Lines. London Underground Ltd had the right to object to, but not veto, changes in Infraco ownership. MPs complained that the companies involved in this ownership change had 'obviously spent some time and money trying to structure a deal that got round our power to do something about it'.[367]

The Infracos' owners were certainly making money. But what of those who were doing the actual work? The next section looks at how Infraco staff fared under the PPP.

PPP VERSUS THE WORKFORCE: 2003-2007

London Underground workers had campaigned against the PPP's introduction, partly motivated by fear for their job security and working conditions should the policy come into force. This section examines what happened to workers under the PPP, whether those fears proved well-founded, and what workers did to defend themselves.

It did not take long for the Infracos to begin reducing their employees' rights. Shortly after taking up the PPP contract, Tube Lines closed its section of the London Transport Pension Scheme to new entrants, meaning that newly-recruited Tube Lines employees could not join the scheme and instead joined Tube Lines' newly-established alternative pension scheme with inferior benefits for members. Tube Lines took this step despite the London Transport Pension Scheme amending its rules to allow the Infracos to participate, despite being indemnified against pension cost rises over the first 7½-year Review Period, and despite having its contribution to the Scheme's deficit refunded in respect of those staff employed at the transfer date. I spoke to several Tube Lines RMT representatives, all of whom regretted that the union did not oppose this attack on workers' pensions more strongly. One said:

It was a mega mistake. At the time there was no-one around who really understood the implications, and it just went through on the nod. It would probably only have taken one day of action from us to make them walk away, because they were so focused on profits and still quite nervous about having the contract taken away from them. It was only later that the old gits like me realised that if we didn't do something about it, then when they came for our pension fund to close it, we'd have no-one there to back us up.

Following Tube Lines' example, Metronet also closed final-salary pensions to new entrants – 'a disaster', according to one RMT representative. The pension change was just one way in which significant differences in benefits opened up between people working for the same Infraco, and between workmates who used to share the same employer, London Underground Ltd. Within a year of PPP's implementation, Infraco staff had worse travel benefits than their LUL counterparts. Even workers doing the same job found themselves being paid at different rates. Adam started working for Tube Lines in 2004, and told me:

> I knew early on that the people who had been in the company before the move over to PPP had more benefits than me. But when I started, the Tube Lines pension wasn't that bad compared to other jobs that I'd been in. I didn't realise at the time that it was so much less than people had previously. At that point, the vast majority of staff had those benefits, but as time progressed, people understood the differences better. It became clear that it's a two-tier system with us doing exactly the same work but getting less benefits, and we're still owned by the same company!

We have already noted Metronet's awarding of work to its own shareholder companies. Metronet also repeatedly attempted to transfer its employees to those shareholder companies. But having recently been transferred to one private employer, workers did not want to be transferred again to another. In 2003, Metronet gave a £3.4bn contract to Bombardier Transportation Ltd to supply 1,738 new carriages for sub-surface and Victoria line trains,[368] and sought to transfer its Victoria line train maintainers to the employment of Bombardier Ltd too. This set up the first battle between the RMT trade union and an Infraco. For RMT representative Sam, 'By then, we were in the private sector, the fight against PPP was long gone and over, but we saw an opportunity to stop this transfer. We passed a resolution to oppose it and set up the Metronet strike committee.' The union prevailed, and the workers remained employed by Metronet.

Metronet tried again in late 2005, this time planning to transfer its fleet engineers to the employment of Bombardier Ltd. RMT balloted its members for industrial action. With over 80 per cent of Metronet staff being RMT members, and an overwhelming majority voting to strike, Metronet backed down. It agreed not to 'outsource' any current work to another company without the union's agreement and that a proposed reorganisation would not involve any compulsory redundancies. A union representative explained that: 'we agreed an arrangement whereby the stock would be maintained by Metronet staff, who would be directed technically by Bombardier but would be managed by Metronet. So staff wouldn't be transferred out, they'd stay with Metronet.'

But Bombardier Ltd was unhappy about Metronet agreeing with RMT not to give it any work without the union's permission. Bombardier Ltd challenged the dispute settlement, wanting to employ those who would maintain the new trains it was building for Metronet's lines. In 2007, Metronet again tried to transfer staff to its shareholder company, and again came into conflict with RMT. A union overtime ban put pressure on the Infraco, and on the eve of a three-day strike, it abandoned the transfer plan.

Metronet developed a new strategy through 2004 and 2005. 'The Metronet Way' was 'founded on a new organisational culture that focuses on performance, achievement and delivery', its key values 'enshrined in a Metronet vision for "Getting London to Work"'. It promised to make Metronet 'a great place to work', while admitting that is staff 'have been subjected to significant change since their transfer from London Underground'.[369] One of those staff, though, described 'The Metronet Way' to me as 'just a corporate fad management initiative.' Metronet staff took strike action in the summer of 2004, prompting the Infraco to increase a pay offer of 2.4 per cent to 3.6 per cent. For RMT representative Sam, 'Metronet were testing the water by seeing if we would fight for more or not, so we knew we had to'.

Metronet also dropped plans to sell the Railway Engineering Works at Acton, which it claimed had 'falling workstreams'. RMT said there was 'no credible evidence' for this claim, and even alleged that 'there have been alarming reports that Metronet may be deliberately scaling down repairs on the existing stock to save money in anticipation that the new trains will arrive on time'.[370] At Ruislip depot, Metronet's contractor Balfour Beatty plc tried to impose new rosters that cut wages, but withdrew them after protests and an unofficial walkout by workers. Balfour Beatty plc then wanted some workers based at the depot to work compulsory overtime every rostered Friday, but backed down when RMT balloted for industrial action. It was a similar story at Northfields depot in 2006 when Tube Lines tried to compel train maintenance staff to work on Saturday nights. [371]

The Infracos did not seem to show a great regard for contract workers, even when they did a great job. Contractor GrantRail completed its 7½ - year contract with Tube Lines in three-and-a-half years. But the seventy workers, instead of being rewarded or at least kept on, lost their jobs. Tube Lines even refused RMT's plea that it take on no new contractors while those facing redundancy could do the work.[372]

Moreover, the stations that the Infracos were not improving were also losing their staff. London Underground Ltd insisted that a 2006 reduction in its station staff's working hours should be 'self-financing', and so reduced overall staffing levels. Around the same time a similar reduction was made in the working hours of service control staff. It was accompanied by a reorganisation that cut costs and worsened working conditions. Although the trade unions won shorter hours for members, they proved ineffective in preventing this coming at a hefty price.

PRIVATE FINANCE PROBLEMS: 2003-2006

London Underground had Private Finance Initiative (PFI) projects in place, which predated the Public-Private Partnership (see **TABLE 1** page 12). How did these projects fare alongside the PPP? Here, we consider three examples: London Underground's power supply; Connect radio; and Northern line train maintenance. During the PPP, all were involved in significant incidents and problems on the Tube.

On 28 August 2003, London's electrical power supply failed from 6.20pm until 7pm. It stopped 62 Underground trains between stations, forced 1,200 passengers to leave eight trains via the track and made 17,000 people wait on board 54 other trains. Previously, London Underground Ltd could have used its own power supply to move the stranded trains. However, the 1998 Power PFI had seen its Lots Road power station's site sold to Taylor Woodrow and become a development of shops and flats. So the Underground no longer had a back-up power supply and the trains did not move.

Another PFI project – Connect – was running seriously late in its task to provide a modern radio communication system that could work underground. It should have been in place before 7 July 2005, but on that tragic date, it was not available when it was needed most. Jihadi suicide bombers brought death and destruction to London's transport, killing 52 people and injuring over 770 more, with three explosions on Underground trains and one on a bus. Fourteen days later, an attempted repeat attack failed, and the day after that, hyped-up police officers shot dead innocent Brazilian electrician Jean Charles de Menezes at Stockwell Tube station. London Underground workers were on hand in the immediate aftermath of the bombings, supporting the injured and evacuating around a quarter of a million people within an hour. Workers repaired the structural damage and got the full Tube service restored within just four weeks. Tim O'Toole said that, 'Our people handled that so well, they did a spectacular job'.[373] Transport Secretary Alistair Darling commended Tube staff's courage and professionalism.[374] But London Underground workers wanted protection more than praise. Bakerloo driver Jock explained that:

> For a few days afterwards, there would be very few people around your station, lots of people gave the Tube a miss, passengers were worried about further terror attacks. And the train radio wasn't reliable, so there was general anxiety from drivers about the ability of London Underground to support us if we were dealing with any of these issues.

As an RMT delegate, I told the Trades Union Congress in September 2005 that if the government and employers really respected London Underground staff, they would reverse the PPP, fund the Underground and stop planned staffing cuts.

Six years later, in 2011, the inquest confirmed what London Underground and emergency workers knew at the time: that radio communications equipment was not good enough. Desmond Fennell, author of the report into the King's Cross fire, reacted to the finding with 'dismay, disappointment and despair'. Developing a radio system that worked below ground was, he said, 'central to my recommendations ...

[and] central to dealing with any catastrophe in London Underground'. He found it 'incomprehensible' that 'technological problems could not have been overcome in that period of time if the money was available'.[375] The answer lay with Connect PFI, which was supposed to deliver a state-of-the-art radio system by October 2003, but which was already running four years behind schedule (and over budget). Transport for London complained that 'performance by the contractor is not good enough'.[376]

In their hurry to restore the service after the bombings, some London Underground Ltd managers tried to have trains run without working radios,[377] but the company agreed to union demands that without a working radio, a train must not run. When further bombs failed to explode on Tube trains two weeks later on 21 July 2005, LUL suspended the lines involved but expected others to keep running. However, Underground train drivers had heard Police Commissioner Ian Blair's advice to the public not travel into London, and knew that the emergency services were busy at the bomb sites. They refused to drive their passengers into danger.

Drivers would also refuse to drive their trains because of safety fears on the Northern line later in 2005, resulting from the failure of another PFI project to ensure that equipment worked safely and properly. The Northern line was London Underground's most heavily-used line. It was also the only one to operate below performance targets without exception throughout the first two years of the PPP. It had by far the most signal, points and track failures, and only 61 per cent of the benchmark number of trains available for service, despite having one of the newest fleets of trains.[378] One major reason was the delay to the Connect PFI, but now there was another reason related to the Northern line train maintenance PFI – brake failure.

When a London Underground signal is red, a 'trainstop' sticks up from the track next to it, so that if a train passes the red signal, a 'tripcock arm' suspended from the underside of the train knocks the trainstop and applies the emergency brake. It is a failsafe system that brings any train that passes a red signal to a halt, preventing it running into another train. It keeps millions of passengers safe. From 9 September 2005, the system began to fail on the Northern line. After the fourth failure, inspections found nearly ten more trains with defective tripcocks. Trade unions ASLEF and RMT insisted on a second person travelling with every driver and each train being checked daily.[379] The following week, London

Underground Ltd issued an Emergency Direction, a contractual mechanism which required Tube Lines to audit the work of its PFI train maintenance contractor Alstom plc and produce a plan to rectify faults. But even after modifications, the emergency braking system failed again, and drivers refused to drive trains which they knew were not safe. LUL managers sent four drivers home without pay, RMT and ASLEF jointly announced a ballot for industrial action, and LUL reinstated the drivers' pay and suspended the line for three days while every train's tripcock mechanism was fixed.

One supporter of private enterprise argued that, 'The Northern line problem is not necessarily a failure of the private sector, but of the public sector's ability to understand how to manage its relationships with the private sector.'[380] Bob Kiley demanded the termination of Alstom plc's PFI contract, and complained that lines of authority were not clear under the PPP: 'It isn't right you can truly be responsible for train operations without having responsibility for the maintenance and renewal of the physical plant.'[381] MPs submitted a motion[382] asserting that 'identifying and fixing the fault has been made more difficult by the fragmentation of train maintenance resulting from the ill-conceived part privatisation of the Tube', and London Underground Ltd admitted that repairs had been more difficult because of PPP and PFI's 'complex contracts'. ASLEF General Secretary Keith Norman blasted, 'It looks more like insanity than complexity to me. It is ludicrous that safety depends on a private contractor who then sub-contracts. Once you're trying to control the private contractor's sub-contractor, you know you're going to get nowhere fast.'[383] LUL Chief Operating Officer Mike Brown reckoned that the only way to sort out the problems was to ignore PPP:

> We just put our engineers straight into Alstom and bypassed Tube Lines where necessary. I lost patience with them and said that we can't mess around with this, I want to get our engineers to get stuck in. If we'd messed around going through the PPP contract, it probably still wouldn't have been fixed today.

The Northern line's problems continued into 2006, with London Underground Ltd accusing Tube Lines of having 'failed to maintain the Northern line to the standards we and the PPP contracts demand'.[384] LUL issued the Infraco with a Corrective Action Notice in December 2006 for 'persistent poor performance' (PPP?!), 'manifest in repeated track, signal and rolling stock failures'.[385]

From these three examples, we can see that the combination of the Public-Private Partnership with the pre-existing Private Finance Initiative was causing serious problems on London Underground.

EAST LONDON LINE FOR SALE: 2004-2007

In 2003, once the PPP was fully in place, Transport for London (TfL) and Mayor Ken Livingstone took over control of London Underground. Livingstone did not want Londoners to expect too much of the Underground, warning that PPP would 'make the management and improvement of the system more difficult.'[386] His appointee Tim O'Toole was 'very worried that the enthusiasm for fighting the PPP was actually going to make the job impossible [and decided] to make sure that people did not use the excuse of PPP for not getting better. I told everyone, 'Forget about PPP, that is not your job, we have people to worry about that.'[387]

We saw in chapter 2 that Livingstone had moderated his opposition to the PPP during its preparation. With PPP now in place and Livingstone now in office, would we see the Mayor further accommodate private-sector involvement in London Underground, and move further from his previous stance and his reputation as a left-winger? This section examines the evidence presented by the project to extend the East London line.

By the time that work started on the project in 2005, Livingstone had been re-elected as Mayor, this time as a Labour candidate. The party had re-admitted him once he passed a 'loyalty test'. Livingstone had also fallen out with the RMT, after he urged the union's members to cross RMT picket lines during strikes about pay in 2004. Bob Crow resigned from the TfL Board in protest.

London Underground's East London line ran from New Cross to Shoreditch, but for several years there had been a plan to extend it both northwards through Hackney and southwards to Croydon. That plan was repeatedly delayed – de-prioritised behind the Jubilee Line Extension, held up by planning challenges, then declared 'at risk' because private money might not be available.[388] By 2005, the plan – endorsed by Mayor Livingstone – was to close the East London line, extend it, reopen it packaged together with the already-private North London line as

'London Overground'. Transport for London would pay a private company to operate it. 157 staff stayed with London Underground by transferring to other lines, and when the line reopened, it would be staffed by private, rather than public, employees.

Trade unions and others campaigned against this privatisation. An opinion poll found that 74 per cent of Londoners wanted the line to stay public.[389] I was President of Hackney Trades Union Council at the time, and together with the rail unions, we leafleted, protested, held a public meeting and argued with the project's bosses on the pages of the local newspaper. East London Line Project Communications Manager Peter Boxall insisted that our safety concerns were 'without substance and misplaced' and that 'What matters to people is not the branding, but whether you can turn up and ride without looking at the timetable'.[390] But the policy's advocates did not explain why the public sector could not operate the extended East London line, especially as London Underground Ltd had offered to do so. There was no physical or technical reason why London Overground could not be joined up under full public control. Hackney South and Shoreditch Labour MP Meg Hillier argued that since British Rail privatisation, 'like it or not ... the expertise now lies with the private sector companies'. But RMT's John Leach disagreed:

> The real expertise lies with the dedicated staff who work on the East London Line and the North London Line and you won't find one of them who wants to be privatised! ... All our experiences of railway privatisation are that the train operating companies' expertise lies in creaming off profits at the expense of quality services.[391]

Ken Livingstone claimed that the transfer of a public railway to a private operator was not privatisation – just as John Prescott had insisted that PPP was not privatisation. Also, as with PPP, the advocates of moving the East London line into the private sector claimed that the improvements mattered rather than the identity of the operator, while campaigners countered that both were important. But this time Livingstone was on the opposite side of the argument. He had a convert in Hackney North and Stoke Newington Labour MP Diane Abbott. Having signed an Early Day Motion calling for the East London line to remain in public hands, Abbott changed her mind after Livingstone assured her that it was the way forward. [392]

The trade unions called no strikes to stop this privatisation, and by the time that MTR Laing Ltd – a joint operation between Hong Kong metro operator MTR Corporation and Laing Rail Ltd – won the bidding war in 2007, campaigning had faded. As the East London line approached closure, RMT held a protest 'wake', *Tubeworker* mourning that 'the line has closed without the unions having fired a metaphorical shot in anger'.[393] The line closed in December 2007 and reopened two-and-a-half years later as part of London Overground, now half-owned by Deutsche Bahn after the latter bought Laing Rail Ltd.

POWERLESS TO PREVENT POOR PERFORMANCE

PPP's complex contractual provisions were supposed to prevent the poor performance that passengers were enduring. Did they succeed? And if not, why not? This section shows that problems arose because: London Underground Ltd had to go 'beyond the contract' to get work done; the PPP's performance regime incentivised the Infracos to make choices that did not benefit railway operations; and the formal mechanisms that were meant to correct shortcomings were ineffective. So alarming incidents continued and Infracos continued to make money while failing to deliver.

London Underground Ltd wanted the Infracos to speed up improvements by investing more sooner. However, the PPP contracts denied LUL the power to insist that the Infracos do this, leaving it in the Oliver Twist role of pleading for more. The Greater London Authority's Transport Committee reported in 2005 that LUL made 33 requests for additional heavy maintenance work on track, signalling and train stock,[394] and paid extra fees to the Infracos for work 'beyond the contract'. Metronet picked up an extra £70m for twenty improvement projects,[395] but lost out to a cheaper bid from Birse Ltd for the Walthamstow Central congestion relief project.

Trade union TSSA claimed that after the White City derailment in May 2004 (see pages 109-110), Metronet used the time while investigations took place not to fix the damage but to balance its books. By improving Ambience rather than carrying out repairs, it was able to win bonuses that offset any penalties it might incur for not fixing faults.[396] This did not make railway sense, but it made business sense: PPP's performance regime not only allowed, but incentivised the Infraco to tidy up stations rather than repair damaged track.

Transport for London tried to keep the faith with PPP. Its third annual report acknowledged some 'notable improvements', mentioning the rebuilding of Wembley Park station and the lengthening of Jubilee line trains to seven cars. Line upgrades were 'showing tangible progress'. Tube Lines had proved that it could deliver projects, and – perhaps damning with faint praise – Metronet was 'not without accomplishments'. Tim O'Toole still believed that 'with the right focus from the Infracos, the contracts can deliver the step changes in asset condition that they set out to'.[397] But there was more critical evidence: for example, 15.6m customer hours were lost in 2005/06, a total that amounted to 1780 years of a Tube passenger's life. Ambience scores fell short of the Infracos' bid promises, and facilities did not perform as well as the contracts demanded. The number of speed restrictions was still rising, and 24 trains or engineering vehicles had derailed in depots.

Transport for London acquired a new Commissioner, when its former Managing Director of Surface Transport, Peter Hendy, was promoted to replace the departed Bob Kiley. An 'absolutely furious' Hendy called Metronet's failure to carry out basic maintenance work a 'shambles' that 'must cause people to question their professional ability'. But he said that he could do little about it other than imposing fines and telling Londoners that it was Metronet's fault.[398] Formal measures were taken against Metronet – including a Regulatory Notice in December 2005, an Emergency Direction and a Railway Inspectorate Enforcement Notice in May 2006 and a Corrective Action Notice (CAN) in June 2006 – but they proved ineffective. Metronet challenged the CAN in court and, as Tim O'Toole reported: 'they got it blocked and we were told by the court, 'No, you are limited under this contract [to] sitting there and collecting your abatement; you are not allowed to use a corrective action notice in this situation.'[399]

So the problems continued. In May 2006, a Metronet signal failure trapped Victoria line passengers in the tunnel near Highbury and Islington station until 3am.[400] The next month, 800 passengers were stuck in the Central line tunnel between Bank and Liverpool Street for more than two hours when a train's current-collecting 'shoe' fell off.[401] The 'acid test' for Metronet, according to TfL, would be the Waterloo and City line upgrade.[402] But in September 2006, the line reopened over a week late, and closed the next day when signals failed and a train stalled. Within weeks, Metronet had to grind the line's rails, but did not clear up the mess, causing further closures when drivers could not see through clouds of dust.[403] If this was the acid test, Metronet had failed it.

London Underground Ltd admitted that the Infracos 'continue to disappoint in many respects'. Metronet in particular had not performed very well. It had renewed only 12.7km of the expected 30km of track on the subsurface lines, with unit costs higher than its bid predicted. It had completed only 14 of 35 station upgrades due by March 2006, all of them late. Metronet BCV completed the three stations due in 2004/05 on average 33 weeks late. All 14 station upgrades due in 2005/06 were running behind schedule, by an average 24 weeks. Metronet SSL completed eight stations six months late, and those still in progress were also late. In September 2006, a Central line train pulled down 250m of the wires that run along tunnels to enable train drivers to communicate and to switch off the current in an emergency, after salt from the road above seeped through and loosened brackets, apparently unnoticed by Metronet's inspection regime. The same month, a loud bang under a train revealed cracks in the wheel sets of some Piccadilly line trains. And one November morning, the first Victoria line train hit a set of points in its way out of Seven Sisters depot, because a bolt of the wrong size had been fitted there.[404] As it stumbled on into a snowbound New Year 2007, Metronet chose not to de-ice Central line points during a freezing night. Twenty sets of points failed, causing massive disruption and raising suspicions that the Infraco had figured that paying the fines might be cheaper than doing the work.[405]

Despite this performance, Metronet made £34m post-tax profit (17 per cent of turnover) in Year Three of the PPP, bringing its total since the contract started to £69m. The Tube Lines consortium made £50m post-tax profit (16 per cent of turnover) in Year Three, bringing its total to £89m. By the end of Year Three, LUL had paid the Infracos £3.3bn in performance-adjusted Infrastructure Service Charge (ISC). In 2006, Tube Lines increased Chief Executive Terry Morgan's pay by 18 per cent to £534,000, but increased its workers' pay by only a fraction above inflation.[406] Tube Lines' shareholders received £18m in dividends, and both Infracos' shareholders received interest and also benefited from what TfL described as 'lucrative supply relationships with the Infracos'. The companies that formed the consortia owned the Infracos, so made money as dividends; lent to the Infracos, so made money as interest; and awarded themselves work with the Infracos, so made money as fees. Lucrative indeed.

The three Infracos expected to earn a net bonus of £22m by the end of Year Three; instead, they had a net abatement of £34.3m. TfL explained that the Infracos were 'underperforming', a fact that was already obvious to London Underground passengers and workers. But they were certainly not underperforming in the money-making department.

Surely this could not go on.

CHAPTER 4 – TERMINATING HERE: PPP COLLAPSES, 2007-10

In the previous chapter, we saw how London Underground's Public-Private Partnership (PPP) worked out in practice, and how, by 2006, things were going seriously wrong. This chapter describes the painful collapse of the PPP. Of the two infrastructure companies (Infracos), Metronet fell first, going into administration in 2007. Three years afterwards, Tube Lines followed it back into public ownership.

TIMELINE: THE FALL OF METRONET 2005-2010

2005

13 April: John Weight resigns and Andrew Lezala becomes the third Metronet Chief Executive in two years.

2007

6 February: Ken Livingstone and Tim O'Toole call on Metronet to seek Extraordinary Review.

29 June: Metronet BCV applies for Extraordinary Review.

5 July: Mile End derailment.

16 July: PPP Arbiter's Interim Determination awards Metronet £121m of the £551m increase it asked for.

18 July: Metronet goes into administration.

24 August: TfL registers formal Expression of Interest in taking over the contracts.

3 September: RMT strike starts.

21 September: Arbiter awards Metronet BCV £140-170m of the £992m ISC claimed; SSL £230-600m of the £1.1bn claimed.

25 October: TfL announces formal bid for Metronet.

31 October: Administrator withdraws reference for Extraordinary Review.

6 November: TfL confirmed as only bidder for Metronet.

2008

4 May: Boris Johnson replaces Ken Livingstone as Mayor of London.

27 May: Metronet comes out of administration.

December: Metronet becomes part of LUL.

2009

June: 48-hour RMT strike on LUL and TfL against 1,000 jobs losses arising from Metronet's reintegration into LUL.

September: TfL announces that Metronet's work will continue as part of London Underground Ltd.

3 December: Metronet's work becomes part of LUL.

22 December: Court order to wind up Metronet Rail SSL and BCV Ltd.

2010

2 March: House of Commons Public Accounts Committee reprimands Department for Transport for failure to heed National Audit Office warnings about Metronet's management.

COMING OFF THE RAILS: 2007

In September 2006, London Mayor Ken Livingstone called Metronet 'a consortium of nightmares'.[407] After Metronet caused delays to thousands of passengers' journeys on a single day in November, Livingstone declared that, 'to say to Londoners that there will be another 12 years of this is inconceivable'.[408] Metronet faced a possible £1m abatement for that particular day's disruption. But this was a similar figure to the Infraco's weekly profit, so was unlikely to bring Metronet to heel.

The standard of Metronet's work continued to disappoint. Metronet's efforts at Putney Bridge station were described by London Underground Ltd's District line General Manager Bob Thorogood as 'very disappointing and unacceptable ... It seems to me beyond belief in this day and age that we cannot find a contractor who can lay a decent floor surface ... I would not accept such a poor standard of work at my house. Why do my people have to put up with it at work?' Metronet's explanation did not impress Thorogood, who commented with a hint of irony, 'It appears that [Metronet] are suggesting the unacceptable condition of the floor surface is because people have been walking on it.'[409]

Then, another train came off the rails. At 9.01am on 5 July 2007, a Central line train full of passengers was travelling at 65kph (41mph) westwards from Mile End towards Bethnal Green. It struck a roll of material lying on the track. The driver applied the emergency brake and the train dragged to a halt over 148m, with two carriages derailed.[410] Passenger Chris Christofi described it:

We felt a massive jolt underneath the train which caused the train to move up and down and sideways. There were some windows that seemed to blow in and explode and there was some soot that came into the carriage. There were a lot of people crying and upset, a lot of people falling over. We thought there'd been a bomb.[411]

By 11am, 520 passengers had been evacuated from the derailed train along the tunnel in temperatures of 26-31C to Mile End station, where a train stalled in the westbound Central line platform became a temporary medical centre. Another 369 passengers walked along the tunnel from another stalled train to Stratford station. Twenty people received medical treatment, five going to hospital. Fortunately, the train's wheels dropped into the narrow gap between the running rails they had fallen off and the conductor rails that carried the current that powers the trains. Only this prevented the train careering into the tunnel wall causing more serious injuries – or worse. London Underground Ltd's Howard Collins reassured Londoners that this was the first derailment of a passenger train for 'a number of years'.[412] That number was three.

The roll of material struck by the train had been blown out of the passageway between tunnels by strong winds. Following work on the track the previous night, the material had been used to cover bags of fast-setting concrete, but it was not fully secured in place. The Department for Transport's Rail Accident Investigation Branch published its report into the derailment the following year,[413] and blamed incomplete training, guidance and documentation, and lack of consideration of wind and other risks. It noted that the gang which carried out track work the night before the derailment included employees of several contractors: Metronet shareholder Balfour Beatty Rail Projects was the principal contractor, and it used staff from subcontractors and agencies alongside its own employees. At least six companies were providing staff, and the different companies had different policies and procedures. Moreover, the plan for the night's work had changed at the last minute. The report declared that the underlying cause was a lack of comprehensive risk analysis, and pointed out that when the Infracos took over the contracts at the start of the PPP, they simply continued using the risk assessments they had inherited rather than update them in line with the latest guidance.

Metronet should have seen this coming. There had been six incidents of trains colliding with objects since March 2006, three on the same section of track westbound between Mile End and Bethnal Green, all three involving material blown out of storage locations. RMT representatives warned London Underground Ltd of the dangers each time, and in April 2007 demanded an investigation. LUL claimed that it had investigated, but did not involve union safety representatives and seemed to settle for assurances from Metronet that it would sort the problem out. The Mile End incident, three months later, revealed how unreliable these assurances were.[414]

Immediately following the derailment, London Underground Ltd issued an Emergency Directive and an Engineering Regulatory Notice to Metronet. But London Underground staff knew that LUL itself was responsible for ensuring their and their passengers' safety, and *Tubeworker* commented: 'Slagging off Metronet, though justified, is becoming a convenient excuse for LUL ... the PPP set-up causes these appalling incidents, and LUL management continually urge us to 'make it work' rather than urge the government to scrap it.'

INTO ADMINISTRATION: 2007[415]

Less than two weeks after the Mile End derailment, on Wednesday 18 July 2007, Metronet called in administrators, saying it could no longer afford to meet its obligations. We need to look into the background to see how Metronet began its slide into this financial failure.

In November 2006, the PPP Arbiter's Annual Report on Metronet revealed that the Infraco was on course to spend £750m more than it should in the first 7½-year Review Period, which was due to end in 2010. The Arbiter's report declared that Metronet had not performed in an overall economic and efficient manner or in accordance with 'good industry practice'. Why had this worrying information not come to light sooner?

Despite appearing three-and-a-half years into Metronet's tenure, this was the Arbiter's first 'Annual' Report on the Infraco. A report was deemed unnecessary for Metronet's first year, and London Underground Ltd and Metronet agreed not to trouble the Arbiter for a report on its second year in 2005. Arbiter Chris Bolt described this decision by LUL and Metronet as 'detrimental', as an earlier report would have prompted earlier action. LUL disagreed, and argued that a 'trial run' report would have been sufficient if the Arbiter had compelled Metronet to hand over information about its costs and performance. But Metronet refused to do so, on the basis that only 'the effectiveness of its business processes' was relevant. When the eventual Annual Review in November 2006 revealed that Metronet expected its costs to overrun, Metronet asked the Arbiter how he would treat seven categories of cost if it were to ask for an Extraordinary Review ahead of the scheduled Periodic Review due in 2010. Arbiter Bolt asked Metronet for a maximum one hundred lines of data, and when Metronet refused to hand over the financial details it gave to its own lenders, Bolt did not exercise his power to compel the Infraco to disclose these details. Transport for London later argued that, 'As a result, Metronet's true position remained unknown for several months'.[416]

In February 2007, Ken Livingstone and LUL Managing Director Tim O'Toole called on Metronet to apply to the Arbiter for an Extraordinary Review. The technical formula was that if legitimate extra costs (known as Net Adverse Effects), exceeded a level set in the contract (the Materiality Threshold), the Arbiter could increase the Infrastructure Service Charge paid by London Underground Ltd to the Infraco. Put more simply, if the Arbiter thought that an overspend was not Metronet's fault, he could make LUL pay Metronet more; if it was Metronet's fault, the Infraco would have to bear the burden itself. Unsurprisingly, LUL blamed Metronet (for inefficiency) and Metronet blamed LUL (for making it do extra work).

Instead of asking for the Extraordinary Review, Metronet sought ways to rescue its finances. It announced that it would: award half-a-dozen station upgrade contracts to companies other than its own shareholders; convert its track renewal programme to an alliance of Metronet and Balfour Beatty plc; and invest £80m in a new engineering train fleet. It appointed three 'independent' senior advisers and a new, non-executive Chairman, Graham Pimlott, a former Director of Tesco and Barclays but never of a railway company. Metronet froze recruitment and planned to axe 290 clerical posts and up to 200 temporary and agency jobs. A follow-up reorganisation threatened depot closures, large-scale job cuts and dramatic changes to shift patterns, work locations and workloads.[417] An eagle-eyed planner suggested that Bombardier Ltd could supply Metronet with 165 rather than the planned 180 trains for the sub-surface lines, saving about £12m. More trains would have meant a better service, but cutting numbers cut costs.[418]

In May 2007, Metronet admitted that its overspend would reach £1bn over the first Review Period. Livingstone swiped, 'My best advice to them is they should go into liquidation, we can take it back and they can go off into a quiet room and take a suicide pill as far as I am concerned'.[419] Metronet's bank lenders turned off the money supply and finally, on 28 June, Metronet asked the Arbiter for an Extraordinary Review. Metronet put the case to the Arbiter that London Underground Ltd was to blame for the Infraco's overspend because LUL had a 'wasteful approach to job specifications' and mistakenly thought that PPP contracts were fixed-price rather than flexible. Metronet asked the Arbiter to make LUL give it £992m for BCV alone, and to increase the Infrastructure Service Charge by £551m over the next twelve months.[420] Pimlott declared himself 'extremely confident that we shall be paid a large sum of money'.[421] His confidence was misplaced. Arbiter Chris Bolt's Interim Determination awarded Metronet just £121m of the £551m increase it asked for. On 18 July, Metronet filed for insolvency, for both the BCV and the SSL contracts, with debts of £2bn. Gordon Brown had replaced Tony Blair as prime minister on 27 June, his flagship PPP policy sank just three weeks later. On the same day as Brown became prime minister, he appointed Ruth Kelly as his new Secretary of State for Transport; she called Metronet's end a 'terrible failure'.

Ken Livingstone claimed that he 'never expected overpaid private sector managers to screw up so badly so quickly',[422] and MD Tim O'Toole similarly felt that, 'this thing fell apart amazingly quickly. When you think of how long this was planned, how big these companies were, for this to have gone pear-shaped this fast is stunning.' RMT, though, was 'not surprised', saying that Metronet had 'collapsed under the weight of its own inefficiency'.[423] The union's workplace representatives condemned Metronet's four-year lifespan for 'poor project management, chaotic financial control and the deskilling of their work'. Metronet Chairman Graham Pimlott admitted that things got 'out of hand' on Metronet's stations project. He was annoyed that London Underground Ltd had refused to sign off some station refurbishments as complete when it was dissatisfied with Metronet's work. Metronet had responded to this by refusing to even start a station refurbishment until every detail was agreed with LUL. According to Pimlott, Metronet 'decided that the only way to get sign-off was to agree up front what it was they were supposed to do'. Note that Pimlott refers to Metronet as 'they', as if the deceased

Infraco were a third party rather than the company he chaired. Clive Efford MP berated him: 'It is not really good enough to sit there and say, "Not me, guv! It all happened before I took over in the chair", is it?' LUL's Chief Operating Officer Howard Collins believed that:

> What killed Metronet was that they thought they could claim hundreds of millions of extra cost they had spent on places like Queensway. We went to the Arbiter and for once we had a smart enough legal team and commercial team. We said we owe you £150m as opposed to £800m, then they worked out that for their shareholders and banks, that was too hard.

So, how had Metronet got into such dire straits?

TRANS4MING PUBLIC MONEY INTO PRIVATE [424]

TfL contended that Metronet had three really serious failings – its basic maintenance performance; its inability to plan and execute works effectively; and significant structural issues in its management.

All told these factors covered most of its activities. London Underground Ltd Managing Director Tim O'Toole focused on just one, 'a unique flaw in its structure', namely the Trans4m set-up.

From the beginning of its PPP work in April 2003, Metronet contracted most of its work to Trans4m, a 'consortium within a consortium' formed by four of Metronet's five owners – Balfour Beatty plc, Atkins plc, Seeboard plc (now part of EDF Energy) and Thames Water plc. Metronet contracted its fifth owner company, Bombardier Transportation UK Ltd, to carry out rolling stock work. Trans4m's contract with Metronet required Metronet to pay bills when Trans4m presented them, with no right to withhold payment if it had not done the job properly. Metronet's owner companies had created a structure to extract money without having to deliver quality work. Trans4m was a conveyor belt carrying Metronet's income from the public purse to its private owners' pockets. A former Metronet worker gave his inside story:

> My colleagues and I witnessed the placement of multi £m contracts with Balfour Beatty Construction Ltd (BBCL) sub-contractors, who were not fit to be scrap dealers let alone competent premises refurbishment contractors. BBCL managed works went on average

approx. 2.5 times over the original budget with all costs fully reimbursed through Trans4m / Metronet ...

In one instance a security company obtained over £19m of LUL Stations refurbishment works from BBCL despite this company having no prior experience in this sector. BBCL also engaged a lot of their supply chain on a day works basis, which is crazy for this type of work and wholly commercially inefficient. ...

It was obvious internally as early as 2004 that ... the business was going to be unsustainable ...

Directors at BBCL/EDF and Trans4m simply would not listen to concerns stated to them and expected the cash cow to be fed by Metronet on a never ending basis ...

If someone gives you a contract indemnifying you for 95 per cent of all losses no matter what the reason for the losses, then an unscrupulous contractor is going to milk it.[425]

London Underground Ltd's Howard Collins believed that:

> The worst thing about the Metronet set-up was that the shareholders were also the suppliers, and that made the Chief Executive's position impossible. John Weight, decent guy, knew how to run an industry, getting pilloried by us because he'd again flooded the Underground, or his guys had done the wrong job and ruined or shut down the Central line again. He would be going back to the guys who had caused this and giving them a bollocking, but the shareholders were saying 'We don't want you to do that because it's ruining our business reputation, and by the way, we own your organisation.' It was an impossible situation.

In the wake of Metronet's collapse, the House of Commons Transport Select Committee enquired into its causes. Metronet Chairman Graham Pimlott admitted in evidence to the Committee that the contract with Trans4m gave Metronet 'very little in the way of leverage'. Also giving evidence, Transport Secretary Ruth Kelly called the Trans4m arrangement a 'poor governance arrangement', but fellow Labour MP Graham Stringer retorted, 'That might strike you as a "poor governance arrangement"; it seems to me corrupt.' London Underground Ltd's Mike Brown told me that Metronet 'started to go wrong from Day One':

They had a flawed model and it backfired on them. They were trying to do things in a way that rewarded their shareholders irrespective of how competent they were to deliver. They did some ludicrous pieces of work, for example on the south part of the Circle line, where they did a huge amount of track work but didn't do the drainage. We had to go back after they'd collapsed and do the drains. A ridiculous application of money and spend. Metronet got away with it because PPP allowed it to happen.

PPP's supporters were keen to restore the dented credibility of their policy, and asserted that it was Metronet, not the PPP, which had failed. The Confederation of British Industry presented arguments to the Select Committee that 'the tube PPP has paved the way for the largest improvement programme it has ever seen' and maintained that 'the collapse of Metronet should not be used as a premise to undermine the model of PPPs'. Giving evidence to the Committee, Arbiter Chris Bolt maintained that PPP's 'principle of an output-based contract' remained sound. Ruth Kelly pleaded that PPP could deliver value for money, 'in theory at least'. Her Department highlighted a few decent performance figures, blamed 'ageing' equipment for the epidemic of failures, and played down the scale of the problem – for example, the Victoria line's performance of just 39 per cent of its easy-to-achieve benchmark was merely 'disappointing'. In the face of the evidence, the Department for Transport contended that the PPP still 'struck a balance between the level of risk' between the public and private sectors. Even Tim O'Toole had 'softened his attitude to PPP', according to MPs. Transport for London stated that while PPP was not its policy of choice, it was 'not unworkable'.

The evidence for this optimism? Tube Lines, apparently, was doing fine. GLA Transport Committee Chair Roger Evans declared that 'Tube Lines has shown that PPP can work'; MPs claimed that 'Tube Lines' performance provides an example of private sector innovation and efficiency'; and the Arbiter saw 'no reason why [Tube Lines] should not continue to succeed'. In a lengthy memorandum to the Transport Select Committee, Tube Lines boasted a long list of achievements; excused its shortcomings (for instance, the Wembley Park station upgrade was late, but no matter, as the new stadium's opening was even later); and predicted great things for the future. It said that the Jubilee line upgrade would be completed in 2009, the Northern line upgrade in 2011 and the Piccadilly line upgrade in 2014 (none of these predictions would come true). Tube Lines praised the PPP which it argued was 'enabling upgrades which had been put off for years to be completed'. Chief Executive Terry Morgan 'believe[d] quite strongly that PPP is working. Risk is transferred, investment has increased and performance has improved'.

But not everyone agreed. Andy Young of the TSSA trade union called the difference between Metronet and Tube Lines only that 'One is in less crisis than the other'. It would have been extraordinary if both companies had collapsed in exact synchronisation; Tube Lines' failings were escaping scrutiny as they were drowned out by those of its calamitous fellow Infraco. But failings there were: the Camden Town and Barons Court derailments, the Piccadilly line cracked wheel sets, the Northern line emergency brakes – all were on Tube Lines' turf.

London Underground Ltd had reported concerns about the quality and timeliness of Tube Lines' track project work, caused by a lack of experienced staff. Workers told of Tube Lines blunders: an overnight contractor leaving signals failing at Chalk Farm station; a platform public address system at Tottenham Court Road station that failed after being revamped; and a subcontractor whose night work on Euston station left a floor so uneven that at least two people were injured by the end of the next morning's rush hour.[426] The Railway Inspectorate launched an investigation when Tube Lines stored explosive detonators at Golders Green without permission.

The Transport Select Committee concluded that 'the [PPP] model itself was flawed and probably inferior to traditional public-sector management ... the failure of Metronet fatally damages the Government's assumption that the involvement of the private sector will always result in efficient and innovative approaches to contracts'.

So by late 2007, Metronet was in administration, Tube Lines was healthier but making mistakes, and the PPP was struggling to maintain credibility.

MIDWIFE AND UNDERTAKER: 2007 [427]

Administrators took over the two Metronet Infracos, BCV and SSL. Their task was to keep Metronet's business going while putting its finances in order in preparation for new owners. London Underground Ltd, London Mayor Ken Livingstone and the administrators assured passengers that

Tube services would not suffer. Trains kept running, stations stayed open and problems continued. In September 2007, emergency brake problems caused the suspension of the Hammersmith and City, Circle and District lines. Drivers could not reset the failsafe 'deadman's handle' (a device which applies the brakes if the driver becomes incapacitated), and refused to take trains into service. Central line drivers also refused to operate their trains, insisting that the whole fleet be checked after the 'shoes' that pick up traction current fell off several trains.[428] London Underground Ltd admitted that there would be some delays to maintenance and Managing Director Tim O'Toole told MPs he was 'not confident' that there would be no scaling-back of capital investments. In particular, Trans4m 'just cancelling and walking off' meant that the stations improvement programme had 'kind of sat down'.[429]

The administrators were Ernst and Young LLP, erstwhile scrutinisers of the PPP's 'value for money', now guardians of its wreckage. The company received around £50m for its part in setting up PPP, with the Department for Transport confirming that 'Ernst and Young independently judged LU's approach to be robust'.[430] Administrators cost around £750 per person per hour, so the 45 administrators running Metronet cost the public over £1m per week. Ernst and Young LLP was both midwife and undertaker to PPP, and was paid handsomely on both counts.

On the day the administrators moved in, 18 July 2007, Prime Minister Gordon Brown told the Commons that another company would be found to take Metronet's place. The BBC speculated as to whether the Infraco should be 'split up into more manageable chunks, re-let to another private company, or brought back "in-house" to London Underground'. It commented that the latter would be a 'severe embarrassment' to the Prime Minister. Would the Tube Lines consortium bid for the contracts? Its Chief Executive Terry Morgan gave non-committal answers to MPs, but did express 'concern' about Metronet's work going in-house, 'because it feels like the way it used to be. It is the old model.' Londoners seemed quite keen on the 'old model' though, with 76 per cent telling ICM pollsters that they wanted London Underground to carry out its own maintenance, only 13 per cent wanting a private company to do it.

In August 2007, the administrators engaged the Rothschild bank 'to carry out independent valuation of the Metronet companies in order that the market might be tested for interest from potential purchasers'. But despite the Arbiter ruling that TfL must give £1bn to Metronet's successor, no private sector interest was forthcoming. Administrator Alan Bloom concluded that marketing Metronet would be fruitless. RMT General Secretary Bob Crow said, 'any attempts to dress up the corpse of Metronet as if it has still got some life in it are pointless ... Metronet is not resting, stunned or pining for the fjords, it is stone dead, and the only solution is to bring its maintenance contracts back into the public sector'.[431]

Mayor Livingstone wanted maintenance in-house but contracts awarded to private companies for upgrades and major investment work. Transport Secretary Ruth Kelly said that both she and the mayor accepted that it was right to have private-sector involvement, and she was 'open-minded' as to 'the appropriate way of doing that'.

THE COST OF COLLAPSE: 2007-2008 [432]

At first, no one seemed able to figure the cost of Metronet's collapse. None of the many witnesses to the Transport Select Committee would name the price, and London Underground Ltd's Tim O'Toole warned that, 'I cannot sit here looking at a catastrophe of this dimension and say, "Don't worry, it is not going to cost anyone anything"'. Six months after Metronet went into administration, Transport Secretary Ruth Kelly was still 'uncertain' as to the cost of failure and how much of the tab would be picked up by tax-payers and fare-payers.[433] Eventually figures came out. The direct loss to the public purse of Metronet's failure was between £170m and £410m.[434] But there was much more. Transport for London was liable for 95 per cent of Metronet's debts, so the government gave £1.7bn to the Infraco's lenders as part of TfL's funding settlement in 2008.[435] Metronet's collapse meant that LUL's legal bill for 2008 was £20.3m, many times greater than a more typical year, for example £4.3m for 2005.[436] The cost to LUL and TfL of running Metronet's business during administration was £13m per week, with TfL advancing £900m to Ernst and Young LLP. As well as money lost, there was money wasted: TfL paid £1.2bn for station renovations that Metronet had not carried out. The National Audit Office reckoned that the cost of the debt repayment and loss to tax-payers amounted to up to 10 per cent of the work actually delivered.[437]

Who should foot the bill? London TravelWatch – the independent, statutory watchdog for passengers – argued that Metronet's shareholder companies should pay for the losses and the government should fund the extra Arbiter costs. GLA Transport Committee Chair Roger Evans argued that, 'because this was imposed on London then the Government that imposed it should be the people who pick the bill up'. Mayor Ken Livingstone agreed, and briefed his publicity machine accordingly, telling staff that 'no-one was to say "we told you so". Journalists pressed me to denounce [Gordon] Brown but I just droned on about "working together to solve the problem".'[438]

Metronet's shareholder companies lost only their stake of £70m each, a sum that MPs called 'relatively modest'. The companies seemed comfortable: Balfour Beatty plc's pre-tax profits were up £76m in the six months to 30 June 2007; EDF Energy made £402m in the year before Metronet's failure; Thames Water plc made £256m;[439] and Atkins plc recorded an 'exceptional accounting gain' of £17.2m directly from the discontinuation of its Metronet activities.[440] Ruth Kelly seemed convinced, however, that 'Metronet's failure has cost its shareholders significant sums'. She argued that it had 'damaged the reputation of those companies involved', and pledged that the 'terrible failure' would be taken into consideration should the shareholders bid for government jobs.[441] Any reputational setback seems to have been minimal though, as Metronet's former owners between them now hold many government contracts, with Atkins plc, Bombardier Ltd, EDF and Balfour Beatty plc holding several lucrative deals with TfL and London Underground Ltd.[442]

SPECIAL SHARES

John Prescott had argued forcefully that the PPP would transfer risk from public to private sector. PPP's critics disputed this claim, and Metronet's demise offered evidence that the critics were right.

The Arbiter identified four elements of risk for Metronet's shareholders – the £70m equity that each invested; 5 per cent of Metronet's borrowing; the first £50m of efficient cost overruns; and Metronet's own inefficiency. For this minimal wager, the companies expected returns described by MPs as 'out of all proportion'. For those who lent money to Metronet, the story was similar. The Transport Select Committee reported that 'what minimal risk was borne by Metronet's lenders was disproportionately well rewarded, at the expense of tax- and fare-payers'.[443] Metronet's lenders charged around

£450m more than they would have charged for lending directly to the government.

So little risk was transferred to the private Infracos that shortly after Metronet's collapse – on 24 September 2007 – the Office for National Statistics (ONS) decided that Metronet (and Tube Lines) had been a public sector outfit all along.[444] In 2006, the ONS 'discovered' the existence of London Underground Ltd's Special Shares in the Infracos, and concluded that these gave LUL sufficient control over the Infracos to classify Metronet and Tube Lines as public bodies. As the Special Shares were included in the PPP contracts, we might think it remiss of the ONS not to have noticed them sooner. The financial 'big idea' behind PPP – that it would remove borrowing to fund London Underground improvements from the government's books – lay in tatters. This had been more of an accounting trick than a genuine big idea, but now even its most basic premise – that private companies supplied the finance – had been nullified as those private companies were reclassified as public. Borrowing to spend on public services had been tossed in the direction of the private sector, but had returned like a boomerang to the public sector. That borrowing now nested in the Public Sector Net Debt (the new name for the Public Sector Borrowing Requirement).

The Special Shares gave London Underground Ltd several powers. LUL could veto dividends and other payments to shareholders, and would receive up to 50 per cent of the net gain if any of the Infracos' founding companies disposed of their holding during the first Review Period. LUL could give or refuse consent to any refinancing during the first eleven months and to the Infracos giving loans or guarantees over £5m at any time. LUL could also nominate a Director of each Infraco. Using (or rather, not using) its powers, London Underground Ltd allowed Tube Lines to pay a dividend of up to £1,658,109 in May 2006.[445] In 2004, LUL consented to a £20m dividend resulting from Tube Lines' refinancing, and received a payment of £54m for giving its approval. Tube Lines' shareholders received another dividend of £4m in respect of tax losses surrendered by Jarvis plc, with LUL paid £2m for its consent.[446] Without fanfare or press release, LUL appointed one Elizabeth Noel Harwerth as its 'Partnership Director' on each Infraco's Board. Harwerth was Chief Operating Officer of Citibank International plc and director of several companies,[447] but appears to have had little railway experience. Will Hutton's report in 2000 had recommended such a post, in order to reduce 'the risk of investment "hold-up" and the Infracos acting as front companies for their shareholders',[448] and the Shareholder Agreement described its role as 'to act in a public interest capacity' and to help address conflicts of interest. It is hard to find evidence of Hawerth achieving this.

COLLAPSE CAUSES CUTS AND CASUALISATION: 2007-2009

We have considered how and why Metronet collapsed and went into administration. Now we need to look at the impact that this collapse had on Metronet's workers, and on other workers and service provision in London Underground.

When Metronet went into administration, trackworker Sam and his workmates 'knew we were on our way back to London Underground. There was euphoria, people were laughing. Then management said that they could only guarantee to pay 90 per cent of our pension. We didn't want to take any chances, so we put these three demands.' The unions demanded no loss of pension rights, no job losses, and no forced transfers to another employer. All three trade unions – RMT, TSSA and Unite – balloted their Metronet members for strikes. Of the 2,700+ workers balloted, just 70 voted not to strike. RMT and Unite called two three-day strikes, the first starting on 3 September 2007, the second a week later. TSSA planned to join in from the second day. Metronet gave some slightly stronger assurances on the issues of pensions, jobs and transfers, and TSSA and Unite declared themselves 'satisfied' and called off their action. RMT, though, pressed ahead. The big majority of Metronet workers were in RMT, and a solid strike saw most Underground lines close. London Underground Ltd seemed more willing than usual to shut its own services during the action, perhaps knowing that many of its staff were ready to refuse to work on safety grounds given that the staff who would rectify faults were out on strike. Sam recalled to me that:

> We were on the picket line and management asked to see us. We said we'll meet you while we're still on strike, so we came off the picket line and went to the meeting with red flags and picket armbands on. Our union officer was trying to negotiate, and Tim O'Toole kept cutting across him, so we told the chair to tell him to have more respect.

Despite all this bluster, that's when the Mayor wrote the letter saying that the pension should be restored to the full amount.

Just one day into the strike, previously 'impossible' guarantees became possible. Ernst and Young LLP pledged that there would be no job losses or transfers during administration and Transport for London secured Metronet staff's pension in full.

But most Metronet workers still did not have the conditions and security they would have had if they had never left the employment of London Underground Ltd. Even into the following year, 2008, there was still no guarantee that when Metronet returned to Transport for London, all its employees would return with it, especially as Bombardier Ltd was insisting that it 'owned' a few hundred of them. Metronet workers went into dispute with their employer, and demanded: membership of the TfL Pension Fund; staff travel passes; the backdated 0.75 per cent pay rise they were owed; and no transfer to Bombardier Ltd. 751 RMT members (81.5 per cent) voted for industrial action, and the union called a 48-hour strike from 28 April 2008. The strike threat prompted Metronet to guarantee to protect staff and meet all the union's demands.

London Underground cleaners also pursued a battle to save their jobs and improve their pay and conditions. By 2008, Tube cleaning had been in the private sector for more than two decades. Most cleaners were paid at or near the legal minimum wage of just £5.52 per hour, in contrast to a Tube Lines' director's salary of £336.54 per hour.[449] RMT explained how privatisation had brought this situation about: 'When a cleaning contract expires, companies compete to see which can get away with the lowest bids and exploit their workers the most. This system of 'reverse bidding' drives down standards as well as exploiting workers.'[450]

In 2007, Tube Lines tried to save money by cutting the price it paid to its cleaning contractor ISS Facility Services Ltd by 27 per cent. ISS responded by announcing that it would cut over 200 cleaners' jobs. The level of cleaning would obviously suffer as a result. But the maximum fine for breaching cleaning standards under the PPP was just £200,000 per year, and Tube Lines stood to save £3.5m by cutting the price of the contract.[451] Under pressure from RMT and public opposition, though, ISS withdrew its threat. In June 2008, London Underground cleaners voted by a majority of over 99 per cent to strike for better wages, sick pay and holiday pay. The union called strikes on four cleaning contracts (those held by ISS Ltd, Initial Transport Services Ltd, ICS Ltd and GBM Services Ltd). RMT's action won a commitment to introduce the London Living Wage,† then £7.20 per hour. Metronet – by now in public ownership – would be first to ensure that its contractors delivered the wage rise. Tube Lines found pretexts to repeatedly delay the increase, until – following further protests – its contract cleaning staff finally achieved this pay level in 2010.[452]

In 2008, Metronet planned to halve the frequency of signal maintenance, but this was met by a warning from RMT that it would strike. In autumn 2008, RMT balloted its Metronet members for industrial action when the company disciplined RMT representative Andy Littlechild, levelling charges against him that Bob Crow claimed 'would embarrass the Spanish Inquisition'. Andy kept his job and the dispute concluded.[453] In 2009, London Underground Ltd cut maintenance on the former Metronet lines by around £60m. RMT argued that 'The result of Metronet's failure is that the travelling public and the public purse is being forced to pay twice; firstly by having to pick [up] the huge debt and secondly by facing cuts to vital upgrade work owing to budgetary constraints caused by the debt inheritance'.[454]

Also in 2008, a strike threat forced Tube Lines to increase its employees' pay rise, and shift testers on the Powerlink PFI contract took strike action over Christmas to reclaim ground they had lost in pay and conditions in the ten years since their job was transferred to a private employer in 1998.[455] Tube Lines workers felt the ripples of Metronet's implosion. Emergency response worker Tom recalled that:

> Pensions really became an issue for Tube Lines workers when Metronet went under, because all the guys who worked for Metronet – and good luck to them – immediately went back and got full pensions, full protection, full travel, and all the other benefits that they hadn't had, and we were left out there. Someone said to me, the reason they called it JNP was Just No Pensions. It didn't seem fair. With Metronet being twice the size of Tube Lines but still going under, people genuinely thought Tube Lines would be going the same way, and that we would all be going back as one big happy family again.

† A figure calculated by the Mayor's Living Wage Unit as 'the minimum amount needed to live free from poverty in London'.

As Metronet returned to the public sector, so, separately, did a small number of stations. In November 2007, ownership of stations between Queen's Park and Harrow and Wealdstone on the Bakerloo line, plus Kew Gardens and Gunnersbury on the District line, transferred from the private Silverlink Trains Ltd to the public London Underground Ltd. These stations were served by both Tube and mainline trains, and changed ownership as the North London Line franchise was broken up and reallocated. London Underground Ltd delayed raising the pay and conditions of its new employees to the level of its existing staff.[†]

Also in 2007, Mayor Ken Livingstone announced plans to close thirty London Underground ticket offices and cut the opening hours of many more, with the loss of 270 jobs. Transport for London claimed that it was responding to changes in passengers' ticket-buying habits, but critics claimed that it was driving those habit changes, as it had been promoting alternative outlets, increasing the range of tickets available from machines, and offering free iTunes downloads to online buyers. Addressing 2007's TUC Congress, I urged delegates to vote to oppose the ticket office closures, which they did. Union members also campaigned, petitioned and leafleted, and ticket office closures were among several issues which led RMT and TSSA to jointly call a three-day strike against 'casualisation' in spring 2008. The company withdrew enough of its plans to convince the unions to also withdraw the strike threat, although not all workplace union representatives were satisfied, seeing the outcome as slowing rather than halting the creeping cuts.

The ticket office closure plan was shelved when Ken Livingstone lost the mayoral election in May 2008. His Conservative rival, Boris Johnson, signed a petition against the ticket office closures, knowing it would win him votes. Livingstone, never much liked by the right, had by now lost favour with the left too, and with many working-class Londoners. He admitted that, 'I used to believe in a centralised state economy, but now I accept there's no rival to the market in terms of production and distribution'.[456] During his time as mayor, Livingstone had courted big business, set up London 'embassies' in Brussels, Beijing and Shanghai,

---

[†] It has since used these stations to test practices it might wish to import from the private railway: mobile staff supervising several stations at the same time; private security guards instead of LUL station supervisors at night; and the use of agencies to supply ticket-selling, gateline and platform staff. Soon after the 2007 transfer, staff whose job was to ensure that trains going out of service at these stations were empty of passengers went on strike in a protest against LUL's plan to require them to work alone.

and sent himself and his senior staff on foreign trips costing around
£370,000. His annual salary was £137,579.[457] RMT's John Leach
recalled to me Livingstone's relationship with the union:

> During our campaign against the PPP coming in, he came to a
> meeting of the RMT Executive and said "Don't go on strike, it won't
> help me in my fight against PPP". He would often put things in
> personal terms. Livingstone had regular meetings with the unions.
> He'd clear the meeting of officials and talk to us with maybe only his
> personal political assistants. On the eve of the first election between
> him and Boris, after we'd discussed Metronet going belly-up, he said
> "Now there's something else I need to talk to you about: we've got to
> win this election, is there anything you can do to help me? If you think
> I'm a bastard, this guy wants to wipe you out", pointing at a dossier
> he had about Boris Johnson.

Johnson won the election for Mayor of London with 53 per cent of
the vote in the final round. In the Greater London Assembly election, no
party won an overall majority, but the Conservatives remained the largest
party, gaining two seats to reach a total of eleven. Labour increased its
representation by one seat to eight; the LibDems lost two seats and now
held only three; the UK Independence Party lost both its seats; the Greens
stuck at two seats; and the fascist British National Party won its first seat,
later expelling the successful candidate. New Mayor Boris Johnson
appointed Tim Parker as Chair of Transport for London. Parker had
earned the nickname 'Prince of Darkness' by cutting jobs during spells in
charge of the Automobile Association, Kwik-Fit Ltd and Clarks Ltd.
Parker resigned from his TfL appointment after less than three months in
the post.

A SLOW RETURN: 2007-2009

With Metronet in administration and no private company interested in
taking it over, the responsibility for London Underground's Bakerloo,
Central, Victoria and Sub-surface lines' infrastructure was heading back
to the public sector. But it would be a long process.

Administrator Alan Bloom announced in November 2007 that
Transport for London was the only company that wanted to take over
Metronet. London Underground Ltd Managing Director Tim O'Toole

wanted Metronet to exit administration 'as soon as possible'.[458] But the target date of 18 January 2008 was missed and administration continued, now costing £14.4m per week.[459] Despite being in administration, Metronet was charging London Underground Ltd handsomely for use of its workers. LUL paid from £48.10 per hour for a night track operative to £79.19 for a skilled signal technician, with only a portion of this being passed on to the workers in wages. Managers were more expensive, a programme manager costing LUL £124.50 per hour, equivalent to £226,000 per year.[460]

Metronet's period in administration ended in May 2008, when its responsibilities transferred to Transport for London. The two Infracos formerly run by Metronet were now known as LUL Nominee BCV Ltd and LUL Nominee SSL Ltd, and remained as separate entities from London Underground Ltd. Mayor Boris Johnson welcomed this development, and promised £1.4bn investment over the coming year, including station works and the Victoria line upgrade. TfL publicised improvements already made during administration. 114km of track had been renewed and a further 38km was scheduled for renewal within a year. The first new Victoria line train entered service on schedule on 21 July 2009. Plans now envisaged nearly 200 new air-conditioned trains entering service on the sub-surface lines by 2010, to be manufactured by Bombardier Ltd,[461] which would thus continue to profit from the PPP. In June 2009, TfL claimed that track reliability had risen by 42 per cent, service disruption had fallen by 13 per cent, and that its renegotiation of several Metronet contracts had saved some £2.5bn.[462] The recently-formed London Underground Ltd Line Upgrades Directorate boasted progress towards improving the sub-surface and Victoria lines. Director David Waboso argued that 'The former Metronet team becoming part of LU and working as one team has been a major factor ... we could cut out the unnecessary layers and just get on and do it'.[463]

In December 2008, Metronet's employees transferred to London Underground Ltd. But this was an interim arrangement, and a committee of representatives from LUL, TfL and the government pondered the permanent policy for another ten months before announcing in September 2009 that it would remain this way. By then, more than two years had passed since Metronet had collapsed.

Dubious Metronet practices now came to light. Metronet manager Ed Maloney – seconded from Balfour Beatty plc – used his position as project director to give work at Oxford Circus station to contractors who many thought were poorly-suited to the work – he had a financial interest with them. When he was convicted of fraud in 2011, his sentence – for cheating and potentially endangering the public – was community service and a suspended jail term.[464] Other Metronet managers exploited the public purse without being accused of breaking the law. The Bond Street modernisation project team held routine managers' meetings during working hours on a hired Thames pleasure boat, with a free bar paid for by the PPP contract. Metronet and its contractors held 'golf days' for senior managers, where the player who got his or her ball closest to each hole got a prize such as a DVD player. Hundreds of managers were taken to Premiership football matches, including hospitality suites and private boxes for some. Tim O'Toole had even sent an email asking, 'How do we prevent the contractors plundering our stations, by the way?' He was concerned that Metronet and its contractors were taking heritage features such as roundels, signs and furniture.[465]

Such excesses should perhaps have been identified and curbed by the National Audit Office. But the NAO's credibility suffered when the tax-payer-funded extravagances of its head, John Bourn, came to light. In 2007, reports emerged of his chauffeur-driven journeys to work each day, and a three-year expenses spree of £375,000 on travel; £27,000 on meals; plus trips to the opera, polo and grand prix.[466] In early 2008, Bourn resigned.

In March 2008, Parliament debated a report from the Transport Select Committee that was highly critical of the London Underground PPP. David Taylor MP asked Transport Secretary Ruth Kelly whether there was 'a serious risk that ... Tube Lines will go the same way as Metronet'. Taylor suggested that to prevent this, Tube Lines should return to public ownership, but Kelly responded that Metronet collapsed because of its own corporate failure rather than any fault of PPP.[467] Was this confidence or complacency?

TIMELINE: THE RETURN OF TUBE LINES, 2008-2010

2008

April: London Underground Ltd asks the Arbiter for Initial Ranges Guidance on the price of the second Review Period (RP2).

December: LUL tells Tube Lines its Restated Terms for RP2.

2009

31 March: Original completion date for the Jubilee line upgrade.

30 June: Tube Lines submits pricing proposals to LUL for RP2.

16 December: Tube Lines announces that Chief Executive Officer Dean Finch is to leave and join National Express.

17 December: Arbiter's Draft Directions.

31 December: Tube Lines misses the (extended) deadline to complete the Jubilee line upgrade.

2010

25 January: QC rejects Tube Lines' claim against LUL for £327m.

10 March: Arbiter's Final Directions on cost of RP2.

25 March: Jarvis plc goes bankrupt.

27 April: Arbiter's Final Directions on Infrastructure Service Charge (ISC) and funding due, but postponed.

6 May: General Election.

7 May: TfL announces purchase of Tube Lines.

UPGRADES GO DOWNHILL: 2006-2010

We noted previously (see pages 136-137) that while Tube Lines had not suffered the ignominious collapse that had befallen Metronet in 2007, it was experiencing problems with its performance in maintaining and improving the Tube's infrastructure. These problems continued. One example was at Hampstead station, which had the deepest lifts on London Underground. These lifts were old and worn, but Tube Lines decided to keep them running. By summer 2009, the lifts were getting stuck in their shaft, causing the station to close several times each day. After local community protests, management agreed to requests for extra staff and a senior Tube Lines engineer to monitor the situation.

Later that year, Tube Lines prepared to cut the frequency of routine checks on the condition of infrastructure. The Infraco had to apply for a formal concession as its plans breached safety rules. RMT saw this as proof of TfL's financial 'black hole' resulting in cuts and compromises, but TfL accused the union of 'scaremongering'.[468] However, it could not so easily dismiss the chaos unravelling on the Jubilee line.

The Jubilee Line Extension had convinced politicians that the PPP was necessary, but the Jubilee line upgrade shattered that conviction. The upgrade aimed to deliver a train-every-two-minutes service, increasing by 40 per cent the capacity of a line that carried 800,000 passengers per day. The upgrade would install a new type of modern signalling, Transmission Based Train Control, which sent information via matrix boards to each train's onboard computer, which read information that kept them a safe distance apart.

Work on the Jubilee line upgrade began in late 2006, and was due to be completed by March 2009. But the work fell way behind schedule, not helped by gaffes including the laying of eight miles of the wrong type of cable.[469] In April 2009, the completion date was put back to 31 December 2009, and London Underground Ltd agreed that the line should close for a dozen weekends in addition to those already planned, in order to enable Tube Lines to carry out its work. Tube Lines initially stated that it needed fifty closures to complete the upgrade, but repeatedly asked for more. In October 2009, it requested another six, in November another six months, in December another 28 closures. By then, Tube Lines had already used 120 closures for upgrade work, including every weekend in 2009.[470] Weekend closures may leave the Monday-to-Friday commute unscathed, but they seriously interfere with travel to the numerous leisure venues served by the Jubilee line. These include Wembley Arena, Wembley Stadium and the O2 Arena. Geoff Symonds of the O2's owners AEG Europe Ltd branded Tube Lines 'clowns' for the 'hugely frustrating' closures.[471] Mayor Boris Johnson wrote a stern letter to Tube Lines Chief Executive Dean Finch, declaring the situation 'unacceptable', then agreed to 22 further days of closures, including eight full line closures up to and including Easter 2010. LUL Managing Director Tim O'Toole blamed the PPP, saying that its structure:

> encourages the use of weekend closures. But better ways should be explored. In Madrid, where they do not close lines at weekends, they do a lot of planning and use an overlay system for new signalling that is installed over the existing one, and it can be turned on and off for testing. Here it is difficult to get people to do things differently as that was the way that the PPP was designed.[472]

In August 2009, London Underground Ltd called on the Infraco to independently review its delivery programme. In September, Boris Johnson met with Tube Lines and its owner company Bechtel Corp. The Infraco pleaded for five more closures and promised to finish on time.[473] But within days, the promise had slipped: it was now to deliver the upgrade 'on time or miss the deadline by the narrowest of margins'.[474] By October, it was clear that the upgrade would not be finished until well into 2010 at the earliest. One Tube Lines worker told me that the Infraco:

> totally underestimated how long it would take. Bechtel, who were supposed to be managing the signalling, were completely useless, the overruns were horrific, they used up all the agreed weekend closures within the first few months, then they were literally grovelling to get more. The cracks started opening up, and people realised that Tube Lines just weren't up to the job.

On the weekend of 3-4 October 2009, London Underground Ltd and Tube Lines were supposed to run 'trial operations' of the new Transmission Based Train Control (TBTC) signalling system. But drivers complained of inadequate training, back-up instructors not being available, and signage not having been commissioned. Nearly all drivers refused to take part. Just one train ran in TBTC, and when the points failed it took two hours to travel just two stations. LUL and Tube Lines declared the trial a success;[475] drivers threatened to continue boycotting testing and training until their safety concerns were addressed.[476]

The report commissioned by Tube Lines shared out the blame between the Infraco (for slowness in responding to problems), its signalling contractor Thales (for having 'significantly underestimated' the scope and complexity of the project) and TfL (for allowing only a 'limited amount' of access). It described a 'low level of trust' between Tube Lines and TfL. Boris Johnson told of 'vivid' conversations in an 'acrimonious relationship'. Dean Finch said that Tube Lines' relationship with London Underground Ltd 'ranged from extreme collaboration to the adversarial'.[477] Finch claimed that, 'On one occasion a [London Underground Ltd] manager only agreed to let [Tube Lines] use the station car park if they installed an air conditioning unit and blinds in his office.'[478] But Finch was departing Tube Lines for new pastures at National Express. Denying that he was leaving due to political pressure,

Finch said that he had 'really enjoyed' his time with the Infraco and was joining National Express just because it was bigger.[479]

Tube Lines had to pay a £10m penalty for each month of 2010 until it completed the upgrade. London Underground Ltd had to pay penalties to the Canary Wharf group – which represented business interests in the Docklands area served by the Jubilee line – but could recover the money from Tube Lines if the Infraco were judged to be responsible for the delays to the upgrade's completion. Tube Lines submitted a multi-million-pound claim against LUL for 'additional works' not specified in the original contract – just as Metronet had done prior to its demise.[480]

ARBITRATION TIME: 2008-2009

We have seen that by 2009, the problems with the Jubilee line upgrade were causing financial conflict between London Underground Ltd and Tube Lines. By then, the time was also approaching for decisions to be made about LUL's ongoing payments to Tube Lines: the Infrastructure Service Charge (ISC). The first 7½-year review period (RP1) of Tube Lines' PPP contract was due to end in mid-2010, and the ISC needed to be set for the second review period (RP2). To kick-start this process, London Underground Ltd asked the PPP Arbiter for an initial estimate in April 2008. LUL told the Arbiter that the price should be £4.1bn; Tube Lines claimed a huge £7.2bn. The Arbiter estimated £5.1-5.5bn.[481]

This created a financial headache for Transport for London, which was already trying to make £2.4bn 'efficiency savings'. The government refused to increase its grant to TfL, claiming that its £39bn ten-year settlement already took into account the possibility that the cost of Tube improvements might rise.[482] A Greater London Authority Transport Committee report in March 2009 warned of a 'huge hole in TfL finances – at least £1bn if the Arbiter's early calculations were accurate'. Tube Lines warned that if it did not get extra money, the 25 per cent capacity increase from the planned Piccadilly line upgrade was at risk and up to 75 station refurbishments could be delayed by seven years.[483] The *Evening Standard* wrote that, 'It is the peripheral projects that are initially at risk – tunnel cooling, congestion relief and schemes to provide step-free access.'[484] But step-free access is not a 'peripheral' issue if you use a wheelchair: it is essential to enable you to access the Underground; and tunnel cooling and congestion relief were both important to the comfort and safety of passengers.

A further GLA report in July 2009[485] revealed a £1.7bn transport income gap as fares revenue fell due to the recession, just as campaigners had warned might happen under PPP. Adding this to Transport for London's existing £2.4bn 'efficiency savings' and the funding argument between TfL and Tube Lines which had now reached £2bn, RMT calculated a cash chasm of over £6bn.[486] But there was still enough money to keep those at the top in comfort. TfL's 2009 Annual Report revealed 123 managers receiving over £100,000 per year, and five over £250,000. TfL chiefs' bonuses had risen by 50 per cent from £3.6m in 2007 to £5.3m in 2009. TfL had spent over £15m on consultants.[487]

Tube Lines insisted that it was 'a healthy business with a strong future ... on target to deliver our financial objectives', and reassured employees that a decision to withdraw hot chocolate, brown sugar and sweetener from its restaurants was 'not in any way linked to our overall financial position'.[488] Tube Lines published glowing reports of the Northern line having 'really upped its game with records galore coming its way', and welcomed a clutch of awards, including the TfL Partnership Project of the Year Award for the collaboration between London Underground Ltd, Tube Lines and Alstom plc.

On 17 December 2009, the PPP Arbiter published his 127-page Draft Directions. The Arbiter used the concept of a 'Notional Infraco', defined as one 'with the same contractual obligations, third party contracts and financing arrangements as the actual Infraco, but which also carries out its activities in an overall efficient and economic manner and in accordance with Good Industry Practice' (an easier standard than 'Best Industry Practice'). The Arbiter compared the real Tube Lines with this 'Fantasy Tube Lines'. Under a series of headings, Tube Lines asked for certain allowances and sums of money, London Underground suggested a figure, and the Arbiter made a determination, usually in between the two numbers.

LUL's Mike Brown agreed with my description of the arbitration process as 'like a pantomime', and added:

But that's what an Arbiter does. I don't criticise him for that, but it was a flawed structure. There was no economic analysis to apply, there were some comparators with other metros around the world, but even that was flawed because every context and every environment is slightly different.

TABLE 5: THE ARBITER'S DRAFT DIRECTIONS ON TUBE LINES REVIEW PERIOD 2

	Tube Lines wanted:	LUL suggested:	Arbiter decided:
Allowance for minor closures (disruptive access during traffic hours)	35.6m Lost Customer Hours (LCH)	15.5m LCH	21.5m LCH
Lifts & escalator closures	9.4m LCH	6.1m LCH	7.8m LCH
Base costs	£5,189m	£3,621m	£3,943m
RP2 overheads	£217m	£113m	£151m
Money in RP2 to prepare for RP3	£21m		£10m
Recovery plan for Tube Lines section of TfL Pension Fund	£60m	nil	£73m
Risk allowance	£302m		£259m (£200m for asset risk; £59m for corporate risk)
Total costs for RP2	£5.75bn	£4bn	£4.39bn

Arbiter Chris Bolt found that the Jubilee line upgrade's problems had begun with Tube Lines signing a contract with Thales UK Ltd for the Jubilee's new signalling system. Thales Ltd – part of the French-owned Thales Group – planned to install its 'SelTrac' signalling system. Significant elements of SelTrac's design would need to be amended to meet London Underground's standards for signalling, but Tube Lines signed the contract with Thales UK before these issues had been settled. The Arbiter ruled that a Notional Infraco would have offered the contract only when it knew what it involved.

Arbiter Bolt assessed that Tube Lines needed just over £170m for 'differential inflation' – the possibility of the real prices of things that it buys, such as materials, rising by more than the inflation measure it used, RPIX (Retail Price Index, excluding mortgage payments) – during RP2. He also added a 'significant risk premium' of £160m. But if prices turned out to be lower, the Infraco would not have to refund this money: it would enjoy a 'windfall gain'. Thus, the PPP required London Underground Ltd to pay the Infraco money to 'insure' it against losses if its gambles failed, but let it keep that money if things went well. Either the Infraco won or the public sector lost.

The Arbiter ruled that Tube Lines' costs should be £4,394m, and then added inflation, Treasury fees and 'fixed amounts', giving a total of £7,104m to be paid in ISC. London Underground Ltd said it could afford £6,412m, and so faced an 'affordability gap' of £463m. Who would pay? Both LUL and Tube Lines 'consider[ed] it would be better value for money for TfL to raise additional finance than for Tube Lines to do so'. Did this not contradict the PPP advocates' core claim that the private sector could raise money for the Tube more easily than the public sector could?! Nevertheless, whichever company raised the finance, the public sector would still pay.

The Arbiter's document reflected badly on Tube Lines. He rejected its claim that London Underground Ltd's Restated Terms were technically unachievable and refused to accept either Tube Lines' assessment of its costs for RP2 or its demands for closures. The Arbiter caught Tube Lines paying secondment fees to its shareholders, Bechtel Corp and Amey plc, which were 'high and potentially outside of market norms'. However, the Arbiter supported Tube Lines' cuts in inspection frequencies, as 'consistent with the Notional Infraco continuing to reduce costs'. He wanted the Infraco to employ a smaller emergency response team, and to run fewer than its ten maintenance depots.

SEARCHING FOR SALVATION: 2009-2010

The Arbiter's determination of what Tube Lines needed for the Second Review Period was £1.5bn less than what Tube Lines said it needed. It was £400m more than London Underground Ltd said it could pay: no small amount. Tube Lines' finances had caught up with it just as Metronet's had, and like Metronet, it demanded more than it was entitled to and more than LUL could afford. London Mayor Boris Johnson said the government should meet the £400m difference between the Arbiter's and LUL's figures; the government said that LUL and Tube Lines should sort out a price between them; London TravelWatch said that passengers should not have to pay through fare rises or service cuts.[489]

The Infraco searched for evidence to change the Arbiter's mind before his Final Directions in March 2010. In an unusual move, it used the Freedom of Information Act to unearth how much London Underground Ltd was spending on upgrading the Victoria line, and how many closures of the line LUL was allowing itself in order to facilitate access to carry out the upgrade work. Tube Lines hoped to persuade the Arbiter that he had judged its work on the Jubilee and Northern lines unfairly in comparison. The Infraco claimed that the data revealed that LUL planned to 'grant itself 50 full line closures on the Victoria line, against the 10 or so we expect on the Jubilee line, which is twice the length', and reckoned that the Victoria line upgrade cost £20m per kilometre, compared with the £10m per kilometre Tube Lines was spending on the Northern line upgrade. LUL was not impressed with Tube Lines' presentation of this data, especially as it had no corresponding right to obtain information from Tube Lines. (Freedom of Information law applies only to 'public authorities', and despite the Office for National Statistics' reclassification of the Infracos as public bodies, apparently did not apply to them.) LUL's Acting Managing Director Richard Parry dismissed Tube Lines' analysis as 'comparing apples with pears', adding that, 'The Victoria line is a much shorter line. You can't split it in half like the Jubilee. The fact is they asked for 400 closures on the Jubilee and withdrew 200 of them themselves because they couldn't make their own programme.' Parry, a London Underground Ltd Director who had stood in as MD since Tim O'Toole's departure in April 2009 to return to the USA, also cast doubts on Tube Lines' motives: 'They want to dig out information on us that we don't think is particularly relevant ... we suspected they could be up to no good with it.[490]

Tube Lines referred its complaint about access to the Jubilee line to carry out its upgrade work to independent adjudication, claiming £327m from London Underground Ltd. In January 2010, the QC who adjudicated dismissed Tube Lines' claim as 'labyrinthine, artificial and unconvincing' and ordered the Infraco to pay LUL's costs. Parry declared LUL 'very pleased to have seen off this attempt to take lots of money from the public purse and drag our reputation through the mud' and told Tube Lines to 'stop making further spurious claims for additional fare payers' and tax payers' money, given the handsome returns already being earned by shareholders Bechtel and Ferrovial, and get on with job in hand.'[491]

This case illustrates a core problem with the PPP. It took a unified London Underground and broke it into parts which it assumed would work together but were in practice doomed to incessant, disruptive, costly dispute. RMT's Oliver New commented that 'PPP was supposed to allow private cash to fund upgrades. In reality it has meant conflicts and delays ... the sooner the PPP is dumped, the better.'[492]

Like Metronet, Tube Lines looked to its workforce's jobs and conditions as a source of financial savings. Before his departure as Chief Executive, Dean Finch declared that Tube Lines needed 'to do some radical stuff now in terms of improving productivity and efficiency'.[493] Plans included: maintenance and cleaning job cuts; more use of agencies and subcontractors; weakening safety measures such as escalator dust tray cleaning; requiring track staff to work every weekend; and putting some workers on a six-day week.[494]

The former Metronet – now part of London Underground Ltd – was also in conflict with its workforce, as signals staff protested against the imposition of new rosters which would leave them thousands of pounds worse off. A one-day strike on 5 February 2010, followed by a work-to-rule on the District line, saw LUL withdraw the rosters and spare itself a series of Sunday strikes. Back at the drawing board, LUL managers held a 'Strategic Planning and Performance Day' seminar, discussing a document which proposed outsourcing maintenance and making significant staffing cuts, noting that 'recession helps'.[495] LUL also planned to reduce ticket office opening hours and cut hundreds of stations jobs. Mayor Boris Johnson approved, despite his previous opposition to ticket office cuts when standing for election. Johnson's Conservative GLA colleagues produced a report advocating driverless London Underground trains.[496]

Mayor Johnson was cranking up the hyperbole against the PPP. In late 2009, despite the chaos with the Jubilee line upgrade, Johnson was 'not going to be tempted to read the last rites over Tube Lines or the PPP'.[497] But by February 2010, he was calling the PPP 'larceny' and 'demented', seeing 'colossal sums ... siphoned out' of the public purse. However, he added – lest anyone expect him to act on his fiery words – 'we are powerless to stop it'.[498] Johnson finally stated explicitly in March 2010 that he wanted the 'catastrophic' PPP to end, but could only suggest to Tube Lines that it 'make a move away'.[499]

That same month – March 2010 – the Arbiter gave his Final Directions on the cost of RP2, and all parties involved responded quickly and forcefully. Arbiter Chris Bolt allowed the Infraco a small increase on his draft figures, but nowhere near what it wanted. He ruled that RP2's work should cost £4.46bn, £1.3bn less than Tube Lines claimed but £460m more than London Underground Ltd said it could afford. Acknowledging that neither side was happy, Bolt shrugged that 'This is just the nature of the business.'[500] The Arbiter instructed LUL to fund the shortfall from its own budget. Tube Lines supported this stance, arguing – apparently without irony – that 'All indications are that public financing is by far the cheapest way forward.' But the Department for Transport refused to reconsider its funding to TfL, and another new Transport Secretary, Andrew Adonis, was 'adamant' that TfL could not borrow more.[501] So London's passengers faced seeing the funding gap plugged by multi-million-pound spending cuts, fare rises and/or significant scaling-back of the long-awaiting upgrades.[502] TfL Deputy Chair Daniel Moylan declared that the Arbiter's suggested cuts 'completely undermin[e] the whole premise of the PPP, that upgrades are delivered by and risk is transferred to the private sector.'[503] LUL's Richard Parry proposed that 'the best way ... to get a true picture is to require Tube Lines to raise finance, and therefore to put a convincing proposition to lenders'.[504] If the Arbiter had compelled the Infraco to raise the finance, and it had failed to do so, Tube Lines could have lost the contract without compensation, and TfL could have reclaimed it for free. However, Arbiter Chris Bolt chose not to do so. TfL complained that 'Despite repeated and insistent requests for him to do so, the Arbiter consistently refused to give any reasons for his position, thereby depriving LUL of the ability to mount an informed challenge.'[505]

The Arbiter was due to give Final Directions on the Infrastructure Service Charge and funding on 29 April. But he announced two days before this date that Tube Lines could not finance the work that London Underground Ltd wanted done on the basis of what LUL said it could afford. He postponed the decision and asked LUL to reconsider both its requirements and the level of charges it could afford.[506]

In March 2010, Mike Brown returned to London Underground Ltd as Managing Director after a brief interlude at the British Airports Authority, ousting Richard Parry. Transport writer Christian Wolmar wrote that TfL had 'played safe' in appointing Brown, describing him as 'an operator – in the old fashioned railway sense of the word who knows how to run a railway – and is good in front of the cameras'.[507] Brown told me that he had 'never intended to come back', but that over several chats, TfL Commissioner Peter Hendy had persuaded him, with talk of the Olympics, expanding into London Rail and investment programmes. Brown returned to a salary of £289,000.

Brown's first month as London Underground Ltd Managing Director would be Tube Lines' last month as a privately-own company.

TUBE LINES BOUGHT BACK: 2010

Rules disallow controversial public sector decisions being announced in the run-up to a general election, to prevent accusations of the announcements being used for political gain. So it was immediately after Labour was voted out of government in the general election on 6 May 2010 that Transport for London announced that it was buying Tube Lines. TfL paid £310m to Bechtel Corp and Amey plc to buy their shares in Tube Lines. Bechtel Corp's involvement in London Underground ended, but Amey plc continued to manage maintenance work on the Jubilee, Northern and Piccadilly lines. Boris Johnson gushed that 'the big winners are the London travelling public and the big losers are the lawyers ... The great advantage is we no longer have to accede numbly dumbly to Tube Lines' requirements.'[508]

But others were not impressed that Bechtel Corp and Amey plc, having been paid to take on the contract, were now being paid to abandon it. Moreover, Transport for London would now assume Tube Lines' debt. RMT London Transport Region President Vaughan Thomas called this 'tantamount to rewarding bad behaviour. The only sensible way to deal with 'cowboy companies' is renationalisation without compensation.'[509]

Former Mayor Ken Livingstone berated Johnson for buying Tube Lines rather than forcing it into administration as he had done with Metronet.[510] But London Underground Ltd's Mike Brown told me that he saw the situation differently: 'Tube Lines was financially in a much stronger position than Metronet. I think it probably would have ended up in a decline, but there was an issue of how long that decline would take and what damage it would do along the way.' For Tube Lines worker Tom, the Infraco 'managed to cling on by the skin of their teeth until they worked out the most fantastic deal in the world and got paid a fortune for doing nothing'. BBC London Transport correspondent Tom Edwards observed that, 'The big question now will be how Transport for London can afford the £310m to buy the shares'.[511] Gordon Brown and John Prescott, who had imposed the PPP, were now out of government, but they had been replaced by a Conservative Party, supported by its LibDem junior partners, which was keen to cut public spending.

On 10 May 2010, Mayor Boris Johnson announced his transport strategy, which included Crossrail, Thameslink, extending the Bakerloo line and Docklands Light Railway, and increasing capacity on Network

Rail Ltd's suburban lines during the morning peak by 30 per cent. But RMT accused the Mayor of designing his policies 'to deflect attention away from swingeing cuts, ticket office closures across the capital and the undermining of safety standards'.[512] Moreover, Johnson was not integrating Tube Lines back into London Underground Ltd, but keeping it as a separate company. Tube Lines electrician Adam recalls that:

> When we heard that TfL was bringing Tube Lines back into public ownership, the mood was very optimistic. Splitting everything seemed like a colossal waste of money and it made perfect sense for us to go back. Everyone thought that we would go back in the same way that Metronet did. But as time went by and we realised that wasn't going to happen, people were more disillusioned than ever. They couldn't understand how we could be owned ultimately by TfL but be treated like second-class citizens.

RMT demanded guaranteed protection of Tube Lines workers' jobs and conditions. When these were not forthcoming, over 90 per cent of RMT Tube Lines members voted for industrial action. The union called two 48-hour strikes in June and July.[513] By this time, Tube Lines had a new Chief Executive – Andie Harper, former Transition Director and Chief Executive of Metronet during its time in administration. Harper replaced Andrew Cleaves, who had been standing in since Dean Finch's departure.

RUNAWAY TRAIN: AUGUST 2010[514]

The once-private Infracos were all now back in public ownership, and the London Underground Public-Private Partnership was practically dead. However, some of its fragmented structure was still in place, and this was to contribute to an alarming incident on Friday 13 August 2010. In the early hours of the morning, a 37-tonne Rail Grinding Unit (RGU) finished its night's work smoothing the southbound Northern Line track between Highgate and Archway. The Unit's crew could not start its engine, so an empty passenger train came to rescue it. The two vehicles joined together using an emergency coupling device, the Unit's braking system was deactivated and the passenger train began towing it northwards. It was still towing when the Northern line's passenger service started. At 06:42, shortly after passing through Highgate, the coupling device broke and the Unit rolled back southwards downhill towards central London. The two crew members jumped off as the Unit ran through Highgate station, and it continued onwards for sixteen minutes, travelling 6.9km (4.3 miles) and coming within one minute of hitting a passenger train before stopping on an upward slope at Warren Street at 06:58.

No-one was hurt, but only because of the swift action of London Underground Ltd staff. Northern line control room staff quickly routed passenger trains onto the line's Bank branch and the runaway Rail Grinding Unit onto the Charing Cross branch, using a 15-second opportunity to switch the points and avoid a collision. Control room staff set points against the runaway Unit at Mornington Crescent station, unsuccessfully trying to derail it but slowing it enough that the Unit could not freewheel over the upward slope at Warren Street. The Department for Transport Rail Accident Investigation Branch's report pointed out that London Underground Ltd staff took life-saving actions despite LUL having provided them with no training or guidance on how to handle this type of situation.

The official report also described the involvement of various companies in the incident. Private contractor Schweerbau operated the Rail Grinding Unit. This particular Unit had broken down on the Jubilee line near West Hampstead on 17 July 2010, and Tube Lines had decided that the emergency coupler's design should be modified. But Tube Lines also decided that until this was done, the existing coupler could stay in use. It was this device that broke on 13 August. Infraco JNP had commissioned this coupler in 2002 from Powerhouse, a private company which had been providing equipment for London Underground since 1992. But neither Infraco JNP nor its subsequent owner Tube Lines had checked Powerhouse's work quality or its competence. The Highgate runaway resulted from multiple mistakes by private companies and the contracting regime that brought them onto London Underground both before and during the PPP. Prosecuted by the Office of Rail Regulation, London Underground Ltd, Tube Lines and Schweerbau all pleaded guilty to endangering passengers and staff. In March 2013, the court fined them £100,000 each.

THE END OF THE ARBITER: 2010

The Infracos were all now back in public hands. But the PPP contracts still governed their relationship with London Underground Ltd, so the PPP Arbiter was still in post – but not for long. LUL and the Infracos withdrew their references for Periodic Review, agreed to make no further references to the Arbiter, and amended the PPP contracts to delete him. In August 2010, the Arbiter announced his own redundancy and the winding-up of his office.[515]

Looking back a year later, Transport for London strongly criticised both the Arbiter and the PPP, publishing a report described by Christian Wolmar as 'difficult to read but utterly fascinating in demonstrating the craziness of the whole idea'.[516] The report accused Bolt of failing to insist on sufficiently detailed information from the Infracos throughout the PPP years, causing an information imbalance in which London Underground Ltd was at a disadvantage.[517] LUL's Mike Brown told me: 'I never questioned [Bolt's] integrity, but I thought it was an horrendous job and no-one celebrated more than he did the end of his role.'

Chris Bolt departed the PPP Arbiter's office and joined the Advisory Board of the Rail Value for Money Study, led by Sir Roy McNulty. The 'McNulty review' delivered its report in 2011, advocating saving money by cutting staffing, fragmenting the structure of the railway and giving more power to private operators. Bolt continues as a member of the Advisory Council of Partnerships UK. He had done well from the PPP, paid £97,821 in his last full year for a three-day week. His office's full-time Director Gaynor Mather received £175,965 and Commercial Advisor James Le Couilliard £171,682. The non-executive Advisory Board members were paid a salary of £17,381 for working just two days per month, considerably more than an Underground cleaner got for more than ten times the hours.[518]

CHAPTER 5 – LEARNING THE LESSONS FROM PPP PAST

In this chapter, I look back at the London Underground Public-Private Partnership (PPP), the criticism and resistance against it, and its imprint on the present London Underground.

A PARTICULARLY POOR POLICY

What were the problems with the London Underground PPP? I suggest that they come in the following main areas: complexity; waste and legal costs; false claims about funding, risks and profits; and a rewards system that incentivised reckless management.

The PPP created a network of management systems which lacked clear lines of responsibility and was dizzying in its complexity, with '300 mathematical formulae and countless volumes of legalese'.[519] The new structures brought no systemic improvements in management and divided a previously-unified underground system which had functioned better than the PPP structures which replaced it. The complexity of management systems obstructed holistic responsibility and encouraged buck-passing.

The waste and cost of the London Underground PPP began with the price of setting up the new structures: a huge £400m+. As the private bidders persuaded the government to refund their costs, the bill rose astronomically. For example, the LINC consortium – a group of companies that made a bid for a PPP contract and reached the shortlist but did not succeed at the final stage – employed seventy people full-time for two-and-a-half years to put together its losing bid, and the public – fare-payers and tax-payers – paid the cost.[520]

The PPP was built on a foundation that was unsound and deluded: that London Underground could become self-financing. It is a simple fact that urban transport systems do not break even, and it was a declaration of war against reality to try to make one do so.

The PPP's other great and false claim was that it would transfer risk to the private sector. Transport writer Christian Wolmar argues that there can never be a real transfer of risk because the government can never let London Underground shut down. But just to be sure, the bidders and the government negotiated terms that so comprehensively removed any trace of risk that there was no way the Infracos could lose even if they performed spectacularly badly – which, as we have seen, they did. Even Denis Tunnicliffe – one of those who devised the PPP as Managing Director and then Chair of London Underground Ltd from 1988 until 2000 – accepted that there was no significant risk transfer to the private sector. He told me that 'Broadly speaking, the private sector doesn't do business where it can take risks, unless it's a bank. The reality of any major involvement that the public sector has with the private sector is that risk migrates to the party of substance, and that is always the public sector.'

Tunnicliffe added that he never claimed that the PPP would transfer big risks to the private sector, 'because we know they won't cope with them'. However, he maintained that it did transfer everyday risks: 'if they can't finish the work by 6 o'clock, they should face a penalty and that will sharpen up their day-to-day management'. But the penalties that PPP imposed for not finishing overnight engineering work by 6 o'clock in the morning were not sufficient to 'sharpen up' the Infracos: the large number of engineering overruns shows that this risk transfer did not work in practice. Those who caused overruns and delays for passengers did not directly face the consequences. The penalties they incurred were low, and their budgets suffered little.

Tunnicliffe had thought the PPP the best policy for London Underground given that public ownership with adequate, reliable funding was apparently not an option, and he can still find grounds on which to defend it. He told me that the Infracos brought in some 'entirely sensible and successful' changes, for example pushing up track work productivity by introducing new techniques; and praised the fact that safety controls remained with the public sector. But his other defences of the PPP were rather more negative: that it was better than the alternatives, such as line-by-line privatisation; and that it was easy to bring to an end: 'Always in my mind was the possibility that things would go wrong and therefore there was no transfer of ownership to the private sector, the freehold ownership was always vested with the public sector.' For Tunnicliffe, the PPP was:

much more successful than people will allow. The period we've lived through has been a success at two levels: one, in the fact that very large amounts of money have gone into capital programmes on the Underground; and two, it has adjusted government's mind, that large amounts of public money by one device or another have to go into the Underground.

There is a problem with this argument. The reason that government has come to understand that it must give large amounts of public money to London Underground is precisely because the PPP failed to bring in the private money that it was supposed to. The 'very large amounts of money' that have gone into capital programmes on the Underground have been public money, when the PPP promised private money. Tunnicliffe's argument is similar to suggesting that an outbreak of measles was 'successful' in convincing the government of the need to provide vaccinations. The PPP did prove that London Underground needs public funding, but we did not need this to be proved in practice, because PPP's opponents made this point before the policy was imposed.

Tunnicliffe accepted that the PPP had flaws: one was that PPP's designers got the contract structure wrong. They failed to learn from the experience of the Channel Tunnel, where a private-consortium constructor contracted to its own shareholders just as Metronet went on to do. Metronet, he admitted:

> was never run holistically and in a sense almost didn't exist as an entity, just as a bunch of suppliers trying to make the best profits that they could. ... I am deeply critical of myself for not putting more intellectual effort into the structure of the Infracos and how they were remunerated. If Metronet had had the right leadership, and if London Underground were mandated to make the relationship work, the PPP could still be in business.

Tunnicliffe particularly blamed Ken Livingstone, accusing him of having:

> an absolute commitment that [the PPP] wouldn't work. The hostility that Livingstone brought to the negotiations and then the subsequent determination to prove the thing didn't work made it very difficult for a partnership-type approach to emerge if the Infracos had wanted it to.

However, today's Managing Director of London Underground Ltd, Mike Brown, is damning of the PPP. He told me that, 'over my dead body would I ever allow something like that happen to this place again. It was a flawed model, poorly executed, poorly delivered, and it will not be the brightest day in London Underground's history.'

Tunnicliffe left London Underground in 2000, midway between the PPP's announcement and its imposition, while the exact structure was still in the process of development. During that process, draft contracts – already generous to the private bidders – became shockingly overgenerous. The companies lobbied in their own interests, their position strengthened by the selection of preferred bidders so early that they had huge leverage in negotiations. If the government did not give them what they wanted, they could walk away and make the process start again: an unthinkable cost to the government of time, money and credibility. The government had put itself over a barrel. The contract prices went up; the rate of return rose; caps on bonuses disappeared; allowances for substandard performance leapt up; the scope of work shrank; and risk practically vanished. The Infracos would be paid more to do less, with smaller penalties when they made mistakes or failed to deliver.

The PPP provided for a contingency fund of up to £360m for each of the three contracts, which could be paid to the Infracos for unforeseen changes in the work. The PPP contracts had a unique provision: if this contingency fund were not spent, the money would go to the Infraco anyway, not back to the public. This provision gave the Infracos a potential profit margin of around 50 per cent. The contracts even allowed the Infracos to walk away at a 7½-year review point and pass their debt to London Underground Ltd. As we have seen, neither Metronet nor Tube Lines reached the first review point due in 2010, but this would surely have been the final infamy. It allowed private companies to suck the public Underground dry and walk away licking their lips. Experience with PPP proved that London Underground needs public investment rather than private predation.

For LUL Managing Director Mike Brown, Metronet was 'an unrivalled disaster'. And although Tube Lines 'did some positive things', such as improving the Piccadilly line fleet's performance, 'the PPP wasn't set up for that, and whatever else Tube Lines did, they never delivered a line upgrade. That was a pretty damning indictment of the whole PPP:

neither Infraco ever delivered a line upgrade.' In 2013, Howard Collins departed his post as Chief Operating Officer of London Underground Ltd to become Chief Executive of Sydney Trains. I asked him if he was going to recommend the PPP model, and he replied: 'I don't think anyone's going to propose PPP, because the world knows that that type of arrangement was a disaster.'

ILL THOUGHT OUT?

Following the demise of the London Underground PPP, those who still support private involvement in public transport argue that this PPP was uniquely bad, and that other models of public-private partnership should not be dismissed on the basis of this PPP's failure. PPP Arbiter Chris Bolt, for example, commented that the Tube PPP was 'a unique arrangement and I think that given the past experiences of both sides ... I believe that it will remain unique.'[521] A 2010 analysis by Trefor Williams argued that 'It is possible to conclude that the London Underground PPPs were not a failure of the PPP form of contract, rather they were an inappropriate application of PPP because the undertaking was so complex.'[522]

The Transport Select Committee thought that the London Underground PPP was 'ill thought out'.[523] It probably was, but I would suggest that is a relatively small matter. 'Ill thought out' suggests that further consideration by more clever people would make the policy acceptable. Would a better-thought-out Tube PPP have reduced the litany of fiascos that was the real Tube PPP? Maybe. Would it still have prioritised profit over transport, and allowed the private sector to milk London Underground at the expense of service and safety? Yes.

Although the London Underground PPP had several unique features, many of its core problematic features are common to many public-private ventures, and some derive directly from the involvement of private companies in public services. The following paragraphs look at some of these common features.

The false claim that public-private partnerships transfer risk to the private sector is not unique to this particular PPP. Other PPPs and PFIs also claim to transfer risk from public to private sector, but in practice allow private companies to make big profits if things go well, smaller profits if things go badly, with the public sector picking up the bill. The assumption or prejudice that private companies bring efficiency to public services was also not unique to this PPP. The International Monetary

Fund has admitted that while there is extensive literature declaring the private sector's efficiency, 'the theory is ambiguous and the empirical evidence is mixed'.[524] Socialist academic Dexter Whitfield claimed that even official reports from the National Audit Office and the Treasury Taskforce 'made unsubstantiated claims of 10-20 per cent efficiency savings' by PPP and PFI.[525] RMT's Oliver New argued that private companies made money from PPP and PFI schemes not because they were efficient, but because those schemes were designed to guarantee profits:

> It is not efficiency that leads to profits, but setting up the system so that they can't lose. This applies to the maneuvering around Iraqi oil, to third world trade, and to plans for future investment in British public services. PFI and PPP are set up to make profits for the fat cats; it is as simple as that.[526]

In his extensive writing on PFI and PPP, Dexter Whitfield barely mentions London Underground. But the Tube PPP fits readily into his analysis of how these policies work. Whitfield locates PPP as part of a process of 'marketisation' of public services, the negative consequences of which we can readily see in the London Underground PPP. For example, Whitfield accuses marketisation of encouraging contractors to play 'market games' such as ignoring service failures which carry low financial penalties;[527] we can recall Metronet not taking action to prevent points freezing. As another example, Whitfield argues that PPP gives cities less control over their economies;[528] we can recognise this in the lack of control that London's Mayor and GLA had over the PPP.

Moreover, marketisation brushes aside concerns such as equality and social justice. The Tube PPP's appallingly low regard for improving disabled people's access to London Underground illustrates this. Whitfield argues that when the National Audit Office considers public sector comparators, it uses criteria which 'ignore equality, employment and environmental sustainability and socioeconomic factors. Hence, they do not take into account the deeper and wider implications of PPP projects.'[529] PPP contracts cannot take into account broader social factors. When the Tube PPP bidders were asked to suggest a price for graffiti removal over a period of thirty years, the LINC consortium's chairman thought the task difficult 'because the amount of graffiti is actually a product of the extent of the policing of the operator'.[530] However, it is also the product of social issues such as unemployment, social exclusion and youth alienation.

The London Underground PPP was not an exception to a rule of successful partnerships between public and private, but a dramatic example of the destructive and contradictory nature of public-private partnership itself. This, more than the peculiar failings of one policy, is the key issue: aspiring to be a business and a public service do not go together.

Marketisation and privatisation push aside the values that should be at the core of public services to the periphery. Equality, provision for need, accessibility and protection of the public interest take a back seat to protection of the interests of private capital. PPP is an 'access all areas' pass, a permit to enter public services and extract profit. Private companies will always try to drive their costs down, minimise the risk of losses and charge as much as they can get away with. Trying to make them do otherwise, however many volumes of contract you devise, is like trying to make a tiger go vegetarian.

So why did a Labour government pursue such a predatory policy?

HOW LABOUR TURNED PRIVATISER

We saw in chapter 1 how the Conservatives prepared London Underground for privatisation and how 'new Labour' took that preparation and, instead of undoing it, used it as the bedrock for its own version of privatisation, the PPP. From 1979 to 1997, Conservative governments starved public services of the funding they needed. This left people disappointed with the failings of those services and made public provision look incapable. This enabled the Conservatives to present the private sector as saviours. The Conservatives sold those public services that they could, and cut and fragmented the rest. By the time Labour was elected to government in 1997 and inherited responsibility for London Underground, the Tube was in a desperate state. Passengers were frustrated and public ownership was discredited. There was intense pressure for a new funding solution, but Labour's solution was not to keep the Underground in public ownership and increase its funding, but to invite private companies to take over its infrastructure and manage that infrastructure for profit.

Let us look at this situation from a satirical angle. Say you take over ownership of a house left to fall into disrepair by its previous owner and now needing serious renovation. You could do some work yourself and employ skilled craftspeople to do what is beyond you. You could stop giving money to rich relations and instead spend it on the house. Or instead, you could invite a set of people with criminal records to move in, take over the lease, charge you for living there, refuse to do half the work you wanted and take twice as long as planned to do the rest – and if they make mistakes or go over budget, you, not they, foot the bill. Why would a householder – let us call him 'Gordon' or 'John' – do such a daft thing? He is from a socialist family, but never really 'got it' and after some local spivs took him out for a drink, embraced the supremacy of the market with such zeal that even self-evident irrationality would not stand in his way. The householder tells his grumpy aged parent in the dilapidated bedsit to stop moaning, and that the 'good old days' of public ownership and direct employment were no such thing. But it is not just the aged parent who opposes the crazy scheme, but the kids, in-laws, friends, neighbours and family pets. Only the tenants from hell approve.

The London Underground Public-Private Partnership is an indictment of 'new Labour', whose turn away from the working class in search of credibility with capital was not only unprincipled but a spectacular failure.

To assess why Labour did this, we need to look at its history. Trade unions – including RMT's predecessor, the Amalgamated Society of Railway Servants (ASRS) – set up the Labour Party at the start of the twentieth century, with the aim of enabling workers to elect their own representatives to parliament. By 1945, thirty railworkers were Labour MPs, opposite just two railway bosses on the Conservative benches. But the Labour Party, while born of the working-class movement, sought to improve capitalism rather than to overthrow it. A 1922 Communist Party pamphlet argued that 'even before the [1914-18] war, the Labour Party had become quite distinctly a class organisation of the proletariat which was dominated by that section of the middle class whose profession it was to organise trade unions'. Lenin described it as a 'bourgeois workers' party'.[531]

There was conflict between these two poles – bourgeois and working class – for example when Labour's left argued in the 1930s for workers' control of industries such as London Underground rather than Herbert

Morrison's 'public corporation' model.[532] By the 1980s, the fragile balance between the two class poles was wobbling. A rank-and-file attempt to pull Labour towards internal democracy and socialist policies was defeated by the leadership, which instead hauled Labour rightwards, fixated with the view that the Party must jettison left-wing stances in order to be electable. 'New Labour', rebranded by Tony Blair, preoccupied itself with proving that it would be moderate and responsible in government. Journalist Nick Cohen wrote: 'Blair was left holding the 'centre-ground' – a prize plot of land whose mortgage was paid by emptying the Labour Party of meaning.'[533]

'New Labour' was continuing 1980s Conservative Prime Minister Margaret Thatcher's project of driving the working class out of politics. In place of left-wing policies came a lexicon of buzzwords, chief of which was 'modernisation'. As Dexter Whitfield explained:

> The driving force [behind New Labour policy] is primarily 'the modernisation agenda' and the belief that partnerships with private companies are, *per se*, the only way forward. The feast of large multi-million-pound contracts under Labour [made] the Tories' Compulsory Competitive Tendering regime look like a roadside picnic.[534]

'New Labour' privatised services that the Conservatives had thus far left untouched: the Royal Mint, National Air Traffic Service, Belfast Port and more. The Conservatives had not yet privatised London Underground, even when they sold the rest of the railways. Maybe privatising the Tube would have been too complex, too unsafe, more controversial; maybe there were more marginal constituencies and more opponents in London; maybe the private sector itself was not interested. No such obstacles would deter 'new Labour' from its particular brand of privatisation, the PPP. 'New Labour' was repackaging Conservative policies rather than departing from them. Tony Blair's 1995 description of British Rail privatisation – 'a hotchpotch of private companies linked together by a gigantic paper-chase of contracts – overseen, of course, by a clutch of quangos'[535] – became an accurate summary of his own government's policy for London Underground.

Many within Labour's own ranks opposed the Tube PPP. Branches and conferences passed resolutions, MPs and councillors spoke out. But the Party leadership did not listen. The unpicking of Labour Party democracy over the previous two decades had left Labour's members unable to make their leaders do what the Party wanted.

Whitfield remarks that Labour's idea of 'Best Value' contains lots of Cs – clients, commissioning, contracts and more – but adds that 'there is one 'c' word which is missing – class.'[536] 'New Labour' had chosen to serve not the working class that created and elected the Labour Party, but the capitalist class that exploited the working class. Granada chief Gerry Robinson said that 'business can do business with new Labour' (see page 18); he added, 'That in my view is one of the healthiest changes in British politics for a very long time.'[537] For Robinson and other company chiefs, what was 'healthy' was that they once again had two parties competing with each other to represent their interests. 'New Labour' listened avidly to trade associations and lobby groups devoted to the pursuit of business interests, mostly funded by the same corporations that benefited from the results. Of course Jarvis plc, Carillion plc and Amey plc funded the New Local Government Network's lobby for private sector involvement in public services: they stood to make a fortune from it. But it was Labour leaders' own choice to listen and bend to this lobbying while dismissing the views of their own party's members and affiliated unions. London Underground Ltd Managing Director Mike Brown could see the paradox: 'The Treasury in particular was absolutely obsessed with being seen to be the friend of big business, the friend of capitalism, which was ironic for the first Labour government for a long time.'

Tony Blair said in his election victory speech on 2 May 1997, 'We have been elected as New Labour and we will govern as New Labour.'[538] But I would suggest that Labour had been elected because it was not the Conservatives, so should not have governed like Conservatives. Its lifelong tug-of-war between aspiring to represent workers and operating within capitalism had been pulled far over to the capitalists' end of the rope. New Labour was, as Peter Mandelson said, 'intensely relaxed about people getting filthy rich'.[539]

HOW DEMOCRACY FAILED

Five days after the 1997 election victory speech quoted at the end of the previous section, Tony Blair told Labour MPs that, 'We are not the master now. The people are the masters. We are the servants of the people. We will never forget that.'[540] However, chapter 2 clearly showed that the

Labour government did not carry out the wishes of the people when it came to the London Underground Public-Private Partnership: the great majority of Londoners opposed the PPP, and the Labour government imposed it against their wishes.

The PPP had some support when Prescott first announced it, but this withered away as the policy was scrutinised, exposed and opposed. By the time it came into force, only those who designed it and those who would benefit financially from it still said they supported it. Poll after poll – both opinion and electoral – revealed a growing majority opposing the PPP. Opponents raised both action and argument against it, while proponents struggled with both. Even the bloody evidence of fatal rail crashes did not move the government. The government remained resolute that it knew best, and cited a series of spurious justifications for its policy.

Chief among these justifications was the claim that there was no alternative to private finance as public funding was simply not available. Throughout the debate in political and 'expert' circles, public ownership of London Underground with adequate public funding was dismissed. The occasional reference to this alternative was a cursory statement that it was 'unrealistic' or 'impossible', usually with no attempt to expand or prove the point. However, events proved that public money was available: under the PPP, a great deal more public money poured into the Underground than if the government had done the job itself.

The Labour Party enjoyed a huge Parliamentary majority. It could have decided to give London Underground the money it needed, but chose not to. Labour chose instead to keep the rules and policies as they were and then claim that the rules and policies constrained it. The Labour government claimed that it had to stick to Conservative spending plans and economic policies, and that it had to abide by Treasury rules and limits on public sector borrowing. The government restrained itself with handcuffs for which it held the key.

Fiddling the figures was an aspect of PPP. The notorious 'Value For Money' test was fixed, with the 'public sector comparator' – variously described as 'an invention', 'artificial', 'biased', 'partial' and 'ineffective'[541] – synthetically inflated to make the PPP look cheaper.

Events proved that as far as this policy was concerned, the government did not know best. It was not its greater expertise – its superior knowledge in the face of misguided opponents fearful of change – that enabled it to get its way. New Labour succeeded in imposing PPP on an unwilling London because our society is not fully democratic. Governments are allowed to ignore public opinion even when it is overwhelming against a particular policy. We can only elect our MPs, not tell them what to do, reverse their decisions, or remove them from office short of the next election. Those we elect to local government positions do not have the power to stop central government imposing a policy that the locality's population does not want. Nor do we have democracy in the workplace. If we did have these powers, if democracy were more extensive, then the London Underground PPP would not have happened.

THE SHACKLING OF UNION RESISTANCE

Public opinion was overwhelmingly against the PPP, but as we have seen, public opinion does not make a government back down. Perhaps an effective, trade-union-led campaign might achieve that. But in another illustration of the restriction of our democracy, trade unions are heavily restricted by the law. Twice during the unions' battles against PPP's imposition, the High Court helped the employers by granting injunctions banning strikes. On both occasions – December 1998 and February 2001 – RMT worked within legal guidelines as they stood, only for the judges to tighten the law by means of their rulings and declare the strikes illegal.

How had this legal situation come about? In parallel with their privatisation programme, the Conservative governments of the 1980s and 1990s pursued a legislative programme to restrain trade unions: they introduced exhaustive balloting procedures, bans on 'political' strikes and solidarity action, limits on picketing, and more. 'New Labour' left these laws virtually untouched. Tony Blair boasted that Labour's tinkering with employment law would 'leave British law the most restrictive on trade unions in the Western world'.[542] The law set up a series of hoops which unions must jump through in order to hold lawful industrial action. Those hoops either tripped up the unions as they jumped through them, or slowed the unions and helped the employer to undermine their action. The law (made by Parliament and embellished by judges) required unions to give notice of ballots and of action, and to hand over reams of information to the employer. This made industrial disputes into an unequal contest: David has to give Goliath detailed advanced notice of his battle plans, but Goliath has no duty to reciprocate.

The law may present itself as fair and neutral, but I would argue that it is not. In a class society, it plays a class role. It was lawful for the government to impose a policy on London that barely any of its people supported. It was lawful for private companies to extract huge sums of money from the PPP contracts and walk away from London Underground unpunished from the dreadful job they did. But it was not lawful for RMT to strike when a big majority of its members wanted to, because a judge moved the goalposts when the employer asked him to.

In spring 2001, London Underground workers who were members of the RMT trade union defied the judges and took part in a strike which the court had declared unlawful. Workers are not always in a position to defy injunctions against strikes. But this time, the injunction had enraged rather than cowed the workforce, and there was a 'critical mass' of flexibility and co-operation at rank-and-file level, including between members of different unions. RMT's John Leach explained at the time:

> [N]o matter how good a lawyer you have, or how legally technical your argument, we will ultimately never win in the courts because of the political make-up of the legal system. The antidote to the legal moves against us is solidarity ... We must not confuse the issue about the law. It's not as if we've put on balaclavas and run into a bank waving a gun about. We're not criminals. What we did was the opposite of a crime, it was to make things better for everyone.[543]

THE UNIONS VERSUS THE PPP

The trade unions provided the most determined resistance to the PPP – perhaps not surprisingly, as their members, London Underground workers, were the people most affected by the PPP policy. During the 2001 strikes, ASLEF and RMT members stood side-by-side and the proposed PPP looked at its most vulnerable. After trying for five years to stop the PPP, the trade unions – RMT in particular – continued their efforts once the policy was in place. RMT's workplace representatives pursued an ongoing, effective campaign to stop the Infracos driving down workers' pay and conditions, making it harder for them to maximise profits at workers' expense and even more inevitable that the Tube's maintenance work would eventually crash back into public ownership. London Underground workers were (and still are) hindered by being divided into separate unions. The AEEU (now part of Unite) refused to even oppose the PPP, the TSSA opposed it in theory but did very little in practice, ASLEF joined the fight late and left it early. RMT fought the most vigorous, albeit imperfect, campaign. Trade union representatives, branches and members campaigned doggedly, giving out thousands of leaflets, holding dozens of protests, lobbying decision-makers, compiling facts, figures and arguments, proposing resolutions and taking industrial action. Without stopping the PPP, those unions which fought it discredited the policy and won protections which limited its damage and hastened its demise.

But London daily newspaper *Evening Standard* furiously opposed the unions' campaign even though it also opposed the PPP at first (once it realised how unpopular the policy was). Perhaps the *Standard* expected the unions to take no action but instead rely on the more 'respectable' opposition. Trade unionists happily campaigned alongside other opponents of the PPP (for example, in the Campaign Against Tube Privatisation), but had good reason to be less trustful of some of PPP's critics. The *Standard*'s favoured dissenters were those, like Bob Kiley, who relied on court cases rather than mobilisation and argued for better forms of privatisation rather than for full public ownership. There was also an assortment of journalists, experts and politicians, from Jeffrey Archer to Ken Livingstone, who discovered their opposition to the PPP as they discovered the nonsensical detail of the scheme and, in some cases, the benefit to their popularity of opposing it. London Underground workers learned through experience that parts of the media do not report objectively on industrial action, and that the adage 'The first casualty of war is the truth' applies to class war as it does to military war. Newspapers owned by rich individuals and corporations rarely present a working-class point of view. Bakerloo driver Jock told me that:

> On the whole, press coverage was relatively fine, because they had to reflect that ordinary people were against this privatisation as well. But the exception was the *Evening Standard*, which hates us with a vengeance. Any time that we're in dispute, it doesn't matter what it's about, it could be the most obvious thing in the world, but they would just hate the fact that workers are organised, that we were taking industrial action over it.

For Metronet trackworker Sam, one reason why he and his workmates took up the battle against PPP effectively was 'a feeling that this was more than just a union issue, it was a class issue'. Other factors were that:

> People were willing to resist because they saw what had happened on British Rail. Also, we had agency workers who had taken action against PPP, refusing to cross picket lines, so others thought 'they're fighting it, so we should too'. And RMT representatives got to know each other across the grades, we attended meetings together, and the strike committee was a formalisation of that. We had some really good reps.

Public-private partnerships usually fragment workforces, making trade union organising more difficult. Union membership almost always falls and union resources are stretched as the unions have to negotiate and battle with several employers rather than one. Under the Tube PPP, RMT bucked this trend and survived (in some ways, even thrived) in Metronet and Tube Lines. This was the result of the conscious efforts of political trade unionists at rank-and-file level. Perhaps surprisingly, a well-organised union may have a stronger hand in the private sector, as Sam explained:

> You are up against shareholders, who look at money, rather than the government which has the endless supply of tax-payers' money to take the unions on. The PPP came in because the government set up a slush fund to bail out the companies if it got scuppered: we were outbid by public money. But in the private sector, the employers weren't prepared to take us on if it was cheaper for them to give in. We started winning, and people enjoyed taking Metronet on. Once the workforce and the reps realised we could beat them, it became infectious, and the membership back in the cabins and depots and offices began to realise that we were strong. Small successes led to bigger ones.

PPP'S POISONOUS LEGACY

We have considered what happened before and during the PPP. But what has happened since, and what might yet happen in the wake of the policy? The London Underground Public-Private Partnership may have gone, but it casts a long shadow.

The financial and organisational mess that the PPP left behind has given London Underground Ltd a reason (and a pretext) to administer further bitter pills. Policies with names such as 'Project Horizon' and the 'Operational Strategic Plan' have seen hundreds of station and administrative staff posts cut. LUL continues to scale back essential maintenance checks and loosen the rules which keep its operations safe. It plans to cram service control staff (signallers and line controllers) into a new control centre and scrap nearly 200 of their jobs. The Greater London Assembly's Conservative members repeatedly lobby for 'driverless trains' despite the serious safety risks. Leaked LUL documents revealed plans for an unattended Underground, with a small core of staff supplemented by wandering teams and agency workers.[544] In November 2013, LUL announced plans to close all its ticket offices and shed nearly a thousand station staff, and RMT announced plans for a campaign of political and industrial action to stop this.

There is now a near-consensus that the PPP failed. But there are very different views on how to deal with PPP's poisonous legacy. RMT reminds us that Underground workers and Londoners strongly objected to the PPP: 'We said it would fail and it did. It should not be Tube staff or passengers who pay the price for this failure'. But those in charge of London Underground counter that in tough economic times, money must be saved. There seems to be a cross-party consensus that cuts are unavoidable. But just because an idea has a cross-party consensus does not mean that it is right: there was also a consensus for some of the erroneous ideas that underpinned the PPP.

LONDON UNDERGROUND'S PRIVATE PARTS

Although the PPP is over, London Underground continues to give contracts to private companies. Who benefits?

Even before the PPP, Conservative policies had pushed sections such as cleaning, catering, building and some maintenance into the private sector. These sections – as well as others such as ticket gate maintenance and advert posting – remain private for no obvious good reason. The workers involved generally have much worse pay and conditions than those in the public London Underground Ltd; they may also be short-term, agency, contract or self-employed staff. Many of the workers involved are what the trade union movement and others call 'vulnerable workers', and include many ethnic minority and migrant workers. London Underground Ltd sees no better service from the contractor companies than it would from doing the work itself.

Reminded that cleaners have terrible pay and conditions, London Underground Ltd Managing Director Mike Brown nevertheless refuses to bring them into LUL's direct employment. Rather, he feels reassured that 'they will at least get the London Living Wage', which he 'feel[s] very passionately about'. (In fact, cleaners only get the London Living Wage for half the year, as contracts allow their employers six months to apply increases.) The minimal London Living Wage is very poor compensation for cleaners employed by private contractors who deny them the sick pay, holiday pay, pensions and safety provision that their LUL workmates enjoy.

Brown told me that 'A publicly-owned, integrated metro service for the biggest city by far in the country and indeed the continent is the right thing to happen', and his former fellow Director Howard Collins agreed: 'I'm a great believer in publicly-owned transport, and I see the downsides of the opposite every day using some of the [private, mainline] Train Operating Companies.' Post-PPP, they have brought some sections back in-house, notably the Underground's power supply and Jubilee line train maintenance. But LUL's most senior managers still see a place for private entrepreneurs, Brown arguing that they provide 'specialist skills and resources', like 'world-class signalling engineers' who 'don't want to work for a company'. He 'can't see the day that cleaning will come back in-house because the specialist cleaning companies are now so big and so well-placed to do it'.

Brown, Collins and Tunnicliffe all told me that while 'core' work should be public, extras can be private. They cited some of the work that used to be done in-house – London Transport making its own sausages, bread, cakes, meat pies, griffin tea and mahogany staircases – as though it were self-evidently absurd for this to happen. Collins argued that, 'if you don't focus on the core business, sometimes you end up focusing on the quality of your meat pies whereas the most important thing is getting people from A to B safely under reasonable conditions. When we tried to do everything, we did nothing well.' But a train needs to be cleaned as much as it needs to be driven, and its drivers and other staff need to be fed: all these functions are 'core'. And even if it is better for a baker than a transport operator to bake bread, that baker could still be employed by the public sector. Moreover, while Collins argues that the public sector 'lacks flexibility to allow change', the well-documented transformation of London Underground after the King's Cross fire – achieved within the public sector – suggests otherwise.

If you believe – as London Underground Ltd's past and present senior managers do – that there should be both public and private involvement, then you have to determine where the line lies between the two. Denis Tunnicliffe argues that:

> The less the task can be described and the more amorphous the general good is, the more important it is that it should be in the public sector. The more you can describe an outcome precisely and reward the elements of that output against a formula, the more you can hand it to the private sector and let it use its enthusiasm, greed and reward systems to deliver those outcomes.

However, the PPP's attempts to 'describe outcomes precisely' tied it up in knots and led directly to its failures and injustices; and the private sector's 'greed' led it to extract money at the expense of standards rather than to deliver outcomes. If we learn the lessons of the PPP, then there may be an alternative after all.

CHAPTER 6 – A SOCIALIST ALTERNATIVE

In this final chapter, I set out an alternative policy for London Underground. I begin by revisiting the five factors that have determined the Underground's well-being over its 150-year history, including the calamitous episode that was the PPP. I contend that this history shows that to fulfil its potential and meet London's needs, the Tube must be: unified; publicly-owned; a public service; well-funded; and under the control of an elected London body. International experience backs this up, and provides examples of how it might be funded. The changes of policy that have been made so often since London Underground came into public control eighty years ago – and which have accelerated over the last thirty years – have resulted in wasted spending on changing structures. Consensus that London Underground needs public ownership and adequate funding would allow stability, and that stability would promote effective working and improvements.

Moreover, we must move beyond standard, bureaucratic models of 'nationalisation' and recast the Tube through thoroughgoing democracy and workers' control. Such ideas were vigorously debated by socialists during the 1930s and 1970s, and I will review some of those arguments. I conclude that working-class control, organised through a Workers' and Passengers' Plan, would be a transformational and transitional policy for London Underground: it would see enormous improvements to the Tube, with consequent benefits to society as a whole, while posing a model for a socialist urban transport policy.

A UNIFIED PUBLIC SERVICE

If the PPP debacle and the long history of public-private tug-of-war on London Underground prove anything, it is that **London Underground, all of London Underground, should be owned and funded by the public sector**. It should be unthinkable for the capital's Tube system to be in anyone's hands other than the public's. After nearly fifty years of public ownership of London Underground, it was only the privatisation juggernaut driven by Margaret Thatcher – plus the labour movement's failure to defeat it and the Labour Party's embrace of its ideology – that meant that private ownership even got a look-in. The PPP showed that if the public sector does not own the whole Underground, then it cannot control it. The PPP left the freehold ownership of the Tube's infrastructure and key responsibilities such as safety in public hands, but this meant little in practice – the Infracos' ownership of the lease and their responsibilities to their shareholders made public control a myth.

The PPP also showed that dividing London Underground is disastrous. It created rivalry, secrecy, blame-passing, communication breakdowns, duplication, waste, skewed priorities, conflict, service disruption and serious accidents. In particular, the separation of infrastructure and operations has nothing to recommend it, and was a mistake that should not be repeated. This separation policy began in Sweden in the 1980s, and was brought to the UK rail industry when British Rail was privatised. The European Union has pursued it through its series of 'Railway Packages'. But there are independent and publicly-owned railways in Germany, Denmark, the Basque country and elsewhere which have thus far escaped this policy and have kept their infrastructure and operations integrated, with good results. RMT points out that railways in Europe are cheaper than UK railways for both tax-payers and fare-payers because 'in the main they are in public ownership and less fragmented'.[545] The only argument in favour of separation is that it facilitates profit-making. The decisive argument against it is that integration facilitates running a safe, effective railway. **Infrastructure, operations and all aspects of London Underground must be reunited and fully integrated.**

London Underground is a public service not a business, and should be allowed to operate as such rather than as a private company (or a pretend private company while technically publicly-owned). Public services should work to public needs, not to contracts and profits. Public transport is not a self-contained enterprise. Rather, it impacts positively on many aspects of the society in which it runs. London Underground enables people to work in the centre of a busy city but live somewhere more pleasant; or to live in the inner city but easily visit the countryside. It enhances people's quality of life by providing access to leisure, culture, education, healthcare and social opportunities. It helps people to get out of private transport, reducing congestion, pollution and road accidents, and freeing up space currently taken up by roads for walking, cycling, public squares and green space. Little of this is measurable in pounds and pence. Little can be incorporated into a contract with a private company: look at the mess that PPP got into by trying. Now PPP is undone, a similar fate should befall all the contracting-out, market-testing and 'business ethic' that has toxified the Tube. It is time for London Underground to drop the 'Limited' and for customers to become passengers again. Campaigners for the Kheel Plan – a proposal to expand New York City's public transport and scrap its fares – argue that: 'As a society, we have chosen to make schools, police, and fire protection free because they are "public goods" whose universal use benefits everyone. That's equally true of transit, and it's time we managed it that way.'[546]

In London and the UK, we could add healthcare to that list of public services. But not everyone accepts this comparison. Former London Underground Ltd Managing Director Denis Tunnicliffe told me that he favours transport monopolies being in the hands of society. But, he added:

> I don't take the view that many on the left take that transport is like the health service. I think that the duty of society to look after the health of its citizens is different from the duty of society to transport its citizens. The problem of creating good transport systems is that you then distort other systems, like housing systems and so on.

However, I would argue that it is precisely because transport affects other areas of our social organisation that it should be considered a public good. A socially-planned London transport network would better integrate the Underground with bus, cycle, river, pedestrian, taxi, light rail, tram and air transport. It should also be accompanied by a re-planning of London itself. This could locate services and reorganise work so that while demand for some aspects of public transport would increase, others – such as the cattle-truck peak-hours commute – would be alleviated.

But before a deeper consideration of planning, we must answer the question: how will this be paid for?

PAYING FOR THE UNDERGROUND

There would be savings in the money spent on operating, maintaining and improving London Underground if it were reintegrated under public ownership. Money that has been leaving the Underground as profits and dividends would stay in the system. The costs of conflict, bureaucracy and duplication between separate companies would disappear. RMT estimates that the mainline railway industry saved £400m per year from Network Rail Ltd's bringing maintenance back in-house; London Underground could save a similar proportion of its costs.[547] But this alone is not enough. The Tube needs substantial public funding.

London Underground must not be expected to 'pay its own way'. All experience shows that this aim is unrealistic, and it was soon dropped during the preparations for the PPP. It was extraordinary that 'new Labour', which stressed that it was realistic not ideological, could consider such an aim at all. Further, PPP's proponents – and even some of its opponents – repeatedly stated that adequate public funding was not possible, without offering an explanation. Academic writers Glaister and Travers were among many who predicated their proposals by 'assum[ing] that adequate funds will not be forthcoming from the normal, national public expenditure source' and that London Underground cannot 'expect the massive state hand-outs given by governments in France and Germany towards the metro systems in their cities.'[548] Why not? Why assume? It is the assumption of non-availability of public funding that led to the misconceived PPP, and which allows former Managing Director Denis Tunnicliffe to still believe that PPP 'remains a good [policy] in the political circumstances of the time'. If you assume that the right answer is impossible, then all you are left with is a choice between wrong answers. Successive governments *would not*, rather than *could not*, properly fund the Tube.

It is crucial that serious debates on London Underground's future refuse to accept this mantra, and return the possibility of adequate public funding to its rightful place at the top of the list of policy choices.

The 2013 Spending Round cut government funding to Transport for London by 12.5 per cent from 2015. Unless campaigners succeed in reversing this, the funding cut will inevitably lead to fares increases, deterioration of services and infrastructure, and abandonment of improvement plans. **The government must increase, not decrease, its funding to London Underground and Transport for London.**

There are many options for doing so. Sweden's regional railways are funded largely through local and regional taxation. The Tube brings custom to London's businesses, so those businesses could pay a levy on business rates towards it, as they are doing towards the cost of building

Crossrail. New Tube lines, extensions and stations increase the value of nearby land, so landowners could pay a land value windfall tax towards new developments (without passing it on to tenants and residents who do not see the fruits of the windfall). In 2011/12, £37bn was paid out in bonuses in Britain, 36 per cent of it in the finance sector. With that much cash around the City of London, a fraction of it could be spared to fund the city's transport. For Denis Tunnicliffe: 'London is a golden goose that lays golden eggs. You've got to look after the goose, and the Underground is an essential part of that.'

In France, administrative areas of more than 100,000 inhabitants levy a 'transport tax' on companies with more than nine employees. The tax is levied at a percentage of the payroll. The Paris Metro is largely funded by this tax, with each employer paying 2.2 per cent of its wage bill. Former London Underground Chief Operating Officer Howard Collins acknowledged that, 'The 'Grand Paris' scheme under M. Hollande is throwing huge amounts of money into the public sector – construction, engineering, and particularly Paris railway. I see that that is a way forward.' Managing Director Mike Brown agrees that the Paris Metro 'never have to start their argument with central government at zero: they have a guaranteed amount, that doesn't happen here'. France's transport tax even covers the full cost of maintaining and operating public transport in some areas, enabling the local authority to scrap fares altogether. A spokesperson for one of France's twenty free transport areas, Pays d'Aubagne, reports that since scrapping fares in May 2009, local public transport has seen a 170 per cent increase in usage and a halving of cost per passenger. He explains:

> Free transport means equality, the idea that we are all equal throughout the area ... everyone can use this public service as they need ... there is no city centre reserved for a few, there are no inaccessible villages, the lower-income housing estates are disenclaved, and everyone goes where they want in complete freedom.[549]

There is also a credible proposal to make New York City's public transport free, funded through congestion pricing (charges for motor vehicles to enter and park in the central zone). The 'Kheel plan' is named after its originator, conflict resolution expert Theodore Kheel. Trade unions would naturally be concerned about jobs being lost, but Kheel's thoroughly-costed plan envisages no decrease in the workforce, as increased services create new jobs to replace the revenue-collecting jobs lost. (Trade unionists might also consider that ticket-selling jobs are being lost already, even while fares rise, under the pretext of smartcard technology.) Currently in the USA, publicly-owned urban transport systems receive public funding from various sources: sales tax, petroleum business tax, corporate tax surcharge, bonds secured against fares revenue, grants from general state funds and dedicated transport funds, and federal grants for capital projects.

For London Underground to become a genuine service to the public, all its funding must be public funding. Any raising of private finance through 'partnerships', stockholding, loans or other means diverts accountability away from the public towards the private sector. The early experience of the London Passenger Transport Board in the 1930s illustrates the point. It paid huge dividends to stockholders while providing inadequate services to passengers and demoralising workers. The Act that created the Board stipulated that it must conduct its business in such a way as to meet its obligations to its stockholders: the former private owners still called its tune. In the 2013 Spending Round, the government extended Transport for London's right to borrow money, and allocated £2m to investigate how private money might be used to finance Crossrail 2. It seems that the mistaken thinking behind the PPP is still there. Ministers still want to use private money, despite knowing that it must be paid back with interest.

Whichever exact mechanism is chosen to prise the money from the employers' class, it must be direct, progressive taxation, not any form of ownership or loan. London Underground must receive reliable and adequate public funding without 'strings'.

NATIONALISATION AND BEYOND

After its problematic start, the London Passenger Transport Board (LPTB) made major improvements under the New Works Programme, extending lines and building new stations. When London Underground came under the control of the Greater London Council (GLC) from the 1960s, significant improvements again followed, including new and extended lines. In both cases – the LPTB and the GLC – the improvements slowed and stopped when national government intervened, cutting funding and wresting control away. **London Underground's history shows that it does best when it is under the control of a London body** (see appendix 1).

Many of the world's urban transport systems are run by the city authority. The New York Subway is owned by the City of New York and run by its Metropolitan Transportation Authority, with other US cities running similar systems. Mexico City's public transport is run by the Mexican Federal District. The Paris Métro is operated by the state-owned Régie Autonome des Transports Parisiens (RATP – Autonomous Operator of Parisian Transports). However, while these underground railways belong to an elected authority, most are run by Boards which are appointed rather than elected. Similarly, London Underground Ltd is a wholly-owned subsidiary of Transport for London. TfL belongs to the Greater London Authority (the Mayor plus the 25-seat Greater London Assembly) and is run by a Board appointed by the Mayor. The elected Assembly has no say in the appointment of the Board, and very little say in its policies. In 2010, the Assembly passed a resolution condemning LUL's plans to shed some 800 jobs – mainly on stations – and urging a rethink. The TfL Board and London Underground Ltd ignored the Assembly's vote. London Underground workers' bulletin *Tubeworker* wrote:

> If the GLA actually was the democratic London government that it claims to be, that would be the end of the job cuts, as the decision of London's elected representatives would trump that of unelected TfL and LU managers. But it might not be the end of it, as we can probably look forward to some hand-wringing about how the GLA is some kind of advisory body rather than one whose decisions count. We should not let the politicians get away with that, but should insist that the democratic government of London prevail and the cuts be withdrawn.[550]

Democracy did not prevail, and the job cuts went ahead. As I write, the sixteen TfL Board members (in addition to the Mayor) comprise three Conservative politicians, eight Directors of private companies, a lawyer, a representative each of the taxi and private hire trades, a disability campaigner and a retired trade union leader. The big majority represent the interests of business, not of London's workers, passengers, residents and communities. The Board has a built-in majority for private interests, and continues to support private sector involvement in London Underground. It has overseen above-inflation fares increases and reductions in staffing levels. The sole seat held by a trade unionist is neither elected by, nor accountable to workers or trade unions. Hugely outnumbered, a lone, appointed trade union official makes little impact against the commercially-driven majority.

It was a similar situation in the 1930s: Transport and General Workers' Union official John Cliff left his union post to join the London Passenger Transport Board, which was dominated by the former owners of the private Underground lines. Many socialists at the time rejected this policy – Herbert Morrison's model of 'public utility corporations' such as the LPTB – which the 'Busman's Punch' (a rank-and-file bulletin published by Communist Party members) labelled 'state capitalism'.[551] The Socialist Party of Great Britain argued that 'The London Transport Board is ... in no sense a 'bit of socialism' as certain misguided persons have pretended, but it is also in no sense a 'public body' for the public has no control over it'.[552]

A similar assessment could be made of London Underground and Transport for London today. **London Underground should be fully in public ownership, but not as an undemocratic 'public corporation'. Instead, there should be democratic control by workers – both those who work on the Underground and those who travel on it.** Speaking in Parliament against the Tube PPP when Prescott announced it in 1998, John McDonnell MP counterposed democratic public control:

> We must now seize this opportunity to install new management in London Underground, which involves representatives of the workforce, passengers and the community as a whole, accountable to the new strategic authority for London and committed to providing a public service and protecting our environment.[553]

There have been proposals for more representative boards of railway operators before. In the 1920s, Canada's Congress considered a scheme supported by the rail unions, under which the Canadian State Railway Board would comprise fifteen members: five chosen by the president to represent the public; five operating officials; and five elected by employees.[554] In the 1930s, some socialists argued for the new London Passenger Transport Board to be chosen by London's borough councils.

The Communist Party suggested that the Board should comprise five representatives of London municipal authorities and two employee representatives.[555]

Genuine workers' control must be more thoroughgoing than simply a more representative board presiding over a London Underground which retains an otherwise unchanged organisational structure. Even with a greater share of the board's seats, workforce and community nominees – distanced from those they represent – would end up playing the role of senior managers. Such a model of public ownership might remove the particular, profit-driven chaos of PPP or privatisation, but it would retain many of London Underground's shortcomings, and it would miss an opportunity to radically improve the Tube, and might even be counter-productive. In the 1970s, a rank-and-file London Transport workers' group took this view and included in its demands, 'No trade union representatives on the LT [London Transport] Executive ... The unions must represent their members not help management do their job for them.'[556] During the '70s, the trade union movement and socialists discussed ideas of workers' control of industry much more than they do now. (This interest sadly faded after the election of Margaret Thatcher's Conservative government in 1979.) These London Transport workers were not alone in rejecting trade union appointees on company boards: others too saw this as a charade, designed to derail the growing demand for genuine workers' control and industrial democracy.

London Underground workers know how to run the system safely and effectively, and share with passengers an interest in it running this way. At Labour Party conference in 1932, trade union officer Harold Clay, proposing to mildly amend Herbert Morrison's plan to appoint businessmen to the Board, argued that workers 'are as public-spirited as any employer', and 'can teach [the Board] more about the job than they ever know'. Clay said, 'I am a socialist. I believe in political democracy, but I do not believe that can become complete until you have industrial democracy.'[557]

Industrial democracy would involve an end to the separation between those who do the work and those who exercise authority: workers and managers, respectively. London Underground's daily functioning – the running of its stations, its trains, its ticket offices, its track maintenance gangs – is carried out by workers, with managers not involved. As a 2006 article in rank-and-file railway workers' publication *Off The Rails* commented, 'Much, maybe most, of what they [managers] do is not about running the railway. Rather, it is about keeping us in line.' The article continued:

> But aren't there some 'management' tasks that need doing?
> Yes, there are. But they do not have to be done by people paid a lot more than everyone else and with extra power and privileges.
> It is common for railworkers to see management cock-ups and to say that we and our workmates could do a better job of it. We know that staff who actually do the frontline work would also make a better job of planning and overseeing it. ...
> In the railway industry ... management tasks could be done by ordinary workers, perhaps on a rota system of release from your normal duties. We could decide policies, plan new projects, keep the accounts, work out rosters, organise training. No problem. [558]

This is not a proposal for managerial tasks to be given to workers on top of their current duties, nor for giving disciplinary power to one rank of worker over another. Managerial tasks can be divided among workers, with a corresponding rise in the number of workers (which would provide employment for those managers whose jobs are no longer needed). Workers running each part of the Underground would elect recallable delegates to regular assemblies and the main governing body, to sit alongside similarly-delegated representatives of passengers and the community. Putting workers, passengers and communities in charge would gear London Underground to meeting working-class needs.

Many of those who comment and write about London Underground are frustrated by decades of unpredictable funding, repeated changes in the Tube's governance and failed schemes such as the PPP. Various governments, authorities and politicians have been responsible for these unhelpful policies, so some have concluded that politics should be kept away from London Underground. Tony Travers and Stephen Glaister argued for the 'need to preserve independence from government in order to allow the business to be managed'.[559] Christian Wolmar wrote that 'transport is unsuited to decisions dictated by the necessarily short-term considerations of politicians ... [but] while transport remains a vital part of the infrastructure, politics will always be involved'.[560]

The damaging effect of 'politics' on the Underground is not caused by policy-makers being elected. Rather, it stems from the particular politics of the politicians making those decisions, and the lack of real political and industrial democracy. London Underground's problems do not come from it being run too democratically, but rather from it not being run democratically enough. The PPP was the product of the rise of 'new Labour' and its project to drive the working class out of politics. So the progressive alternative is to assert working-class representation in politics, including in the governance of services that we work on and use. If private companies, bureaucratic public management and those meddling politicians cannot save and improve our Tube, then who can? Those who have a direct, human stake in making it run well: those who work and travel on it and those who live in the communities it serves. We need a Workers' and Passengers' Plan for London Underground.

A WORKERS' AND PASSENGERS' PLAN

London Underground must provide services to meet people's needs, so its operation and development must be planned. The PPP showed, as private ownership had shown more than half a century earlier, that the 'market' cannot meet London Underground's needs. In 2008, RMT General Secretary Bob Crow wrote:

> Market forces cannot deliver the long-term planning and investment the railways need if they are to play their key environmental and economic role. Without addressing control – and that necessarily means ownership – the dream of an 'integrated transport system' will remain just that.[561]

Moreover, public ownership without planning is hollow. A 1962 Communist Party pamphlet reported that rail nationalisation had been an extreme disappointment to railworkers, and that, '[a] nationalised industry can be wrecked if it is not allowed to plan but is restricted in the alleged interests of private enterprise'. The pamphlet argued that great industries such as public transport should be 'socially owned and coordinated in a national economic plan, designed to achieve the fastest possible rate of economic development, as a basis for the sharp and steady rise in living standards'.[562] But there is something missing from the Communists' vision, perhaps not surprisingly considering the regimes they backed. There may be breakneck development, but there is no mention of democracy. **Only democratic planning can make London Underground meet public needs.**

Workers and passengers have a common interest in London Underground providing as good a public service as possible. (I include in the scope of 'passengers' those who wish to be passengers but are currently excluded – those who would travel by Tube if it were cheaper, more physically accessible, and if it served the areas they travel to and from.) Passengers want a service that is reliable, safe and accessible. Many of London's workers travel to work by Tube, and London Underground workers have the knowledge of how to make the system work to its maximum effectiveness. Both groups are motivated by improving London Underground, neither by accumulating private profit.

To draw up and carry out their plan, the first thing our workers' and passengers' governing body would need is full access to London Underground's financial information. The PPP and other private schemes kept finances shrouded from public scrutiny. Metronet refused to divulge its financial information. The cap on Alstom plc's penalties is 'commercially confidential'. RMT obtained a copy of the London Underground power PFI contract, only to find that the entire section on finance was redacted – hidden behind blocks of black ink. Academic Dexter Whitfield identifies this as a common feature of PPPs:

> Most partnerships are cloaked in secrecy with limited democratic accountability. The state and private contractors collude to protect intellectual property rights using 'commercial confidentiality' to minimise disclosure, participation, assessment of deals and public accountability. In this context, partnership is little more than negotiated privatisation.[563]

To plan London Underground's future direction, we need full public access to, and scrutiny of, its finances and structures. That way, a democratically-run Underground can identify how much funding it needs, and can identify waste which can be eliminated – money draining away from Tube services into private companies' profits, excessive salaries for top managers, or duplication and bureaucracy caused by sub-dividing London Underground's functioning. As Russian revolutionary Leon Trotsky advocated in his 'Transitional Programme' in 1938: 'The abolition of "business secrets" is the first step toward actual control of industry ... transport should be placed under an observation glass.'[564]

Alongside political and industrial democracy, this openness and scrutiny will allow knowledge of London Underground's operation to spread among workers and passengers, enabling the working class to apply that understanding collectively to the running of the Tube. Already, many Londoners – frustrated by the Underground's shortcomings, or imagining a better transport system serving a better London – find themselves saying, 'If we ran the Tube, ...'

What might workers and passengers plan? Large-scale investment to upgrade the Underground; significant cuts in fares; expansion of the network with new and extended lines; enough staff to run the system effectively; better safety standards; new technology designed to be used by staff rather than to replace them; prompt repairs. A Workers' and Passengers' Plan could organise those projects currently in the pipeline (such as Crossrail 2; extensions to the Bakerloo, Northern and Central lines) and those that ought to be (making the entire network fully accessible to disabled people). The Plan could prioritise those projects that better serve working-class communities rather than jumping to the dog-whistle of big business' latest luxury location. It could plan effectively for London's expected population growth.

Moreover, London Underground is a good candidate for 'public works' designed to both improve services and create jobs: to revive the economy at a time of recession. Under pressure of working-class demands, governments in the 1920s and 1930s did this – why not now? New work could be carried out by a TfL Major Works Department, with secure, directly-employed jobs and apprenticeships for young Londoners.

London Underground needs a Workers' and Passengers' Plan, drawn up and overseen by a democratically-elected governing body of workers, passengers and the community. This would lead to significant improvements in Underground services. It would also see a seismic shift in power towards the class of people who travel, rely and work on the Tube and away from the class that uses it merely as a source of profit. A Workers' and Passengers' Plan would be a popular democratic exercise which would massively extend the debate about London Underground's future, and would turn working-class people into decision-makers not just service users or wage slaves.

During the twentieth century, RMT's forerunner the National Union of Railwaymen (NUR) repeatedly called for the union to have 'a due measure of control' (1914), 'equal representation' (1917) and 'workers' participation' (1945) in the running of the railway. But while this might have been a step forward, workers and passengers need something more. In 1953, NUR General Secretary Jim Campbell set out a more inspiring vision when speaking at Labour Party conference. Public ownership, he said, could be more than simply the rescue of unprofitable industries or a means for treating workers a little better: rather, he said, 'it could be a preliminary to socialism, and it is in this context that democratic self-management becomes a realistic proposition'.[565]

If workers and passengers are to run London Underground, then workers and passengers must lead the campaign to achieve this policy. Those who currently control London Underground, and extract profit from it, will not willingly give up the reins. The Underground trade unions need to unite and organise an effective battle, alongside service users and as part of the working-class movement. We can devise this campaign by learning from both the strengths and the flaws of the fight against the PPP. It needs to be active, rank-and-file-led, militant and outward-looking. And it needs to put its faith in our own self-organisation. Genuine allies are welcome, but we learned from bitter experience that we cannot rely on political opportunists or quangos.

It was New Labour's retreat from working-class and socialist policy that brought about the calamitous PPP. A return to these things can begin to save it. We need a more rational way of organising London Underground, as part of a more rational way of organising society.

APPENDICES

APPENDIX 1 – THE 'FIVE FACTORS' IN LONDON

YEARS	OWNERSHIP public/ private	INTEGRATION	GOVERNANCE London/national Elected?	
1863-1908	Private	Private companies established different underground railway lines; from 1902, the Underground Electric Railways Company (UERL) became the holding company for several of them	No public governance: fully privately-owned.	
1908-1921	Private	The different companies worked together on advertising and promotion; branded the service as 'the Underground'; introduced the roundel; Underground typeface designed (1916)	No public governance: fully privately-owned.	
1921-1933	Private	The 'Underground group' co-ordinated the different private companies	No public governance: fully privately-owned.	
1933-1948	Public corporation with private stockholders	Separate railways became lines of one, united 'London Underground'; Tube map designed by Harry Beck introduced	London – the London Passenger Transport Board	
1948-1963	Public	Remained integrated as London Underground	National – under the control of the British Transport Commission	
1963-1984	Public	Remained integrated as London Underground, part of London Transport	London – under the control of London Transport Board (from 1963), then London Transport Executive, appointed by the elected Greater London Council (from 1970)	

UNDERGROUND'S HISTORY

ETHOS Public service or business?	FUNDING	SIGNIFICANT EVENTS
Business	Private	Metropolitan Railway opened; followed by several other railway lines and extensions
Business	Private	Further extensions and new lines built
Still private business, but government grants enabled improvement works, for social reasons and service improvement	Private, plus government support -1921 Trade Facilities Act gave government financial guarantees for capital projects that promoted employment	Extensions, including to Metropolitan Railway, Hampstead tube, Piccadilly and District lines; 55 Broadway opened as headquarters of the Underground group (1929)
Public control brought the goal of a public service, but with former private owners still having a controlling hand, a business ethos still prevailed	Government grants to enable improvement works	New Works Programme: five-year plan to modernise and extend the Underground, and take over and electrify some mainline routes
National railway was prioritised above London Underground	Public funding reduced	NWP abandoned; no significant new works
Return of London control enabled planned improvements; transport became an issue in GLC elections	Funding improved until the late 1970s, when it began to fall again	Victoria line opened (1968); Jubilee line opened (1979); Piccadilly line extended to Heathrow (1977); Fares Fair (1981)

APPENDIX 1 – THE 'FIVE FACTORS' IN LONDON

YEARS	OWNERSHIP public/ private	INTEGRATION	GOVERNANCE London/national Elected?	
1984-1997	Public/private	Sections are separated off and privatised. e.g. building works, cleaning. catering	National – run by London Regional Transport, appointed by the Secretary of State	
1997-2003	Public/private	Structure maintained while New Labour government develops PPP	National	
2003-2007/2010	Public/Private	Fragmented – under the PPP, control of infra-structure divided into three contracts and leased to 'Infracos'; sections already in private control remained so	London – Greater London Authority (Mayor and Assembly), elected in 2000, took over London Underground in 2003, once the PPP is in place	
present	Public/private	A degree of reunification – two-thirds of infrastructure back in LU; the remaining third in public ownership though not yet reintegrated. Some contracted-out sections brought back in-house, but most remain private and separate	London – GLA and Transport for London in charge	

UNDERGROUND'S HISTORY cont.

ETHOS Public service or business?	FUNDING	SIGNIFICANT EVENTS
Business – London Underground becomes London Underground Ltd (1985); some sections privatised; use of contracting-out, PFI and other schemes	Funding steadily cut; unreliable and paid in annual settlements	Kings Cross fire (1987); Company Plan (1983); several PFI deals
	New government stuck to predecessor's spending plans for two years; gave some extra grants to tide LU over until PPP	Jubilee Line Extension (1999)
Passengers now labelled 'customers'	Public funding increased significantly, but much was squandered on dealing with the flaws of the PPP	Several derailments and other incidents; East London line repackaged as part of London Overground and franchised to private operator
	2013 – Comprehensive Spending Review announced 12.5 per cent to Transport for London	Some line upgrades completed by public sector

APPENDIX 2 – SIGNIFICANT PUBLIC POSTS AND THEIR HOLDERS

MANAGING DIRECTOR OF LONDON UNDERGROUND LTD
Denis Tunnicliffe, 1988-1998
Derek Smith, 1999-2001
Paul Godier, 2001-2003
Tim O'Toole, 2003-2009
Richard Parry, (acting) 2009-2010
Mike Brown 2010-present

CHAIR OF LONDON UNDERGROUND LTD
Denis Tunnicliffe, 1998-2000
Derek Smith, 1999-2001

CHAIR OF LONDON REGIONAL TRANSPORT
Keith Bright, 1984-1988
Neil Shields, 1988-1989
Wilfrid Newton, 1989-1994
Peter Ford, 1995-1999
Malcolm Bates, 1999-2001
Bob Kiley, 2001
Malcolm Bates, 2001-2003

CHIEF EXECUTIVE OF LONDON REGIONAL TRANSPORT
Denis Tunnicliffe, 1998-2000

COMMISSIONER OF TRANSPORT FOR LONDON
Robert Kiley, 2001-2006
Peter Hendy, 2006-present

MAYOR OF LONDON
Ken Livingstone, (independent, then Labour) 4 May 2000 – 3 May 2008
Boris Johnson, (Conservative) 4 May 2008 – present

CHAIR OF TRANSPORT FOR LONDON
Ken Livingstone, 2000-2008
Tim Parker, 2008
Boris Johnson, 2008-present

SECRETARIES OF STATE
Secretary of State for the Department of the Environment, Transport and the Regions
John Prescott, 2 May 1997 – 8 June 2001
Secretary of State for Transport, Local Government and the Regions
Stephen Byers, 8 June 2001 – 29 May 2002
Secretaries of State for Transport
Alistair Darling, 29 May 2002 – 5 May 2006
Douglas Alexander, 5 May 2006 – 27 June 2007
Ruth Kelly, 28 June 2007 – 3 October 2008
Geoff Hoon 3 October 2008 – 5 June 2009
Andrew Adonis, 5 June 2009 – 11 May 2010

MINISTERS OF STATE FOR TRANSPORT
Gavin Strang, 2 May 1997 – 18 June 1998
John Reid, 27 July 1998 – 17 May 1999
Helen Liddell, 17 May 1999 – 29 July 1999
Gus Macdonald, 29 July 1999 – 8 June 2001
John Spellar, 8 June 2001 – 12 June 2003
Kim Howells, 12 June 2003 – 10 September 2004
Tony McNulty, 10 September 2004 – 9 May 2005
Stephen Ladyman, 9 May 2005 – 27 July 2007
Rosie Winterton, 28 July 2007 – 3 October 2008
Andrew Adonis, 3 October 2008 – 5 June 2009
Sadiq Khan, 7 June 2009 – 11 May 2010

PARLIAMENTARY UNDER-SECRETARY OF STATE WITH RESPONSIBILITY FOR TRANSPORT IN LONDON
Glenda Jackson, 1997-1999
Keith Hill, 1999-2001

APPENDIX 3 – WHAT BECAME OF PPP'S PERSONNEL?

As PPP collapsed, Christian Wolmar seethed that:

> [T]hose accountable for this scandal, from [Gordon] Brown through his adviser Shriti (now Lady) Vadera and its inventor, Martin Callaghan now of PwC [Pricewaterhouse Coopers], have never been brought to book. Indeed, all have been promoted or rewarded for this disgraceful episode.[566]

Brown now advises the World Economic Forum and others. Vadera, recruited from the City to strengthen its hold on government, did, as Simon Jenkins predicted, return there. She enjoys a global career and directorship of several companies. Other pillars of PPP, despite their involvement and apparently unrepentant, were given posts elsewhere in the railway industry. Iain Coucher, Chief Executive of Tube Lines 1999-2001, became Managing Director then Chief Executive of Network Rail Ltd, pocketing an estimated £7m-plus in pay and bonuses in his eight years at the publicly-owned, 'not-for-profit' company[567] before leaving in 2010 with a £1.6m payoff. His successor, Terry Morgan, left Tube Lines in 2009 to become the non-executive Chair of Crossrail, receiving a cool £250,000 in 2012/13 for a three-day week. Metronet's 1999-2003 Chief Executive, Rod Hoare, now chairs transport consultancy firm North Star. Andrew Lezala, having steered Metronet into ignominious collapse, left with a £500,000 pay-off from public funds.[568] He now runs Melbourne Metro in the Australian state of Victoria. A scathing article by journalist Tess Lawrence bemoaned Victoria state's habit of recruiting 'failed foreign corporate asylum seekers' like Lezala, who, she claimed, 'is now doing to Melbourne's hapless Metro system what he so excelled in doing to Metronet. It is a seething morass of incompetence and customer frustration.'[569]

Other industries also welcomed fugitives from the wreckage of the PPP. London Underground Ltd's former Managing Director Derek Smith became Chief Executive of Hammersmith Hospitals, then of private health consultancy firm Durrow. Ruth Kelly, Labour Secretary of State for Transport when Metronet went into administration, is now Senior

Manager for Strategy and Global Business for the HSBC bank. Steve Robson, unembarrassed architect of both British Rail privatisation and London Underground PPP, walked away from his Frankenstein's monsters in 2001, onto the Board of the Royal Bank of Scotland. There, he 'sat on his hands' while the bank went to ruin, until being 'purged' along with six other non-executive directors for 'having failed to protect shareholders' interests and failing to stand up to chief executive Sir Fred Goodwin'.[570] The notorious 'Fred the Shred' had presided over the bank's 2008 UK-record loss of £24.1bn and was stripped of his knighthood. Even this, though, was not enough to derail Robson's career: he is now non-executive Director of Partnerships UK and regulatory body the Financial Reporting Council. For Christian Wolmar, Robson is 'that ever so clever fool' who is 'a serial offender when it comes to wasting tax-payers' money'.[571] But for the political establishment, he is worthy of a knighthood. Also decorated are Rod Hoare MBE, Terry Morgan CBE, Lady Vadera, Chris Bolt CB and Baron Prescott. No such glory, though, for Stephen Byers, banned from the Parliamentary estate after being caught by undercover journalists offering to lobby decision-makers for a fee of up to £5,000 per day.

Ken Livingstone poured scorn on two further Lords: Denis Tunnicliffe, now 'comfortably remunerated as director of the Atomic Energy Agency and – alarmingly – the Rail and Safety Standards Board'; and Professor David Currie, 'who claimed that PPP would save £3.3billion [and is] now Lord Currie of Marylebone with a nice little earner chairing Ofcom'.[572] Currie is an economist and was one of the 'six wise men' who advised the Conservative government on economic matters from 1992; he became a Lord in 1996, before the Labour government was elected or had announced its London Underground PPP.

Livingstone is no stranger to the 'nice little earner' for which he derides Currie. He changed the rules to allow political appointees to receive severance packages, so when he departed the Mayor's office in 2008, eight of his advisers departed with him, with an average £200,000 each. When Livingstone sought election again four years later, it emerged that he and his wife had set up a company to channel money from his media appearances and speeches, allowing him to pay 20 per cent corporation tax instead of 50 per cent income tax on his £55,000 fees that year.[573] He again lost the election, to Boris Johnson. By this time, his appointee Bob Kiley had returned to the USA, after leaving his

Commissioner's post in 2005 with a £1m 'golden farewell' and continuing to receive £3,200 per day in consultancy fees (totalling £416,250) from TfL, which was unable to say what he actually did for the money.[574] Tim O'Toole became Chief Executive of transport multinational FirstGroup, paid more than a million pounds in 2012.[575] Livingstone had been carried into the Mayor's office in 2000 on a wave of opposition to PPP and revulsion at New Labour's undemocratic manipulations against him. But although he may have seemed a figurehead of objection to PPP, he did not lead any significant mobilisation against it, preferring legal manoeuvres and technical spats. **The fight against PPP did more for Ken Livingstone than Ken Livingstone did for the fight against PPP.**

Tube Lines worker Tom remains bitter against the cats who got the cream:

> PPP simply created a cash cow for private companies and friends of politicians to take as much as they could out of the public's pockets. It appals me, because every penny came out of taxes, and if it had gone back into London Underground instead, these upgrades would have been finished years ago. They wonder why there's no money to fix their Underground, when it's in the flats and the mooring fees and the cars and the riverboat trips and the expenses that managers get paid. It can't be right to give public money to private companies whose only aim is to make a profit out of it. No private company should ever have that much control again over a public transport service. As long as it is like that, as long as you are allowing these charlatans in to steal our money, it's just not right.

BIBLIOGRAPHY

GOVERNMENT PUBLICATIONS

Department of the Environment, Transport and the Regions, *London Underground Public-Private Partnership: facts and analysis*, 1998.

Government news releases.

House of Commons Hansard.

House of Commons Regulatory Reform Committee, *Proposal for the Regulatory Reform (Fire Safety) Order 2004*, 11th Report 2003-04, HC684, 2004.

House of Commons Transport Committee, *London Underground*, 2nd Report 2001-02, HC387-II, 2002.

House of Commons Transport Committee, *London's Public Transport capital investment requirements*, 3rd Report 1992-3, HC754, 1993.

House of Commons Transport Committee, *The London Underground and the Public-Private Partnership Agreements*, 2nd report 2007-08, HC45, 2007.

House of Commons Transport Committee, *The Performance of the London Underground*, 6th report 2004-05, HC94, 2005.

House of Commons Transport, Local Government and the Regions Committee, *London Underground – the Public Private Partnership: Follow Up*, 7th report 2001-02, HC680, 2002.

Kellaway, Martin and Shanks, Helen, *Metronet, Tube Lines and the London Underground PPP*, NACC decision, Office for National Statistics, 2007.

Office of the PPP Arbiter: Announcements, Press Notices, Reports and Accounts.

UK Government Bill, *The PFI and the Local Government (Contracts) Bill* (Bill 5 1997/98), House of Commons Library Research Paper 97/80, House of Commons Library, 1997.

UK Government White Paper, *Public Transport in London*, Cmnd 9004, HMSO, 1983.

LONDON UNDERGROUND, TRANSPORT FOR LONDON AND INFRACO PUBLICATIONS

London Underground Ltd, *Company Plan, summary 1991: a new dawn for the heart of London*, 1991.

London Underground Ltd, *Annual Report*, 1992-93.

London Underground Ltd, *Statement of Strategy*, 1993.

London Underground Ltd, *Making Vision into Reality*, 1993.

London Underground Ltd, *Moving Forward*, 1994.

London Underground Ltd, *Evaluation of Options*, 1997.

London Underground Ltd, *Public Private Partnership: briefing document*, 1999.

London Underground Ltd, *The PPP's Performance Specification*, 1999.

London Underground Ltd, *Public Private Partnership, Final Assessment Report*, 2002.

London Underground Ltd, *Summary of the PPP contract documents*, 2000.

London Underground Ltd, *On The Move* (in-house magazine).

Metronet Rail SSL Network Planning, *BTUK Intention to Reduce SSL Fleet Size: Initial Assessment for MRSSL*, 2007.

Transport for London, *Outline of a Programme for the Rehabilitation and Management of the London Underground*, 2000.

Transport for London, *Popular Myths about the Tube PPP*, 2002.

Transport for London, *London Underground and the PPP: The First Year*, 2004.

Transport for London, *London Underground and the PPP: The Second Year*, 2005.

Transport for London, *London Underground and the PPP: The Third Year*, 2006.

Transport for London, *London Underground PPP & Performance Report 2008-2009*, 2009.

Transport for London, *Role of the PPP arbiter and lessons for future monitoring*, 2011.

Transport for London, press releases and statements.

Transport for London, list of contracts, 28 June 2012.

Tube Lines press releases.

Tube Lines, *platform* (in-house magazine).

Tube Lines, *Response to the Arbiter's Draft Direction on the Second Review Period*, 2009.

REPORTS

Comptroller and Auditor General, *London Underground PPP: were they good deals?*, HC645, National Audit Office, 2004.

Comptroller and Auditor General, *London Underground: Are the Public Private Partnerships likely to work successfully?*, HC 644 Session 2003-

2004, 2004.

Comptroller and Auditor General, *The failure of Metronet*, HC512, National Audit Office, 2009.

Comptroller and Auditor General, *The financial analysis for the London Underground Public Private Partnerships*, HC54, National Audit Office, 2000.

Deloitte & Touche, *Report into London Underground Public Private Partnership: Emerging Findings*, 2001.

Department for Transport Rail Accident Investigation Branch, *Derailment of a London Underground Central Line train near Mile End station, 5 July 2007*, Report 03/2008, 2008.

Department for Transport Rail Accident Investigation Branch, *Runaway of an engineering train from Highgate, 13 August 2010*, Report 09/2011, 2011.

Ernst & Young, *London Underground Limited: Public-Private Partnership Value for Money Review*, 2002.

Fennell, Desmond QC, *Investigation into the King's Cross Fire*, Department of Transport, 1988.

FirstGroup, *Directors Remuneration Report*, 2012.

Gaffney, Declan, Shaoul, Dr Jean, and Pollock, Professor Allyson, *Funding London Underground: myths and realities*, commissioned by 'Listen to London', 2000.

Health and Safety Executive, *A Health and Safety Review of London Underground and its preparations for the Public-Private Partnership*, Revision 1, 2002.

Health and Safety Executive, *Derailments on London Underground at Camden Town and Hammersmith*, 2005.

Health and Safety Executive, *White City train derailment*, 2005.

Hutton, Will, *The London Underground Public Private Partnership, An Independent Review*, The Industrial Society, 2000.

International Monetary Fund, *Public Private Partnerships*, 2004.

Kiley, Robert, *Report to Mayor Ken Livingstone regarding the Feasibility of the PPP Structure as Currently Proposed*, TfL, 2000.

London Assembly Budget Committee, *A fare decision? The impact of the Mayor's fare decision*, 2009.

London Assembly Transport Committee, *Delays possible: maintaining and upgrading the London Underground*, 2009.

London Assembly Transport Committee, *The PPP: Two Years In – The*

Transport Committee's scrutiny into the progress of the PPP, 2005.

Mayor of London, *74th Mayor's report to the Greater London Assembly*, 2007.

Monopolies and Mergers Commission, *London Underground Ltd*, Cm 1555, HMSO, 1991.

Nurture New York's Nature, *A Bolder Plan: Balancing Free Transit and Congestion Pricing in New York City* ('The Kheel Plan'), 2008.

Office of Water Services (Ofwat), *Report on Leakage and Water Efficiency*, 1998/99.

Office of Water Services (Ofwat), *Report on Levels of Service for the Water Industry in England and Wales*, 1998/99.

Prison Reform Trust, *Prison Privatisation Report International*, 1996.

The Future Tube Priorities Investigative Committee, *Mind The Gap – between what Londoners want and what Londoners get*, London Assembly, 2003.

Tracey, Richard, *Driverless Trains*, 2010.

Treasury Taskforce on Private Finance, *Partnerships for Prosperity – the Private Finance Initiative*, HM Treasury, 1997.

WS Atkins plc, *Annual Report*, 2008.

BOOKS, PAMPHLETS AND PAPERS

Ahern, Tom, *The Railways and the People: an appeal to passengers and workers*, Communist Party, 1962.

Bagwell, Philip S, *End of the Line? The Fate of British Railways Under Thatcher*, Verso, 1984.

Bagwell, Philip S, *NUR 1913-1988: 75 Years of Industrial Trade Unionism*, National Union of Railwaymen, 1988.

Cohen, Nick, *Pretty Straight Guys*, Faber & Faber, 2004.

Croome, Douglas F and Jackson, Alan A, *Rails Through Clay* (2nd edition), Capital Transport Publishing, 1995.

Day, John R and Reed, John, *The Story of London's Underground* (9th edition), Capital Transport Publishing, 2005.

Downton, Arthur, *The London Transport Scandal*, London District Committee of the Communist Party, 1936.

Glaister, Stephen and Travers, Tony, *Liberate the Tube! Radical proposals to revitalise the London Underground*, Policy Study no.141, Centre for Policy Studies, 1995.

Glaister, Stephen, Scanlon, Rosemary and Travers, Tony, *The Way Out:*

An Alternative Approach to the Future of the Underground, LSE LONDON discussion paper no.1, London School of Economics, 1999.

Irvine, Kenneth, *Underground Revolution: Modernizing London Underground through Public-Private Partnership*, Adam Smith Institute, 1997.

Lawley, F E, *Socialism and railways*, ILP Study Courses no.9, undated, probably 1924.

Livingstone, Ken, *You Can't Say That: Memoirs*, Faber & Faber, 2011.

London First, *Funding London's Transport: the way ahead*, 1997.

Lord Morrison of Lambeth, *Herbert Morrison: An Autobiography*, Odhams, 1960.

Mirza, Unjum, *London Underground: I Do Mind Dying – The Politics of Health & Safety*, RMT, 2007.

Osler, David, *Labour Party plc: New Labour as a Party of Business*, Mainstream Publishing, 2002.

Pimlott, Ben, *Labour and the Left in the 1930s*, Allen & Unwin, 1977.

Socialist Party of Great Britain, *Nationalisation or Socialism?*, 1945.

Trotsky, Leon, *The Death Agony of Capitalism and the Tasks of the Fourth International: The Transitional Programme*, Part I, Fourth International, 1938.

Whitfield, Dexter, *New Labour's Attack on Public Services*, Socialist Renewal, fifth series, no.3, Spokesman Books, 2006.

Whitfield, Dexter, *Private Finance Initiative and Public Private Partnerships: what future for public services?*, Centre for Public Services, 2001.

Whitfield, Dexter, *Public Services or Private Profit?*, Socialist Renewal, new series, no.7, Spokesman Books, 2001.

Whitfield, Dexter, *The £10bn Sale of Shares in PPP Companies: New source of profits for builders and banks*, ESSU Research Report no.4, European Services Strategy Unit, 2011.

Wolmar, Christian, *Down The Tube: the battle for London's Underground*, Aurum Press, 2002.

Workers' Liberty, *Tunnel Vision: London Underground's Public-Private Partnership and the Fight against it*, 2004.

ARTICLES AND PAPERS

Baldock, Hannah, Getting the Tube to Work, *Building journal*, 9 February 2001.

Bolt, Chris, *Regulating London Underground*, Beesley regulation lecture, 2003.

Crow, Bob, Rail privatisation – a failed experiment, *Building the new common sense: social ownership for the 21st century*, Left Economics Advisory Panel, 2008.

Glatter, Pete, 'London Busmen: Rise and Fall of a Rank and File Movement', *International Socialism*, no.74, 1975.

Glaister, Stephen, Scanlon, Rosemary and Travers, Tony, 'Getting Public Private Partnerships Going in Transport', *Public Policy and Administration* vol. 15 no. 4, Winter 2000.

Trefor Williams, 'Analysis of the London Underground PPP Failure', *Working Paper Proceedings*, Engineering Project Organizations Conference, South Lake Tahoe, CA, November 4-7, 2010.

NEWSPAPERS AND JOURNALS

Action For Solidarity
Building
Camden New Journal
Daily Mail
Daily Telegraph
The Engineer
Evening Standard
Financial Mail on Sunday
Financial Times
The Guardian
Hackney Gazette
The Independent
The Independent on Sunday
The Metro
Modern Railways
Morning Star
The Observer
Prospect
The Rail Engineer
Rail magazine
Rail Technology Magazine
Scotland on Sunday
Solidarity
Sunday Times
The Times

Tribune
Workers' Liberty

WEBSITES
BBC website
BBC News
BBC Water Week webpage
CBC News
christianwolmar.com
Commission for Integrated Transport (archive)
CorporateWatch
guardian.co.uk
independentaustralia.net
Mail Online
New Civil Engineer
PA News
ppparbiter.co.uk (archive)
pppbulletin.com
Railway Gazette
railway-technology.com
rmtlondoncalling.org.uk
Seattle Times
tallinn.ee
telegraph.co.uk
The Age theage.com.au
thisislondon.co.uk
Tubeworker's blog

TRADE UNION PUBLICATIONS
ASLEF letters to members.
ASLEF press releases.
ASLEF/RMT/TSSA, *London Underground Public-Private Partnership: Your Questions Answered*, undated, probably 2000.
Campaign Against Tube Privatisation newsletters, bulletins, leaflets and minutes.
Campaign Against Tube Privatisation newspaper, 2000.
Campaign Against Tube Privatisation, *The Trade Unions and New Labour: CATP discussion document*, 2003.

Listen to London Campaign Bulletins.

Listen to London, 'time to think again: the future of London Underground', 1999.

Neasden Flyer (RMT branch newsletter), 2009.

RMT leaflets, letters to members, minutes of meetings, circulars to branches.

RMT News.

RMT press releases.

RMT, *Issues Arising From the London Bombings*, Evidence to Home Affairs Committee, undated, probably 2005.

RMT, *Memorandum to the GLA Transport committee investigation into Industrial Relations on the London Underground*, 2005.

RMT, *Paying for Privatisation: RMT briefing on the McNulty Report in the Railways*, 2011.

RMT, *Putting People First: The London Underground Public Private Partnership and RMT's proposals for protecting staff*, 1998

RMT, *Response to Transport Select Committee*, October 2009.

RMT, *Submission to GLA investigation into PPP on London Underground*, 2008.

RMT, *The Public/Private Partnership for London Underground: Discussion Paper for RMT Strategy to Protect members*, 1998.

Unison Bargaining Support Group reports.

LETTERS

Letter, Boris Johnson to Dean Finch, 4 December 2012.

Letter, Deputy Prime Minister to Malcolm Bates, 30 March 2001.

Letter, Jackie Darby to John Biggs, 27 May 2002.

Letter, John Monks, TUC General Secretary, to Vernon Hince, RMT Senior Assistant General Secretary, 2 May 2001.

Letter, John Prescott to London Underground / London Transport staff, 20 March 1998.

Letter, Ken Livingstone to Alistair Darling, February 2003.

Letter, Tim O'Toole to Lynne Featherstone, GLA Transport Committee, 13 May 2005.

Letter, Tube Lines to Caroline Pidgeon AM, 22 February 2010.

Letters, London Underground Ltd to the Office of the PPP Arbiter, 1 August and 23 August 2010.

Open letter from Denis Tunnicliffe to London Underground staff, 20 March 1998.

CORRESPONDENCE/INTERVIEWS WITH THE AUTHOR
Mike Brown
Howard Collins
Gwyneth Dunwoody MP
Oona King MP
John Leach – RMT
London Underground workers Jock (driver), Paul (Station Supervisor), Adam (electrician), Sam (trackworker), Ronnie (lift engineer), Tom (emergency response worker) – names have been changed to protect anonymity
John McDonnell MP
Gavin Strang MP
Lord (Denis) Tunnicliffe

RANK-AND-FILE TRANSPORT WORKERS' PUBLICATIONS (current/recent, unless otherwise indicated)
Across The Tracks
Busman's Punch, 1930s
Off The Rails
The Live Rail: organ of the United Efforts Movement, 1936
The Platform, 1977-78
The Red Line
Tubeworker

OTHER
Britain at Work project newsletter, 'Going Underground: tales from the tube', 2013.
Conservative Party election leaflet, 1997.
Freedom of Information requests.
General Election manifestos.
Green Energy League, Friends of the Earth.
Washington State Department of Ecology press release, 1997.
Opinion polls – IPSOS/MORI.

NOTES

1   Department of the Environment, Transport and the Regions, *London Underground Public-Private Partnership: facts and analysis*, 1998.

2   Jonathan Prynn, 'Taking a new line to get Tube back on track', *The Guardian*, 4 March 1998.

3   Jonathan Prynn, *The Guardian*, 4 March 1998.

4   Lord Morrison of Lambeth, *Herbert Morrison: An Autobiography*, Odhams, 1960, p. 41.

5   Socialist Party of Great Britain, *Nationalisation or Socialism?*, 1945.

6   See, for example, Ben Pimlott, *Labour and the Left in the 1930s*, Allen & Unwin, 1977, pp. 66-67; and *The Live Rail*, 1936.

7   Quoted in Britain at Work project newsletter, 'Going Underground: tales from the tube', 2013.

8   Arthur Downton, *The London Transport Scandal*, London District Committee of the Communist Party, 1936, p. 1.

9   John R Day and John Reed, *The Story of London's Underground* (9th edition), Capital Transport Publishing, 2005, p. 146.

10   Christian Wolmar, *Down The Tube: the battle for London's Underground*, Aurum Press, 2002, p. 31.

11   Christian Wolmar, (2002), p. 37.

12   Britain at Work project newsletter, (2013).

13   *The Platform*, March 1977.

14   Bus travel increased by 13 per cent, Underground travel by 7 per cent – Philip S Bagwell, *End of the Line? The Fate of British Railways Under Thatcher*, Verso, 1984, p. 150.

15   Bus journeys fell by 16 per cent, Underground journeys (excluding OAPs) by 13 per cent, and peak period car traffic rose by 5 per cent – Philip S Bagwell, (1984), p. 155.

16   John R Day and John Reed, (2005), p. 187.

17   UK Government White Paper, *Public Transport in London*, Cmnd 9004, HMSO, 1983, p. 71.

18   House of Commons Hansard, 26 July 1983.

19   Philip S Bagwell, *NUR 1913-1988: 75 Years of Industrial Trade Unionism*, National Union of Railwaymen, 1988, p. 52.

20   Desmond Fennell QC, *Investigation into the King's Cross Fire*, Department of Transport, 1988.

21   Monopolies and Mergers Commission, *London Underground Ltd*, Cm 1555, HMSO, 1991.

22   London Underground Ltd, *Company Plan, summary 1991: a new dawn for the heart of London*, 1991.

23   London Underground Ltd, *Making Vision into Reality*, 1993.

24   House of Commons Transport Committee, *London's Public Transport capital investment requirements*, 3rd Report 1992-3, HC754, 1993, p. 26.

25 London Underground Ltd, *Annual Report*, 1992-93; London Underground Ltd, *Statement of Strategy*, 1993.

26 London Underground Ltd, *Moving Forward*, 1994.

27 Jonathan Prynn, *The Guardian*, 4 March 1998.

28 Stephen Glaister and Tony Travers, *Liberate the Tube! Radical proposals to revitalise the London Underground*, Policy Study no.141, Centre for Policy Studies, 1995, p. 52.

29 Christian Wolmar, (2002), p. 11.

30 *Evening Standard*, 19 August 1998.

31 *Evening Standard*, 19 January 1999.

32 Christian Wolmar, (2002), p. 11.

33 *RMT News*, March 2001.

34 Christian Wolmar, (2002), pp. 4-5.

35 Christian Wolmar, (2002), p. 91.

36 Christian Wolmar, (2002), p. 82.

37 *Evening Standard*, 9 November 1998; *The Guardian*, 14 February 1998.

38 Christian Wolmar, (2002), p. 87.

39 House of Commons Hansard, 20 March 1998.

40 Christian Wolmar, (2002), p. 90.

41 BBC News website, 25 September, 1998.

42 *The Observer*, 8 November 1998.

43 Christian Wolmar, (2002), p. 90.

44 Conservative Party election leaflet, 1997.

45 *RMT News*, no.31, April 1997.

46 'Tube Faces Sell-Off', *Workers' Liberty*, March 1997.

47 *RMT News*, April 1997.

48 *The Independent*, 12 April 1997.

49 Labour's net gain of 25 seats in London was its highest of any region; Research Paper 138, House of Commons Library, 29 March 2001, Table 7.

50 *The Guardian*, 2 May 1997.

51 House of Commons Hansard, 20 March 1998.

52 *The Guardian*, 3 September 1998.

53 UK Government Bill, *The PFI and the Local Government (Contracts) Bill* (Bill 5 1997/98), House of Commons Library Research Paper 97/80, House of Commons Library, 1997, p. 6.

54 *Daily Telegraph*, 3 December 2000.

55 *The Independent*, 13 September, 1997.

56 *The Guardian*, 4 March 1998.

57 Comptroller and Auditor General, *London Underground PPP: were they good deals?*, HC645, National Audit Office, 2004, para.1.7.

58 David Osler, *Labour Party plc: New Labour as a Party of Business*, Mainstream Publishing, 2002, pp. 232, 96.

59 DETR, (1998), p. 4.

60 London Underground Ltd, *Evaluation of Options*, 1997.

61 David Osler, (2002), pp. 35, 230.

62   Comptroller and Auditor General, (2004), para.1.9.

63   Christian Wolmar, (2002), p. 109.

64   *Evening Standard*, 17 November 1997.

65   Comptroller and Auditor General, (2004), para.1.17.

66   *The Guardian*, 4 March 1998.

67   House of Commons Hansard, 20 March 1998.

68   *Daily Telegraph* website, 9 July 2009 and 25 July 2009.

69   House of Commons Hansard, 20 March 1998.

70   Treasury Taskforce on Private Finance, *Partnerships for Prosperity – the Private Finance Initiative*, HM Treasury, 1997.

71   House of Commons Hansard, 20 March 1998.

72   October 1997 review of Price Waterhouse report, cited in Comptroller and Auditor General, (2004), para.1.15.

73   Christian Wolmar, (2002), p. 121.

74   House of Commons Environment, Transport and Regional Affairs Committee, Seventh Report: London Underground, 8 July 1998.

75   *Evening Standard*, 26 August 1998.

76   DETR, (1998), p. 8.

77   House of Commons Hansard, 20 March 1998.

78   *Evening Standard*, 1 May 1998.

79   *Evening Standard*, 19 August 1998.

80   *Evening Standard*, 16 April 1998.

81   House of Commons Hansard, 20 March 1998.

82   London First, *Funding London's Transport: the way ahead*, 1997.

83   Kenneth Irvine, *Underground Revolution: Modernizing London Underground through Public-Private Partnership*, Adam Smith Institute, 1997.

84   Jonathan Prynn, *The Guardian*, 4 March 1998.

85   Employee Communications bulletin no.640, 20 March 1998.

86   Open letter from Denis Tunnicliffe to staff, 23 March 1998.

87   *Evening Standard*, 22 April 1998.

88   Commissioned by and reported in the *Evening Standard*, 28 April 1998.

89   *Evening Standard*, 14 August 1998.

90   House of Commons Hansard, 20 March 1998.

91   *RMT News*, June 1998.

92   RMT leaflet, 1997.

93   *The Times*, 7 May 1998; *The Guardian*, 7 May 1998.

94   *Evening Standard*, 23 March 1998.

95   *Evening Standard*, 10 March 1998.

96   *The Guardian*, 7 May 1998.

97   *Daily Telegraph*, 7 May 1998.

98   *Tribune*, 2 October 1998.

99   *The Guardian*, 16 June 1998.

100 *Daily Telegraph*, 28 June 1998.

101 *Evening Standard*, 30 July 1998.

102 *Evening Standard*, 19 August 1998.

103 RMT, London Transport Regional Council leaflet, 1998.
104 London Underground Ltd, *Public Private Partnership: briefing document*, 1999, para.4.5.
105 Notice of Judgment, Mr Justice Sullivan, 22 December 1998, 4.31pm.
106 RMT, letter to members, 21 April 1999.
107 *Evening Standard*, 15 February 1999.
108 Letter, Jimmy Knapp to RMT members, 18 February 1999.
109 *Evening Standard*, 16 February 1999.
110 *Evening Standard*, 23 February 1999.
111 *Financial Times*, 9 March 1999.
112 *Evening Standard*, 30 March 1999.
113 *Evening Standard*, 20 April 1999.
114 *The Observer*, 11 April 1999.
115 *Evening Standard*, 20 April 1999.
116 *Financial Times*, 9 March 1999.
117 *Evening Standard* feature, 19 January 1999.
118 Declan Gaffney, Dr Jean Shaoul and Professor Allyson Pollock, *Funding London Underground: myths and realities*, commissioned by 'Listen to London', 2000, pp. 10-11.
119 Letter, John Prescott to London Underground / London Transport staff, 20 March 1998.
120 Comptroller and Auditor General, (2004), Appendix 3: Evidence to the GLA Bill Standing Committee, February 1999.
121 Listen to London, 'time to think again: the future of London Underground', 1999.
122 House of Commons Hansard, 15 June 1999, col.137.
123 Declan Gaffney, Dr Jean Shaoul and Professor Allyson Pollock, (2000).
124 *The Guardian*, 28 December 2001; House of Commons Transport Committee, *London Underground*, 2nd Report 2001-02, HC387-II, 2002.
125 London Underground Ltd, *The PPP's Performance Specification*, 1999.
126 London Underground Ltd, *Public Private Partnership, Final Assessment Report*, 2002, p. 10.
127 Quotes from London Underground Ltd, *Public Private Partnership: briefing document*, 1999.
128 Christian Wolmar, (2002), p. 122.
129 *Evening Standard* editorial, 26 September 2000.
130 Christian Wolmar, (2002), p. 131, 122.
131 House of Commons Transport Committee, HC387-II, (2002), LU03A, Supplementary Memorandum by Transport for London.
132 House of Commons Transport Committee, HC387-II, (2002), LU11B, Supplementary Memorandum by London Underground Ltd.
133 *The Economist*, 7 December 2000.
134 London Underground Ltd, *Summary of the PPP contract documents*, 2000.
135 Chris Bolt, 'Regulating London Underground', Beesley regulation lecture, 2003.
136 Comptroller and Auditor General, (2004).
137 House of Commons Transport Committee, HC387-II, (2002), Q.517.

138 *The Economist*, 7 December 2000.

139 *Daily Telegraph*, 16 November 2001.

140 *Evening Standard*, 8 July 1999; Christian Wolmar, (2002), p. 8.

141 *The Independent*, 31 January 1999.

142 London Transport page, *The Metro*, 21 July 1999.

143 *Evening Standard*, 16 July 1999.

144 Barrie Clement, 'London Goes Down The Tubes', *Independent on Sunday*, 4 July 1999.

145 *The Guardian*, 13 October 1999.

146 *The Observer*, 10 October 1999.

147 *Evening Standard*, 6 October 1999.

148 *The Guardian*, 8 October 1999; *Morning Star*, 8 October 1999; *Evening Standard*, 7 October 1999.

149 *Evening Standard*, 7 October 1999.

150 *Morning Star*, 8 October 1999.

151 Prison Reform Trust, *Prison Privatisation Report International*, 1996; The Age, 19 January 2004.

152 Washington State Department of Ecology press release, 1997; Seattle Times website, 26 July 1997.

153 BBC Water Week website; Office of Water Services (Ofwat), *Report on Leakage and Water Efficiency*, 1998/99.

154 CBC News website, 7 August 2002.

155 RMT press release; PA News, 11 December 2000.

156 Unison Bargaining Support Group report on Balfour Beatty plc; PA News, 5 July 2000; BBC website, 22 March 1999; Kate Geary, CorporateWatch website.

157 PA News, 13 September 2000.

158 PA News, 21 February 2000; 20 September 2000; Ofwat, *Report on Leakage and Water Efficiency*, 1998/99; Ofwat, *Report on Levels of Service for the Water Industry in England and Wales*, 1998/99.

159 Health and Safety Executive, case no. F030000254; The Green Energy League, March-July 1998.

160 Campaign Against Tube Privatisation newspaper, 2000.

161 PA News, 25 August 2000; Christian Wolmar, (2002), p. 182.

162 Unison Bargaining Support Group report on Brown & Root.

163 According to Dr Bill Ryder, chair of the regional consultants' committee – Unison Bargaining Support Group report on AMEC plc, including information from *Scotland on Sunday*, 26 May 1996.

164 CorporateWatch website.

165 *Daily Telegraph*, 29 July 2000.

166 *Morning Star*, 8 October 1999.

167 *Daily Telegraph*, 19 August 2000.

168 BBC News website, 18 August 2000.

169 *RMT News*, September 2000; House of Commons Transport Committee, HC387-II, (2002).

170 Keith Harper, *The Guardian*, 12 December 2000.

171 Letters, *The Guardian*, 13 December 2000.

172 *RMT News*, April/May 2001.

173 House of Commons Transport Committee, HC387-II, (2002) – LU04, Memorandum by Capital Transport Campaign, Ev.77.

174 MORI/Commission for Integrated Transport, July 2000.

175 IPSOS, August 1999, research survey conducted for the Jeffrey Archer campaign; the transport issues were public transport (unspecified), traffic congestion/roads, trains (not underground) and Tube/Underground.

176 BBC News website, 19 January 2000.

177 BBC News website, 19 January 2000.

178 *Evening Standard*, 16 November 1999.

179 Ken Livingstone, *You Can't Say That: Memoirs*, Faber & Faber, 2011, p. 395.

180 BBC News website, 21 Februay 2000.

181 *Daily Telegraph*, 26 February 2000.

182 *The Economist*, 7 December 2000.

183 Ipsos/MORI, 16 November 2000.

184 BBC News website, 28 January 1999; *The Guardian*, 13 October 1999.

185 *Evening Standard*, 7 March 2000; *Daily Telegraph*, 26 February 2000.

186 House of Commons Hansard, 13 November 2000.

187 CATP bulletin no.7 – August 2000.

188 *The Guardian*, 21 February 2005.

189 Christian Wolmar, (2002), p. 224.

190 Christian Wolmar, (2002), p. 217.

191 Stephen Glaister, Rosemary Scanlon and Tony Travers, *The Way Out: An Alternative Approach to the Future of the Underground*, LSE LONDON discussion paper no.1, London School of Economics, 1999.

192 Stephen Glaister, Rosemary Scanlon and Tony Travers, Getting Public Private Partnerships Going in Transport, *Public Policy and Administration* vol. 15 no. 4, Winter 2000.

193 Christian Wolmar, (2002), p. 202.

194 *Evening Standard* feature, 19 January 1999.

195 Editorial, *Evening Standard*, 17 February 1999.

196 *Evening Standard* editorial, 26 September 2000.

197 www.thisislondon.co.uk/savethetube (no longer available); referenced in *Evening Standard*, 16 July 2001.

198 Cited in *The Economist*, 7 December 2000.

199 Listen to London, (1999).

200 *The Economist*, 7 December 2000.

201 Poll conducted by Electoral Reform Society, commissioned by Listen to London, reported in Listen to London Campaign Bulletin no.5, February 2000.

202 Letter, RMT London Transport Regional Council to RMT branches, 27 October 2000; CATP letter to supporters, November/December 2000.

203 CATP bulletin no.1, March 1999.

204 *Tubeworker*, 11 May 2000.

205 Bernard Jenkin, House of Commons Hansard, 13 November 2000.

206 Will Hutton, *The London Underground Public Private Partnership, An Independent Review*, The Industrial Society, 2000.

207 *Evening Standard*, 26 September 2000; BBC News website, 25 September 2000.

208 House of Commons Hansard, 13 November 2000.

209 BBC News website, 9 October 2000.

210 *Daily Telegraph*, 20 October 2000; *Evening Standard*, 20 October 2000.

211 *Solidarity*, 7 December 2000.

212 *RMT News*, November 2000.

213 Ken Livingstone, (2011), p. 440.

214 *RMT News*, November 2000.

215 *The Guardian*, 9 December 2000.

216 *Daily Telegraph*, 16 December 2000.

217 *The Guardian*, 10 October 2000.

218 Robert Kiley, *Report to Mayor Ken Livingstone regarding the Feasibility of the PPP Structure as Currently Proposed*, TfL, 2000.

219 Transport for London, *Outline of a Programme for the Rehabilitation and Management of the London Underground*, 2000.

220 House of Commons Transport Committee, HC387-II, (2002).

221 BBC News website.

222 Christian Wolmar, (2002), p. 140.

223 Christian Wolmar, (2002), p. 170.

224 *Daily Telegraph*, 16 December 2000; *Independent on Sunday*, 17 December 2000.

225 Ken Livingstone, (2011), p. 443.

226 *Evening Standard*, 26 January and 29 January 2001.

227 eg. *The Guardian*, 3 February 2001; *The Times*, 3 February 2001; *Evening Standard*, 2 February 2001.

228 *Evening Standard*, 2 February 2001.

229 Letter, Jimmy Knapp to RMT members, 9 February 2001.

230 *Tubeworker*, 3 January 2001.

231 *Tubeworker*, 31 January 2001, 3 February 2001.

232 *Evening Standard*, 5 February 2001.

233 *Action for Solidarity*, 9 February 2001.

234 *Evening Standard*, 5 February 2001.

235 *Daily Telegraph*, 6 February 2001.

236 *Daily Telegraph*, 19 March 2001.

237 Letter, Deputy Prime Minister to Malcolm Bates, 30 March 2001.

238 BBC News website, 17 April 2001.

239 Letter, John Monks, TUC General Secretary, to Vernon Hince, RMT Senior Assistant General Secretary, 2 May 2001.

240 *Evening Standard* editorial, 25 April, 2001.

241 House of Commons Transport Committee, HC387-II, (2002), LU10 – Memorandum by Metronet.

242 *Evening Standard*, 3 May 2001.

243 House of Commons Transport Committee, HC387-II, (2002), LU13 – Memorandum by Tube Lines, para 4, Ev.99 and para 38, Ev.103.

244 *Evening Standard*, 3 May 2001.

245 *Evening Standard*, 27 April 2001.

246 Ken Livingstone, (2011), p. 445.

247 House of Commons Transport Committee, HC387-II, (2002), LU15, Memorandum by Linc consortium, ev.105-6.

248 *Daily Telegraph*, 5 May 2001.

249 BBC News website, 3 April 2001.

250 Christian Wolmar, (2002), p. 179.

251 Ken Livingstone, (2011), p. 445.

252 *RMT News*, July/August 2001.

253 Westminster City Council vs. Unison, 3 April 2001.

254 Railway Gazette website, 1 August 2001.

255 Letters, *The Guardian*, 14 July 2001.

256 *Daily Telegraph*, 6 July 2001.

257 Railway Gazette website, 1 August 2001.

258 Railway Gazette website, 1 October 2001.

259 Nick Cohen, *Pretty Straight Guys*, Faber & Faber, 2004, p. 202.

260 HC387-II, (2002).

261 Comptroller and Auditor General, *The financial analysis for the London Underground Public Private Partnerships*, HC54, National Audit Office, 2000.

262 Deloitte & Touche, *Report into London Underground Public Private Partnership: Emerging Findings*, 2001.

263 BBC News website, 24 August 2001.

264 Ernst & Young, *London Underground Limited: Public-Private Partnership Value for Money Review*, 2002.

265 House of Commons Transport, Local Government and the Regions Committee, *London Underground – the Public Private Partnership: Follow Up*, 7th report 2001-02, HC680, 2002, paras 6 and 7.

266 House of Commons Transport, Local Government and the Regions Committee, HC680, (2002).

267 Comptroller and Auditor General, (2004), paras 2.10 and 2.11.

268 House of Commons Hansard, 4 July 2002, written answer; Comptroller and Auditor General, (2004), para 6.

269 *Sunday Times*, 25 March 2001; 18 March 2001.

270 Hannah Baldock, 'Getting the Tube to Work', *Building journal*, 9 February 2001.

271 *The Times*, 20 March 2002.

272 Comptroller and Auditor General, (2004), table 7.

273 Comptroller and Auditor General, (2004), para 2.9.

274 *Tubeworker*, 1 March 2002.

275 *The Guardian*, 14 February 2002.

276 Letter, Jackie Darby to John Biggs, 27 May 2002.

277 *Solidarity*, 15 February 2002.

278 *Tubeworker*, 24 September 2002.

279 *Evening Standard*, 24 October 2002; *The Guardian*, 20 October 2002.

280 House of Commons Transport Committee, HC387-II, (2002).

281 Letter, Ken Livingstone to Alistair Darling, February 2003, cited in House of Commons Transport Committee, HC387-II, (2002).

282 Hannah Baldock, (2001).

283 Comptroller and Auditor General, (2004).

284 *The Guardian*, 21 February 2005.

285 House of Commons Transport Committee, HC387-II, (2002).

286 Press Notice 03/03, Office of the PPP Arbiter, 9 September 2003.

287 Chris Bolt, (2003).

288 The PPP Arbiter: Report and Accounts 2003/04; 2009/10.

289 www.ppparbiter.co.uk.

290 He had been an engineering director in the Rover Group and with BAE Systems plc.

291 BBC website, 2 January 2003, 8 January 2003.

292 Tube Lines press release, 6 March 2003.

293 *The Engineer*, 20 June 2003.

294 Volkerrail.co.uk

295 BBC, 4 April 2003.

296 *The Guardian*, 6 October 2004; House of Commons Transport Committee, *The Performance of the London Underground*, 6th report 2004-05, HC94, 2005, Ev 24.

297 House of Commons Transport Committee, HC94, (2005).

298 Transport for London, *London Underground and the PPP: The First Year*, 2004.

299 Christian Wolmar, *Rail* magazine, 7 May 2009.

300 *The Guardian*, 31 January 2004.

301 *The Guardian*, 6 October 2004.

302 Comptroller and Auditor General, *London Underground: Are the Public Private Partnerships likely to work successfully?*, HC 644 Session 2003-2004, 2004.

303 This and other references in the remainder of this section are from Transport for London, *London Underground and the PPP: The Second Year*, 2005, unless otherwise stated.

304 *Tubeworker*, 25 October 2004.

305 BBC News website, 8 December 2004.

306 *The Guardian*, 21 February 2005.

307 *RMT News*, March 2004.

308 BBC News, 11 February 2004.

309 *RMT News*, March 2004.

310 *RMT News*, December 2005; RMT press release, 1 November 2005.

311 *Tubeworker*, 19 March 2005.

312 London Assembly Transport Committee, *The PPP: Two Years In – The Transport Committee's scrutiny into the progress of the PPP*, 2005, para 1.2, p. 4.

313 References in this section are from Transport for London, *London Underground and the PPP: The Third Year*, 2006, unless otherwise stated.

314 House of Commons Hansard, 13 February 2002.

315 Transport for London, *Popular Myths about the Tube PPP*, 2002.

316 House of Commons Transport Committee, HC94, (2005), Ev.15: Tim O'Toole.

317 Transport for London, (2002).

318 Letter, Tim O'Toole to Lynne Featherstone, GLA Transport Committee, 13 May

2005.

319 Transport for London, (2005).

320 *Evening Standard*, 18 March 2008.

321 *Tubeworker*, 19 September 2006.

322 BBC News website, 25 January 2003.

323 BBC News website, 27 January 2003.

324 House of Commons Transport Committee, HC94, (2005), LU03: Memorandum by RMT.

325 *RMT News*, May 2003.

326 *RMT News*, February 2003.

327 *Tubeworker*, 30 January 2003.

328 *RMT News*, May 2003.

329 London Assembly Transport Committee, (2005), Appendix E: Metronet evidence to GLA.

330 *RMT News*, May 2003.

331 *RMT News*, September 2003.

332 Rotherham, November 2002; King's Cross, 16 September 2003; BBC website, 10 October 2003.

333 *RMT News*, December 2003 / January 2004.

334 BBC website, 18 October 2003.

335 BBC website, 19 October 2003; 20 October 2003.

336 *RMT News*, December 2003 / January 2004.

337 Health and Safety Executive, *Derailments on London Underground at Camden Town and Hammersmith*, 2005.

338 BBC News website, 20 October 2003; *Camden New Journal*, 30 October 2003.

339 *Camden New Journal*, 30 October 2003.

340 *RMT News*, November 2003; December 2003 / January 2004.

341 BBC website, 27 October 2003.

342 House of Commons Transport Committee, HC94, (2005), LU03: Memorandum by RMT.

343 BBC News website, 28 October 2003.

344 *RMT News*, December 2003 / December 2004.

345 BBC website, 3 December 2003.

346 HC94, para 22.

347 Health and Safety Executive, *White City train derailment*, 2005.

348 BBC News website, 19 August 2004.

349 ASLEF press release, 28 July 2005.

350 Unjum Mirza, *London Underground: I Do Mind Dying – The Politics of Health & Safety*, RMT, 2007, pp. 12-14.

351 Unjum Mirza, (2007), p. 14.

352 Unjum Mirza, (2007), pp. 14, 15.

353 Unjum Mirza, (2007), pp. 15-16; *Tubeworker* 18 July 2006.

354 House of Commons Regulatory Reform Committee, *Proposal for the Regulatory Reform (Fire Safety) Order 2004*, 11th Report 2003-04, HC684, 2004.

355 Spokesperson for the Office of the Deputy Prime Minister, BBC News website, 14

July 2004.

356 *RMT News*, July/August 2005.

357 RMT press release, 25 November 2005.

358 House of Commons Hansard, 25 January 2006.

359 *RMT News*, March 2007.

360 All figures in this section from Transport for London, (2005), unless otherwise stated.

361 *Financial Mail on Sunday*, 16 February 2003; BBC website, 16 February 2003.

362 *RMT News*, February 2004.

363 *RMT News*, December 2004 / January 2005.

364 RMT press release, 21 March 2004.

365 House of Commons Transport Committee, HC94, (2005).

366 *The Guardian*, 21 February 2005.

367 House of Commons Transport Committee, HC94, (2005), paras 32, 30.

368 www.railway-technology.com

369 London Assembly Transport Committee, (2005), Appendix E: Metronet evidence to GLA.

370 *RMT News*, July/August 2005.

371 *Tubeworker*, 27 July 2005; 12 September 2005; 21 August 2006.

372 *Tubeworker*, 25 May 2007.

373 Christian Wolmar, *Rail* magazine, 7 May 2009.

374 *RMT News*, July/August 2005.

375 BBC News London website, 6 May 2011.

376 Transport for London, (2005).

377 *Off The Rails*, July 2005.

378 London Assembly Transport Committee, (2005).

379 RMT and ASLEF press releases, 6 October 2005.

380 Letter to *The Guardian*, from the Director, Institute of Local Government Studies, Unversity of Birmingham, 20 October 2005.

381 *RMT News*, October 2005.

382 EDM 794.

383 ASLEF press release, 13 October 2005.

384 Transport for London, (2006), accompanying press release.

385 RMT press release, 31 December 2006.

386 BBC website, 15 July 2003.

387 Christian Wolmar, *Rail* magazine, 7 May 2009.

388 *Hackney Gazette*, 18 April 2002.

389 Ipsos MORI; *RMT News*, October 2006.

390 *Hackney Gazette*, 22 January and 8 January 2004.

391 *Hackney Gazette* letters, 18 January and 1 February 2007.

392 *Hackney Gazette*, 16 November 2006.

393 *Tubeworker*, 21 October 2007.

394 London Assembly Transport Committee, (2005), para.5.13, p. 16.

395 London Assembly Transport Committee, (2005), paras.5.20 and 5.21, p. 17.

396 House of Commons Transport Committee, HC94, (2005), Ev5.

397 References from here to the end of this section are from Transport for London, (2006), unless otherwise stated.

398 BBC News website, 4 May 2006.

399 House of Commons Transport Committee, *The London Underground and the Public-Private Partnership Agreements*, 2nd report 2007-08, HC45, 2007, Q271, Ev.32.

400 BBC News website, 31 May 2006.

401 *Evening Standard*, 16 June 2006.

402 Transport for London, (2006).

403 BBC News website, 4 and 5 May, 12 September 2006.

404 *Tubeworker*, 19 September, 11 October, 23 November 2006.

405 BBC News website, 24 January 2007; *Tubeworker*, 10 February 2007.

406 RMT press release, 15 December 2005.

407 BBC News website, 5 September 2006.

408 BBC News website, 21 November 2006.

409 Email quoted in *Evening Standard*, 18 March 2008.

410 Information in this section on the Mile End derailment from Department for Transport Rail Accident Investigation Branch, *Derailment of a London Underground Central Line train near Mile End station, 5 July 2007*, Report 03/2008, 2008, unless otherwise stated.

411 BBC News website, 5 July 2007.

412 BBC News website, 5 July 2007.

413 Department for Transport Rail Accident Investigation Branch, *Derailment of a London Underground Central Line train near Mile End station, 5 July 2007*, Report 03/2008, 2008.

414 *RMT News*, August/September 2007.

415 References in this section from House of Commons Transport Committee, HC45, (2007), unless otherwise stated.

416 Transport for London, *Role of the PPP arbiter and lessons for future monitoring*, 2011.

417 *Tubeworker*, 9 June 2007; 5 July 2007.

418 Metronet Rail SSL Network Planning, *BTUK Intention to Reduce SSL Fleet Size: Initial Assessment for MRSSL*, 2007.

419 BBC News website, 18 May 2007.

420 Mayor of London, *74th Mayor's report to the Greater London Assembly*, 2007.

421 BBC News website, 18 July 2007.

422 Ken Livingstone, (2011), p. 576.

423 RMT, *Response to Transport Select Committee*, October 2009, p. 2.

424 References in this section from House of Commons Transport Committee, HC45, (2007), unless otherwise stated.

425 *New Civil Engineer* website, 20 October 2009 – anonymous reader's comment.

426 *Tubeworker*, 9 June and 21 September 2007.

427 References in this section from House of Commons Transport Committee, HC45, (2007), unless otherwise stated.

428 *Tubeworker*, 21 September 2007.

429 BBC News website, 5 June 2009; TfL press release, 5 June 2009.

430 BBC News website, 5 June 2009.

431 *RMT News*, October 2007.

432 References in this section from House of Commons Transport Committee, HC45, (2007), unless otherwise stated.

433 BBC News website, 31 January 2008.

434 Comptroller and Auditor General, *The failure of Metronet*, HC512, National Audit Office, 2009.

435 BBC News website, 6 February 2008.

436 *Evening Standard*, 22 November 2010.

437 Comptroller and Auditor General, (2009).

438 Ken Livingstone, (2011), pp. 578-9.

439 *RMT News*, October 2007.

440 WS Atkins, *Annual Report*, 2008.

441 *New Civil Engineer*, 20 November 2007.

442 TfL list of contracts, 28 June 2012; LUL awarded the contract for the SSL signalling upgrade to Bombardier Ltd.

443 House of Commons Transport Committee, HC45, (2007).

444 Martin Kellaway, and Helen Shanks, *Metronet, Tube Lines and the London Underground PPP*, NACC decision, Office for National Statistics, 2007.

445 Freedom Of Information request.

446 Letter, Tube Lines to Caroline Pidgeon AM, 22 February 2010.

447 Freedom Of Information request: TfL ref 1300-1213; 1007-1213.

448 Will Hutton, (2000), p. 18.

449 *RMT News*, January 2008.

450 *RMT News*, September 2008.

451 *RMT News*, March 2007.

452 *RMT News*, January 2008, July/August 2008, September 2008, July/August 2009, July/August, 2010.

453 *RMT News*, October 2008.

454 RMT, (2009).

455 *RMT News*, September, October, and November/December 2008.

456 *Prospect* magazine, 2007, quoted in *Solidarity*, 21 February 2008.

457 *Solidarity*, 21 February 2008.

458 BBC News website, 6 November 2007.

459 *RMT News*, February 2008.

460 *Evening Standard*, 18 March 2008.

461 TfL press release, 27 May 2008.

462 TfL press release, 5 June 2009.

463 *On The Move*, October 2009.

464 Mail Online, 13 March 2008; *Evening Standard*, 22 November 2011.

465 *Evening Standard*, 18 March 2008.

466 *The Guardian*, 11 October 2007.

467 *RMT News*, March 2008.

468 RMT press releases, 20 November and 3 December 2009; BBC News website, 3 December 2009.

469 BBC News website, 8 July 2009.

470 *Evening Standard*, 9 October, 24 November and 7 December 2009.

471 *Evening Standard*, 24 November 2009.

472 Quoted by Christian Wolmar, *Rail* magazine, 7 May 2009.

473 *Evening Standard*, 3 September 2009.

474 Letter, Boris Johnson to Dean Finch, 4 December 2012.

475 *Neasden Flyer* (RMT newsletter), October 2009.

476 *Evening Standard*, 9 October 2009.

477 To House of Commons Transport Committee, quoted in *Evening Standard*, 10 December 2009.

478 *Evening Standard*, 10 December 2009.

479 guardian.co.uk, 7 December 2009; *Daily Telegraph*, 17 December 2009.

480 RMT, (2009).

481 London Assembly Transport Committee, *Delays possible: maintaining and upgrading the London Underground*, 2009; RMT, *Submission to GLA investigation into PPP on London Underground*, 2008.

482 *Evening Standard*, 19 March 2009.

483 *Evening Standard*, 19 March 2009.

484 *Evening Standard*, 19 March 2009.

485 London Assembly Budget Committee, *A fare decision? The impact of the Mayor's fare decision*, 2009.

486 *RMT News*, July/August 2009.

487 *RMT News*, November/December 2009.

488 *platform* (Tube Lines in-house magazine), August 2009.

489 BBC News website, 17 December 2009.

490 telegraph.co.uk, 1 January 2010.

491 guardian.co.uk, 25 January 2010; TfL statement, 25 January 2010.

492 Letters, *Evening Standard*, 18 December 2009.

493 *The Guardian*, 4 January 2010.

494 *Across The Tracks*, undated, probably January/February 2010.

495 *RMT News*, April 2010.

496 Richard Tracey, *Driverless Trains*, 2010.

497 BBC News website, 9 December 2009.

498 *Evening Standard*, 3 February 2010.

499 *Evening Standard*, 30 March 2010.

500 *Rail Technology* magazine, June/July 2010.

501 *Evening Standard*, 10 March 2010; *The Guardian*, 8 March and 11 March 2010.

502 *Evening Standard*, 10 March 2010.

503 Letters, *Evening Standard*, 11 March 2010.

504 *The Guardian*, 8 March 2010, quoting correspondence between LUL, the government and the Arbiter.

505 Transport for London, (2011).

506 Office of the PPP Arbiter Press Notice 02/10, 27 April 2010.

507 *Rail* magazine, 1 October 2009.

508 *Evening Standard*, 15 May 2010.

509 Letters, *Evening Standard*, 10 May 2010.

510 Ken Livingstone, (2011), p. 646.

511 BBC News, 7 May 2010.

512 *RMT News*, May 2010.

513 *RMT News*, June, September 2010.

514 Department for Transport Rail Accident Investigation Branch, *Runaway of an engineering train from Highgate, 13 August 2010*, Report 09/2011, 2011.

515 Office of the PPP Arbiter Announcements 02/10 27 May 2010, 03/10 12 August 2010; 4/10 31 August 2010; OPPPA Press Notice 03/10 28 June 2010; letters, LUL to OPPPA, 1 August 2010, LUL to OPPPA 23 August 2010.

516 *Rail Magazine*, 10-23 August 2011.

517 Transport for London, (2011).

518 The PPP Arbiter: Report and Accounts 2009-10.

519 Christian Wolmar, (2002), p. 220.

520 House of Commons Transport Committee, HC387-II, (2002), Evidence from Michael Cassidy, LINC consortium Chairman.

521 *Rail Technology Magazine*, June/July 2010.

522 Trefor Williams, Analysis of the London Underground PPP Failure, Working Paper Proceedings, Engineering Project Organizations Conference, South Lake Tahoe, CA, November 4-7, 2010.

523 House of Commons Hansard, 27 June 2002, column 1016.

524 International Monetary Fund, *Public Private Partnerships*, 2004, cited in Dexter Whitfield, (2006), p. 44.

525 A 1999 National Audit Office Report and the 2000 Andersen report for the Treasury Taskforce, cited in Dexter Whitfield, (2001), p. 22.

526 Campaign Against Tube Privatisation, *The Trade Unions and New Labour: CATP discussion document*, 2003.

527 Dexter Whitfield, (2006), p. 43.

528 Dexter Whitfield, (2006), p. 14.

529 Dexter Whitfield, (2001), p. 25.

530 House of Commons Transport Committee, HC387-II, (2002).

531 Quoted in Workers' Liberty no.52, January 1999.

532 See Ben Pimlott, (1977).

533 Nick Cohen, (2004), p. 23.

534 Dexter Whitfield, (2001), p. 16.

535 Quoted by Ian Jack, *The Independent*, 4 August 2001.

536 Dexter Whitfield, (2006), p. 20.

537 *The Independent*, 12 April 1997.

538 Quoted on BBC website, 11 May 2007.

539 *The Guardian*, 6 October 1998.

540 Quoted on BBC website, 11 May 2007.

541 Dexter Whitfield, (2001), p. 19.

542 Quoted in *The Independent*, 22 May 1998.

543 *Action For Solidarity*, 9 February 2001.

544 www.rmtlondoncalling.org.uk.

545 RMT, *Paying for Privatisation: RMT briefing on the McNulty Report in the Railways*,

2011.

546 Nurture New York's Nature, *A Bolder Plan: Balancing Free Transit and Congestion Pricing in New York City* ('The Kheel Plan'), 2008, p. 10.

547 RMT, (2011).

548 Stephen Glaister and Tony Travers, (1995), pp. 14, 32.

549 Bernard Calabuig, Office of President of Aubagne and Etoile Urban Community, www.tallinn.ee

550 *Tubeworker*'s blog, 20 October 2010.

551 Cited in Pete Glatter, 'London Busmen: Rise and Fall of a Rank and File Movement', *International Socialism* no.74, 1975.

552 Socialist Party of Great Britain, (1945), p. 21.

553 House of Commons Hansard, 20 March 1998.

554 F E Lawley, *Socialism and railways*, ILP Study Courses no.9, undated, probably 1924 – this set-up is known as the 'Plumb Scheme'.

555 Arthur Downton, (1936).

556 *The Platform*, March 1977 and January 1978.

557 Quoted in Lord Morrison, (1960), p. 122.

558 *Off The Rails*, Spring 2006.

559 Stephen Glaister and Tony Travers, (1995), p. 12.

560 Christian Wolmar, (2002), p. 45.

561 Bob Crow, Rail privatisation – a failed experiment, *Building the new common sense: social ownership for the 21st century*, Left Economics Advisory Panel, 2008.

562 Tom Ahern, *The Railways and the People: an appeal to passengers and workers*, Communist Party, 1962, pp. 14-16.

563 Dexter Whitfield, *Public Services or Private Profit?*, Socialist Renewal, new series, no.7, Spokesman Books, 2001.

564 Leon Trotsky, *The Death Agony of Capitalism and the Tasks of the Fourth International: The Transitional Programme*, Part I, Fourth International, 1938.

565 Cited in Bob Crow, (2008).

566 christianwolmar.co.uk, 13 December 2009.

567 *Daily Mail*, 24 June 2011.

568 *Evening Standard*, 25 October 2007.

569 independentaustralia.net, 31 May 2012.

570 Ian Fraser, *Sunday Times*, 15 March 2009.

571 christianwolmar.co.uk, 15 October 2008; 10 February 2009.

572 Ken Livingstone, (2011), p. 577.

573 *Evening Standard*, 4 August 2008; BBC London News, 11 March 2012.

574 *Evening Standard*, 28 September 2006, 24 July 2007.

575 FirstGroup, *Directors Remuneration Report*, 2012.

INDEX